THE MUSLIM BROTHERHOOD

THE MIDDLE EAST IN FOCUS

The Middle East has become simultaneously the world's most controversial, crisis-ridden and yet least understood region. Taking new perspectives on the area that has undergone the most dramatic changes, the "Middle East in Focus" series, edited by Barry Rubin, seeks to bring the best, most accurate expertise to understand the area's countries, issues, and problems. The resulting books are designed to be balanced, accurate, and comprehensive compendiums of both facts, and analysis are presented clearly for both experts and the general reader.

Series Editor: Barry Rubin

Director, Global Research International Affairs (GLORIA)
Center Editor, *Middle East Review of International Affairs* (MERIA)
Journal Editor, *Turkish Studies*

Turkish Dynamics: Bridge across Troubled Lands
By Ersin Kalaycıoğlu

Eternal Iran: Continuity and Chaos
By Patrick Clawson and Michael Rubin

Hybrid Sovereignty in the Arab Middle East: The Cases of Kuwait, Jordan, and Iraq
By Gokhan Bacik

The Politics of Intelligence and American Wars with Iraq
By Ofira Seliktar

Hezbollah: The Story of the Party of God: From Revolution to Institutionalization
By Eitan Azani

Lebanon: Liberation, Conflict, and Crisis
Edited by Barry Rubin

The Muslim Brotherhood: The Organization and Policies of a Global Islamist Movement
Edited by Barry Rubin

THE MUSLIM BROTHERHOOD

THE ORGANIZATION AND POLICIES OF A GLOBAL ISLAMIST MOVEMENT

Edited by
Barry Rubin

palgrave
macmillan

THE MUSLIM BROTHERHOOD

First published in 2010 by
PALGRAVE MACMILLAN®
in the United States—a division of St. Martin's Press LLC,
175 Fifth Avenue, New York, NY 10010.

Where this book is distributed in the UK, Europe and the rest of the world,
this is by Palgrave Macmillan, a division of Macmillan Publishers Limited,
registered in England, company number 785998, of Houndmills,
Basingstoke, Hampshire RG21 6XS.

Palgrave Macmillan is the global academic imprint of the above companies
and has companies and representatives throughout the world.

Palgrave® and Macmillan® are registered trademarks in the United States,
the United Kingdom, Europe and other countries.

ISBN: 978–0–230–10069–5 Hardcover
ISBN: 978–0–230–10071–8 Paperback

Library of Congress Cataloging-in-Publication Data

The Muslim Brotherhood : the organization and policies of a global
Islamist movement / edited by Barry Rubin.
     p. cm.—(The Middle East in focus)
     ISBN 978–0–230–10071–8 (alk. paper)—
     ISBN 978–0–230–10069–5 (alk. paper)
     1. Jam'iyat al-Ikhwan al-Muslimin (Egypt) 2. Jam'iyat al-Ikhwan
al-Muslimin (Syria) 3. Jama'at al-Ikhwan al-Muslimin (Jordan) 4. Jama'at
al-Ikhwan al-Muslimin (Palestine) 5. Islam—Societies, etc.—Political
activity. 6. Islam and politics. I. Rubin, Barry M.

BP10.J383M87 2010
322'.1—dc22   2009038178

A catalogue record of the book is available from the British Library.

Design by Newgen Imaging Systems (P) Ltd., Chennai, India.

First edition: May 2010

D 10 9 8 7 6 5

Printed in the United States of America.

CONTENTS

CONTRIBUTORS

José Escobar Stemmann is a Spanish diplomat. He was a lecturer on Islamic movements in the Instituto Gutierrez Mellado for Defence Studies and is currently in the Spanish Diplomatic School in Madrid. His publications include "Islamic Movements in the Muslim World" in *Perspectivas Exteriores* edited by *FRIDE* and "Middle East Salafism's Influence and the Radicalization of Muslim Communities in Europe" published by the *Middle East Review of International Affairs (MERIA)* Journal. He is a frequent writer for *Política Exterior* about political Islam and the process of democratization in different Arab countries.

Jorge Fuentelsaz Franganillo is deputy chief at the Middle East Bureau of the Spanish News Agency Efe, based in Cairo. He is also carrying out research (PhD) on the Society of the Muslim Brothers and its relationship with the Egyptian regime and political system at the Universidad Autónoma in Madrid.

Hillel Frisch is a senior lecturer in the Departments of Political Studies and Middle East History in Bar-Ilan University, Israel, and also a senior researcher in the BESA Center for Strategic Studies, specializing in Middle Eastern political and security affairs. Among his latest publications are "The Palestinian Strategic Debate over the Intifada," *Terrorism and Political Violence* (2004), "Do Better Fences Make Better Neighbors: Palestinian-Jordanian Relations Since Oslo," *Middle East Journal* (2004), and "Nationalizing a Universal Text: The Qur'an in Arafat's Rhetoric," *Middle Eastern Studies* (2005). A forthcoming book, *Radical Islam: Challenge and Response*, co-edited with Efraim Inbar, will be published by Routledge.

Farhad Khosrokhavar is professor at Ecole des Hautes Etudes en Sciences Sociales in Paris, France. He has published fourteen books on revolutionary Iran and Islam in Europe. He has been a Rockefeller Fellow, a visiting professor at Yale University, and, in 2009, he will be a visiting professor at Harvard University. Two recent books are *Avoir ses vingt ans dans le pays des ayatollahs* (Robert-Laffont, January 2009) and *Inside Jihadism Jihadism Worldwide* (Yale Sociological Series, Paradigm Publishers, December 2008).

Alyssa A. Lappen is a senior fellow at the American Center for Democracy. She is a former senior editor of *Institutional Investor, Working Woman, and*

Corporate Finance. She was previously an associate editor at *Forbes* Magazine and an editor and staff reporter for several other publications. Since 2001, Ms. Lappen has applied her investigative reporting skills to the Middle East and matters of American security. She holds a BA in English Literature and graduated Phi Beta Kappa from Tulane University.

Robert G. Rabil is Director of Graduate Studies and an Assistant Professor of Political Science at Florida Atlantic University. He is the author of *Embattled Neighbors: Syria, Israel and Lebanon* (Lynne Rienner Publishers, 2003) and *Syria, United States and the War on Terror in the Middle East* (Praeger, 2006). The author extends his deep gratitude to the FAU Division of Research for supporting his work.

David Rich is author of "British Muslims and UK Foreign Policy" in *Britain and the Middle East: From Imperial Power to Junior Partner* (2008) and "Jihadism as an Obstacle to Integration" in *Islam in Europe, Case Studies, Comparison & Overviews* (2007).

Professor **Barry Rubin** is director of the Global Research for International Affairs (GLORIA) Center and professor at the Interdisciplinary University. He is editor of the *Middle East Review of International Affairs (MERIA)* journal and of *Turkish Studies.* His books include *The Truth About Syria; The Long War for Freedom: The Arab Struggle for Democracy in the Middle East; Hating America: A History; Yasir Arafat: A Political Biography; The Tragedy of the Middle East; The Transformation of Palestinian Politics; Revolution Until Victory: The Politics and History of the PLO; Cauldron of Turmoil: America in the Middle East; Istanbul Intrigues; Modern Dictators; Secrets of State: The State Department and the Struggle over U.S. Foreign Policy; Paved with Good Intentions: The American Experience and Iran; The Arab States and the Palestine Conflict; Islamic Fundamentalism in Egyptian Politics;* and *The Great Powers in the Middle East, 1941–1947.*

Ana Belén Soage holds two degrees, in politics and translation, from London Guildhall University and the University of Granada respectively and has completed a masters degree in Muslim and Jewish Culture. She has been a regular visitor to the Middle East for the last decade and has lectured at Ayn Shams University and the American University in Cairo. She is also a member of the Editorial Board of Religious Compass (Political Religions section). She is currently in Egypt where she is conducting research (PhD) on the evolution of political Islam.

Guido Steinberg is a senior fellow specializing in Middle East and Gulf Affairs at the German Institute for International and Security Affairs (Stiftung Wissenschaft und Politik, SWP) in Berlin. An Islamicist and Middle East historian by training, he has worked as a research coordinator at the Free University Berlin (2001) and as an advisor on international terrorism in the German Federal Chancellery (2002–2005). He is a frequent expert witness in German terrorism trials and has published widely on the Middle East,

Saudi Arabian and Iraqi history and politics, the Wahhabiya, Islamism, and terrorism.

Lorenzo Vidino is a senior fellow in International Security Studies at the Fletcher School of Law and Diplomacy, Tufts University. His research focuses on terrorism and political Islam worldwide, focusing mostly on Europe (throughout which he travels several months a year). He has testified before Congress on the issue and regularly works with U.S. and European law enforcement agencies. He is the author of the book *Al Qaeda in Europe: The New Battleground of Global Jihad* (Prometheus, 2005) and has published various articles on terrorism in publications such as *The International Herald Tribune, The Wall Street Journal, The Boston Globe, Studies in Conflict and Terrorism, The Middle East Quarterly,* and many others. A native of Milan, Italy, he holds a law degree from the University of Milan Law School and a masters degree in International Relations from the Fletcher School of Law and Diplomacy. He is currently working on a book about the Muslim Brotherhood in Europe and North America.

INTRODUCTION

Barry Rubin

The Muslim Brotherhood is by far the most successful Islamist group in the world: a point often overlooked by those studying such matters. There are good reasons for people not to take note of this point. The Brotherhoods in each country are independent of each other; they usually do not use terrorism; they often follow different policies adapted to their surroundings; and they often try to avoid publicity.

Nevertheless, the organization—or one might better to say this loose collection of organizations with many similarities among them—is well worth studying. The Brotherhood was the first modern Islamist group to be formed, and in many places, it is a large and influential organization. At the same time, it has never quite seized state power anywhere—though one might say it did so at times in Sudan, and Hamas rules the Gaza Strip—though it still aspires everywhere to this goal.

This raises perhaps important questions about the Brotherhood, which is dealt with by every chapter in this book, namely, is it a revolutionary or reformist organization? Does it prefer violent or peaceful means? While following tactics and strategies appropriate for its specific circumstances—and also based on the preferences of its local leaders—the Brotherhood does seek a thoroughly Islamized society and polity in which it exercises state power.

As for violence or terrorism, there is no principled opposition to such tactics. But when faced with strong states that would not hesitate to repress it—as in Jordan or Egypt—or in places where Muslims themselves are a weak minority—as in Europe or North America—extreme tactics are seen as being disastrous. Syria is something of a special case, as the Brotherhood there did try and fail to launch an armed uprising and today lacks any option for open, peaceful operation.

Given this clever tactical sense, however, the Brotherhood faces another consistent characteristic: the constant shedding of radical splinter groups for which the Brotherhood is too cautious. They thus express more radical views and launch wars of revolution that have repeatedly failed. Egypt is the clearest case of this phenomenon. While the radical groups have left the Brotherhood, though, it should be remembered that their members were recruited and indoctrinated by it. Thus, the Brotherhoods are sources of violence and terrorism indirectly, even when they disdain or disavow such measures themselves.

This book takes a comparative approach to Muslim Brotherhoods in different countries. In addition to the differences among countries, there are wide divergences between the Middle Eastern and European Brotherhoods. The first part of the book deals with the Middle East. In chapter 1, Barry Rubin takes the task of "Comparing Muslim Brotherhoods" to evaluate what they have in common, and how adjustments have been made to situations in different countries, particularly Egypt, Jordan, and Syria.

In chapter 2, Ana Belén Soage analyzes the man who is by far the most significant Brotherhood thinker today. Of course, Qaradawi is not part of the organization's power structure, nor is he specifically linked to any individual branch. At the same time, though Qaradawi has very wide appeal throughout both regions and has emerged as one of the leading—perhaps the most influential single leading—Islamist clerics of this era.

The original Brotherhood, and arguably the single largest, is the Egyptian branch. Repressed completely in the early 1950s and repeatedly struck at by the regime thereafter, the Egyptian Brotherhood has been very cautious, especially given its elderly leadership. This story is told in chapter 3 by Ana Belén Soage and Jorge Fuentelsaz Franganillo.

Yet, is its tactical carefulness and strategic modesty a sign of moderation or self-preservation? The indication is that the truth lies with the latter. If the Brotherhood was seemingly approaching the possibility of power—through election or insurrection—its tone could be expected to change sharply.

A parallel situation is examined by Hansi Escobar in chapter 4. While newer than its Egyptian brothers, the Jordanian Brotherhood has enjoyed a great deal of success in its organizing efforts but also has faced the firm hand of a government that will not let it forget that the regime is the boss. The Jordanian government has been more willing to let the Brotherhood act openly, contest elections, and even win many parliamentary seats, though the result is always fixed to ensure a pro-regime government emerges.

The Jordanian situation, however, is somewhere between Egypt—where the Brotherhood is allowed to function in practice but not quite legally as it faces sporadic repression—and Syria, where the Brotherhood is an underground organization with no scope for public action at all. It is this complex Syrian situation taken up in chapter 5 by Robert Rabil.

Hamas is the only Muslim Brotherhood branch that rules a political entity. In chapter 6, Hillel Frisch analyzes as the Palestinian branch of the how Hamas developed, successfully competed with its nationalist rivals, won an election, and then seized power through a coup.

One advantage Hamas has over its brother Brotherhoods is that it has no strong Muslim government to oppose it, and it can build on anti-Israel xenophobia. Thus, it is less of a "domestic revolutionary" than a "national liberation" group. This point, however, should not be overplayed since—like Communist parties in third world countries—its social-ideological agenda is every bit as salient as any "patriotic" orientation. Fatah's reluctance to get into a civil war situation and its poor defense of its own interests, however, also play to Hamas's benefit.

The Brotherhood, however, is not only a Middle Eastern or even a Muslim-majority country phenomenon any more. With the massive migration of Muslims to Europe, the Brotherhood—with its history, organization, cadre, clear ideology, and international connections—was in the perfect position to affect their thinking and compete for their leadership.

Different countries, however, presented varied conditions. Immigrants came from different countries, while the Brotherhood was mainly effective among Arab populations. An important question was whether Muslim life in Europe and America would have to make religious adjustments or attempt to reproduce the situations in the old countries. In chapter 7, Lorenzo Vidino provides a comparative perspective on the Muslim Brotherhood in Europe.

Then follow four case studies (chapters 8 to 11) about the Brotherhood in Britain, by Dave Rich; France, by Farhad Khosrokhavar; Germany, by Guido Steinberg; and North America, by Alyssa Lapin.

What is clear and vital is that while other Islamist groups have made more dramatic appearances, launched huge terrorist attacks, and fought civil wars, the Muslim Brotherhoods have shown more staying power and better organizational skills. The Brotherhoods' ability to maneuver, build bases of support with patience, pose as moderate, and employ both violent and electoral tactics, make them far more impressive political actors. The oldest of modern Islamist groups, the Brotherhoods seem to have the brightest future, albeit their rule would bring tragedy and disaster to the communities they seek to dominate and the societies they seek to rule.

Pages 2 & 3
(Chapter Summaries)

1

THE MIDDLE EAST

COMPARING THREE MUSLIM BROTHERHOODS

Barry Rubin

The banner of the Islamist revolution in the Middle East today has largely passed to groups sponsored by or derived from the Muslim Brotherhood. This chapter examines three key Muslim Brotherhood groups—those of Syria, Jordan, and Egypt— compares their politics and methods, and looks at the relationships among them. Each of these groups, of course, is adapted to the conditions of a particular country.

It is important to understand the Brotherhood's policy toward and relations with jihadist groups (al-Qa'ida, the Zarqawi network, and others such as Hizb al-Tahrir and Hamas) and theorists (such as Abu Mus'ab al-Suri and Abu Muhammad al-Maqdisi). The Brotherhood groups do not have any organizational relationships with Hizb al-Tahrir, which is regarded by them as a small, cult-like group of no importance. Other than in Jordan, they have had little contact with Hizb al-Tahrir.

Regarding al-Qa'ida, the Brotherhoods approve in principle of its militancy, attacks on America, and ideology (or at least respects its ideologues), but views it as a rival. An example of this kind of thinking comes from Rajab Hilal Hamida, a Brotherhood member in Egypt's parliament, who said:

> From my point of view, bin Ladin, al-Zawahiri and al-Zarqawi are not terrorists in the sense accepted by some. I support all their activities, since they are a thorn in the side of the Americans and the Zionists. ... [On the other hand,] he who kills Muslim citizens is neither a jihad fighter nor a terrorist, but a criminal and a murderer. We must call things by their proper names![1]

His final sentence is intended to show the difference between the Brotherhood's and al-Qa'ida's views of strategy and tactics.

Al-Qa'ida has a growing presence in Syria, and it is trying to enlist militants who would otherwise be Brotherhood supporters. In Jordan, al-Qa'ida has operated independently as a small group carrying out terrorist operations, which have been condemned by the Brotherhood there on the grounds that a number of Jordanians and Palestinians have been killed in bombings.

In Egypt, the story is somewhat different as the jihadist group is an al-Qa'ida affiliate and many of the organization's leaders come from Egypt.[2] Again, though the factors such as rivalry and concern over government reactions would make the Brotherhood keep its distance from al-Qa'ida, individuals who have wanted more immediate revolutionary action have joined al-Qa'ida in the past.

When comparing the Brotherhood groups with al-Qa'ida, we must keep three key factors in mind. First, the Brotherhood and the jihadists represent the two main Islamist streams today. They are not enemies, and there has been no violent conflict between them; nor has there been a great deal of ideological friction. Yet, at the same time, they are rivals who follow different strategies are competing for mass support and state power. Thus, it would be misleading to speak of cooperation, except in the special case of Iraq, which is discussed below.

Second, a critical difference between the two groups is that, except in Saudi Arabia and Iraq, the jihadists focus on attacking what they call the "far enemy," that is, Israel, the United States, and the West in general, whereas the Brotherhoods, despite being strongly anti-Israel (and supporting Hamas, see below) and anti-Western, focus on the "near enemy," that is, Arab governments. Thus, for the Brotherhoods, while al-Qa'ida is fighting for the "Islamic" cause, it is also undermining it (except in Iraq) by diverting resources from the struggle for change within the Arab world, which is the Brotherhoods' primary focus.

Third, while the Brotherhood groups are tactically flexible, al-Qa'ida is exclusively focused on armed struggle. The Brotherhood groups view revolution as a long-term . . . process, which involves, amoung other things, providing social services to build mass support; educating and indoctrinating young people through institutions; participating in elections; compromising at times with Arab governments and showing restraint to avoid repression; allying temporarily with non-Islamist groups;. Thus, while al-Qa'ida is far more of a danger in terms of terrorism, it is far less likely to seize state power because of what would be called in Leninist terms its "infantile leftism."

The best example of a short-term turn toward apparent moderation in the cause of carrying out a revolution later is the use of elections. In Jordan and Egypt, Brotherhood groups embraced opportunities to candidates in elections even when they were fully aware that incumbent regime would not count the votes accurately or let them win. In contrast, Al-Qa'ida has condemned election as human voters and parliamentarians in the place of God for the making of laws. For example, the views of the al-Qa'ida leader in Iraq, Abu Mus'ab al-Zarqawi, with those of the influential Brotherhood ideologue Qaradawi. In a statement on January 23, 2005, Zarqawi condemned the upcoming Iraqi elections and threatened to kill those running for office and voting in the elections.[3] In sharp contrast, Qaradawi endorsed the elections, arguing that the majority of voters would back an Islamist party while liberals would get little support. If truly fair elections were to be held, he insisted, Islamists would win by a landslide.[4] This analysis correctly predicted the results of the 2005 Egyptian and 2006 Palestinian elections.

In institutional terms, all the above points apply while discussing the Iraqi insurgency if one were to look at it as a struggle led by al-Qa'ida. However, in terms of the insurgency itself, while the Brotherhood groups strongly support it and view it as an important struggle, there is no institutional involvement in contrast to their backing of the Palestinians.

In addition, the Syrian Brotherhood faces a problem because the government it is fighting is a major patron of the Iraqi insurgency and uses it to strengthen its support among the Islamists who function publicly in Syria. The Syrian Brotherhood support it enthusiastically, but in the short run, at least, it does not benefit them; the Brotherhood would be happier if the leadership did not come from al-Qa'ida.

If one wants a parallel to past experience, one might compare the Brotherhoods' attitude to revolution and armed struggle to the official Communist parties and al-Qa'ida's to Maoist groups in the 1960s and 1970s. The Brotherhoods argue that the time is not ripe for revolution and that a variety of methods be used; the latter are for an all-out revolutionary struggle now.

Thus, the Brotherhood groups have a profile of their own that is self-consciously quite different in strategy and tactics—though very parallel in ideology and goals—from the jihadist groups.

To what extent are the Brotherhood groups coordinating among themselves in the international organization of the Muslim Brotherhood? Does the organization provide strategic orientation, tactical coordination, and financial and/or operational support to these groups?

The Brotherhoods operate in silos rather than collectively, and there is virtually no coordination between them. If asked, Brotherhood leaders in Egypt, Jordan, and Syria would, of course, say that they support each other, but, in practice, it is surprising how little practical backing is offered. For one thing, except on the Palestinian and Iraqi issues, they are all internally oriented rather than internationalist, though some funds raised by Egyptian Muslim Brotherhood–controlled institutions are donated to Islamist struggles abroad.

Aside from their daily focus and largely "national revolution" goals, there are other reasons for this orientation. Conditions in each country are very different; Abd-al-Majid al-Dhunaybat, controller-general of the Jordanian Muslim Brotherhood, said in an interview that the groups in Egypt and Jordan make their own decisions based on local conditions. Indeed, he denied that any international organization existed and said that this was an idea put forth by the Brotherhood's enemies.[5]

At the same time, however, Dhunaybat admitted that the leader of the Egyptian Brotherhood—elected only by that group—is seen as being the supreme guide of the movement as a whole. In his words:

> The brothers in various countries...try to standardize the understanding, ideology and positions regarding the world events involving all the groups. Meetings take place every now and then...without there being any obligation to a certain policy on the domestic level. In other words, each country has its own exclusive organizational and political nature and relations with the state in which it exists. This gathering has no binding capacity regarding any domestic decision.[6]

The individual Brotherhoods have a specific problem with coordinating too openly or extensively. The regimes in Egypt and Jordan would not appreciate a vocal stance of calling for the overthrow of other Arab governments, whereas in Syria the movement is too harried to help anyone else and—except from Jordan—receives little assistance in its life-and-death struggle. For all practical purposes, while these groups respect the same ideologues—for example, Yusuf Qaradawi—they operate independently and in response to local conditions. This is another distinction between the Muslim Brotherhoods and al-Qa'ida, whose effort to create an Islamist International is in sharp contrast to the Brotherhood practice.

Even when the Brotherhoods influence the movement in other places, these contacts are bilateral. For example, Hamas in the Gaza Strip is related to the Egyptian Brotherhood, while Hamas in the West Bank has its links to the Jordanian Brotherhood. Furthermore, to make matters even more complex, the external leadership of Hamas is located in Damascus, where the Syrian Brotherhood is outlawed, and its patron is the regime that persecutes the Brotherhood. At times, in discussing the Hamas victory, Egyptian Muslim Brotherhood sources have said that the "Muslim Brotherhood" won the Palestinian elections. Yet, again, these are parallel and fraternal movements, not truly branches of a transnational organization.

Next, the strategic and tactical orientation of each national branch (objectives, alliances, organizational forms, attitudes toward the political system in the country where it operates, etc.) should be considered.

What is truly remarkable in discussing the Muslim Brotherhoods of Syria, Jordan, and Egypt is how three groups so parallel in origin, ideology, and goals have developed so differently owing to the local situations they face. This fact also reflects the difference between the Muslim Brotherhood and al-Qa'ida groups. The former have proven tactically flexible; the latter have committed to armed struggle as the only proper strategy.

One might sum up the conditions in this way: Muslim Brotherhood groups are as anti-American and extreme in their goals as the bin Ladinist ones. However, they almost always put the emphasis on gaining power within the context of a single country, compared to the international jihadist policy of al-Qa'ida. Equally, Muslim Brotherhood groups are far more likely to seize power than the bin Ladinist ones, but as long as they do not govern countries, they are also less dangerous in terms of terrorist violence. It also should be noted, however, that many violent revolutionary groups—especially in Egypt—have emerged from the more militant end of the Muslim Brotherhood spectrum.

Briefly, the distinction between the Syrian, Jordanian, and Egyptian groups may be summarized as follows.

The Syrian Muslim Brotherhood is a revolutionary underground group because it has been outlawed by the government there. Law number 49 of 1981 declares mere membership in the group to be punishable by death. In 1982, the regime unleashed a huge wave of repression against the Muslim Brotherhood, destroying much of its infrastructure and driving it into exile. The Brotherhood has unsuccessfully tried to regain the right to operate in Syria from the regime. Thus, for example, in 2001, it supported a manifesto backed by a broad spectrum of oppositionists urging the end of single-party rule and supporting democratic elections.[7] Given the failure of these efforts, the Syrian Muslim Brotherhood today is part of a broad coalition of anti-regime groups, members of which include the former vice president of the regime. In political terms, it functions as a leading group—perhaps in the future, as the leader—of the Sunni Arab community, which constitutes roughly 60 percent of the population. Thus, it can be characterized as revolutionary (though not necessarily through its own preference) and communalist. Yet while the Egyptian and Jordanian Brotherhoods are in an optimistic mood and are arguably gaining ground, their Syrian counterpart is frustrated and prevented from exploiting a trend toward Islamist thinking in Syria. In recent years, the regime has cultivated Syrian Islamists by building new mosques, allowing radicals to be preachers, and supporting the Islamist insurgency in neighboring Iraq. For obvious reasons, these cultivated activists have not adhered to the Muslim Brotherhood principles and could also build rival groups, including al-Qa'ida affiliates.

As for the Jordanian Muslim Brotherhood, it is a legal group that uses peaceful methods and participates in elections through its political wing, the Islamic Action Front. It has at times cooperated with the monarchy, though recently its relationships have been strained by its show of sympathy for al-Qa'ida's leader in Iraq, Abu Mus'ab al-Zarqawi, which led to a regime crackdown on the Brotherhood in July 2006. The Brotherhood is not only restrained because of the fear of repression but also moderated by having a share of authority. It controls professional groups and other institutions. However, it also knows that the regime will never let it win the elections. Thus, the key element of its strategy is a willingness to remain permanently as a group that enjoys benefits and privileges but cannot take power or change the country.

While this proposition appeals to many Palestinians, the Jordanian Brotherhood also has a considerable East Bank membership and thus is not a communalist organization. Given the decline of the Palestinian Liberation Organization (PLO) and Fatah (i.e., Palestinian nationalism), the

Brotherhood could well become the main organization gaining loyalty from
Jordanian Palestinians.

The Egyptian Muslim Brotherhood is somewhere in between its two
counterparts. It is not technically legal but is allowed to function normally
most of the time. Leaders and activists are periodically arrested by the government to remind the Brotherhood that it can function only if the regime
finds its behavior satisfactory. Denied the right to have a party of its own,
however, the Muslim Brotherhood has found it easy to work with or even
virtually take over other parties, notably the Wafd in the 1980s, and it is even
willing to work with liberals to press the regime for concessions. In the 2005
elections, when the Brotherhood was allowed to run what amounted to its
own slate, it won 20 percent of the seats in parliament.[8] While it is incorrect
to say that the Egyptian Brotherhood has not been involved with violence—
and many factions have also left the Brotherhood to form terrorist groups—
the movement generally avoids it.

The case of Faraj Fawda is indicative of how the Brotherhood conducts
a culture war. Fawda was a liberal critic of the Islamists. In 1992, Fawda
debated with Brotherhood leader Muhammad al-Ghazali at the Cairo Book
Fair. Brotherhood members in the audience heckled Fawda. When Fawda
was murdered five months later by an Islamist, Ghazali testified at the trial,
saying that the killer had acted properly in killing an "apostate" like Fawda.
After being sentenced to execution, the defendant shouted: "Now I will die
with a clear conscience!"[9]

The Brotherhoods also played a key role in the Danish cartoon controversy. Qaradawi was a key person in spreading the protest movement. The
Egyptian Brotherhood demanded an apology for the publication and urged
a boycott of Danish products.[10] The Islamic Action Front organized a protest
demonstration in Amman.[11] They clearly saw this as a good issue on which
to build a broad base—defending Islam against alleged attacks on it in the
West. Abu Laban, the Danish Muslim cleric who played the leading role in
setting off the issue, himself has strong ties to the Muslim Brotherhood. The
controversy began when he visited Egypt to get the Muslim Brotherhood
network to take up the issue.

To carry out their operations, the Brotherhood groups are reasonably
well funded. Their money seems to come from four major sources. First,
rich adherents to the movements give donations. This is especially true of
Egyptians who emigrated to Saudi Arabia or Kuwait and became rich there.
One such Islamist Egyptian businessman is Hisham Tal'at Mustafa, who is
a partner of the Saudi billionaire Prince al-Walid ibn Talal al-Sa'ud. Second,
the Brotherhoods in Jordan and Egypt control professional and other associations from which funds can be drained for their cause. Third, in Egypt
at least, there are Islamic banks and enterprises—sometimes involved with
major corruption scandals—that are a source of money. Finally, in some
cases, there is international funding from various sources including the Saudi
state and Kuwaiti or Saudi charitable foundations that is passed through
the international organization. The Saudis and Kuwaitis involved are not

so much trying to use the Brotherhoods as state sponsors but rather merely ensuring that they do nothing inimical to Saudi or Kuwaiti interests.

Is the Muslim Brotherhood conducive to a dialogue with the United States, and if so, over what specific issues? If by dialogue what is meant is talking with American officials, the answer is generally yes. However, if what is meant is the possibility of American officials having any effect in changing Brotherhood positions through explanations and mutual understanding or to engage in negotiations that would lead to any cooperation, then the answer is "no."

The Islamic Front in Jordan says that holding such a dialogue is a decision that might be taken by any individual group. Dhunaybat has no objection to his Egyptian colleagues doing it, but notes thus:

> We in Jordan, however, believe that in terms of the situation in the Arab and Islamic world, particularly with regard to Afghanistan, Iraq, Palestine and its role in the region, America does not want a dialogue in which it can listen to others and change its policies. What we see is that it wants to dictate certain terms by promoting this so-called dialogue, which is like giving instructions. Therefore, I believe that there is no benefit in holding a dialogue with the people in charge of the U.S. policy.[12]

Yet, Dhunaybat also has no objection to the Islamic Action Front in Jordan—which his group largely controls—having a dialogue with the United States. This approach is clearly a division of labor in which the Brotherhood maintains the stance of an internationalist revolutionary group, while the Front, as a political party, can have such contacts if it aids its own interests.

There are some specific points on which the Brotherhoods want to influence the United States and think that doing so would be possible. These include the Egyptian Brotherhood's desire that the United States push harder for democratic elections and more civic rights in Egypt. While the Brotherhood would publicly denounce such issues as imperialistic, it does want to widen its sphere for public action. If elections were freer, the Brotherhood could win more seats. Indeed, some of its leaders believe it would win outright in free elections, though this is more doubtful. Of course, another goal of the Brotherhood is to win legal status as an organization.

Syria is clearly the most interesting case. Both the United States and the Syrian Brotherhood view the regime as an enemy. Would this be a case of the adage that the enemy of my enemy is my friend? The answer is likely yes. The Syrian Brotherhood is willing to talk about receiving covert support to fight the Syrian government. Indeed, since it is participating in a wider coalition of opposition groups, it could more easily excuse such a policy as going along with its partners.

It should be stressed, however, that this is a dangerous game. A stronger Syrian Brotherhood might be able to seize leadership of the 60 percent Sunni Arab population and take over the country, transforming Syria into an Islamic republic. Such an outcome could create far worse crises and threats to U.S. influence in the region. In addition, it should be noted that although the Muslim Brotherhoods in Egypt and Jordan are the largest Islamist factors in their respective countries, this is no longer necessarily true for their counterpart in Syria.

The Brotherhoods' view of the United States and its allies is profoundly hostile, especially their act of trying to take over the Middle East and destroy Islam. While they are passionately opposed to U.S. support for Israel, they are no happier with American support for the Egyptian and Jordanian regimes.

In terms of their analysis of and hostility toward the United States, there is not much difference between the Brotherhoods and al-Qa'ida, though their responses to this analysis are very different. One difference in analysis is that al-Qa'ida argues that American support is the main reason why Arab regimes survive. This legitimizes their priority on attacking the United States. The Brotherhoods have a more sophisticated understanding of the sources of power and support for regimes, though they overstate American influence and responsibility in their own countries.

The preceding analysis may seem to apply mainly to Egypt and Jordan. The Syrian Brotherhood has to deal with the fact of American hostility toward Damascus, though it no doubt has some belief in conspiracy theories that America and Damascus are actually secretly allied. At any rate, this does not make them any less anti-American. One response may be to argue that America is a great threat to Syria but that the Ba'thist regime is incapable of handling it and that only an Islamist government could do so victoriously.

Given these positions, the Brotherhoods' support for the Iraqi insurgency is not surprising. All three Brotherhoods have attacked the U.S. presence in Iraq in the most extreme terms and have called for supporting the insurgents. It should be remembered that even if the Brotherhood groups do not have institutional links to the insurgency leadership (which largely comes from al-Qa'ida); they are all Sunni Arab Islamists and in this case seem undisturbed by this distinction.[13]

When Zarqawi, a Jordanian himself, was killed, Zaki Sa'd, the leader of the Islamic Action Front, praised him but also distinguished the Brotherhood from al-Qa'ida in terms of their tactics. Zarqawi, he said, was acting not only legitimately but also as a Muslim must act in fighting the American forces in Iraq, and the Islamic Action Front supported these actions. Yet, it also denounced operations targeting innocent civilians. Zarqawi did not specifically mention Iraqis in this context but quoted the bloody bombing of hotels in Amman by al-Qa'ida forces as examples.[14]

The Brotherhoods have not directly organized units or sent members to Iraq, though it is probable that some of the Jordanians (but fewer of the Egyptians or Syrians) who go there might be rank-and-file members. After all, the leaders of all three groups have told them that fighting the Americans is an Islamic duty. It should also be noted, however, that contrary to al-Qa'ida, the Brotherhoods focus on fighting the American forces rather than the Iraqi Shi'a and the Kurds. For them, the battle in Iraq is against non-Muslims rather than an attempt to take over the country and defeat non-Arabs or non–Sunni Muslims there.[15]

In what direction, then, are the Brotherhood groups evolving? Each Muslim Brotherhood group faces a key question regarding its evolution. For the Egyptians, it is whether to continue in the phase of *da'wa*—recruiting, propagandizing, base-building, and accepting the limits the government places on it—or to move into a more activist phase—demanding political changes and being willing to confront the regime. Given the organization's current high level of confidence, as the younger generation takes over leadership and the government —especially during its transition under a new president—it could well push harder.

In Jordan, the movement faces the same options but is probably even more skewed to the side of caution. The choice it has to make is to either accept the limits of its current operation or push harder on elections and on a real parliamentary system in which the legislature can affect the monarch's policies and decisions. Especially important—and delicate—here is the communal relationship. The Brotherhood could become more dependent on Palestinian support, which would broaden its base while also making it more suspect the regime. It seems likely that caution will prevail.

As for Syria, the Brotherhood there faces the possibility of beginning an active revolutionary armed struggle to overthrow the regime, trying to use the unpopularity of the Alawite-dominated government (the Alawites are not even Muslims) to rouse the Sunni Arab majority to jihad. Given the weakness of the current Syrian leadership, its international isolation, and multiple problems—far greater than in Egypt and Jordan—it is quite possible that a major crisis would be seen by the Brotherhood as creating such a revolutionary situation. Yet, newer groups with stronger bases in Syria, or at least able to operate more freely there, might be the ones who gain most from this situation.

In terms of their stand on different issues, especially regarding international affairs, the Brotherhoods are fairly candid. Inasmuch as they conceal anything, it is to downplay their goal of an Islamist state in which they rule evade discussing specific points, such as the likely treatment of non-Muslims in a country they would rule. The cautious rhetoric of the Jordanian Muslim Brotherhood concerning domestic politics, the Syrian Brotherhood's willingness to participate in a broad anti-regime front, and the Egyptian Brotherhood's declarations of support for democracy all conceal their objectives of monopolizing power and transforming their societies.

Yet, this does not mean that these goals are not often discussed, even publicly. Sometimes, this is done indirectly. For example, such key Egyptian Brotherhood leaders as Salah Abu Isma'il and Muhammad al-Ghazali, and the then head of the organization Omar al-Tilmisani praised Sudan at a time when it had temporarily become an Islamist state.[16] They certainly endorsed the application of Muslim law, *Shari'a*, as the law of the land and have advocated this continually.[17]

In its March 2004 platform, the Egyptian Brotherhood stated:

> Our mission is to implement a comprehensive reform in order to uphold God's law in secular as well as religious matters.... Our only hope, if we wish to achieve any type of progress, is to adhere to our religion, as we used to, and to apply the Shari'a (Islamic law).[18]

In order to achieve this goal, the Brotherhood's mission "is to build a Muslim individual, a Muslim family and an Islamic rule to lead other Islamic states" On specific points, it explains, this means that the media's activities should be censored to conform with Islam's outlook, and the economic and political system should be structured likewise. Equally, the "focus of education," at least in the early years of schooling, "should be on learning the Koran by heart," and "women should only hold the kind of posts that would preserve their virtue." In parliament, Egyptian Brotherhood members have focused on trying to control the culture, with a great deal of indirect success.

The Brotherhood's former leader and guide Mamun al-Hudaybi explained that its purpose is to establish Islamic unity and an Islamic Caliphate, while former Supreme Guide Mustafa Mash'hur stated: "We accept the concept of pluralism for the time being; however, when we will have Islamic rule we might then reject this concept or accept it."[19]

Within the Brotherhood groups there are also examples of pluralism, most obviously in the Egyptian case. Similar to the parties based on Marxism, from the start the Brotherhood had a strategy built on the notion of stages. The first stage is base-building. Individuals and families are indoctrinated with proper thought and behavior, coming to constitute a society within the society based on *Shari'a*. This is the phase of *da'wa*, a historic Muslim word meaning spreading the faith but which here can be likened to mass- and cadre-organizing. As with Communist parties, the key question here too is when this phase should be turned into a revolutionary stage, where active measures are taken to seize state power.

The older leadership, which has a better memory of the massive regime repression during the period from the 1950s to 1980s, is more cautious. An example of this view is the current guide, top leader Muhammad Mahdi Akif, who joined the Brotherhood in 1948 and was imprisoned by the regime in the 1950s and 1960s.

Some of the younger and middle-aged members want a more energetic policy—of not using violence but pushing harder for elections, being more aggressive in demanding legalization, and eventually running a candidate for president. Their experience often comes from involvement in the Jama'at al-Islamiyya (Islamic Group) in the 1970s, a more militant organization that did extensive student and community organizing, after which some of its members joined the armed struggle of the 1990s.[20] Examples here include such Brotherhood leaders as Isam al-Aryan, head of the political bureau, and Abd al-Mun'im Abu al-Futuh.

One issue that has raised several disputes is the likely succession of leadership from President Husni Mubarak to his son Gamal. One view is to make a deal with the government in which the Brotherhood accepts this transition in exchange for legalization, an end to the emergency laws, and fairer elections; the other is to strongly criticize Gamal's becoming president.

In Syria, there are not any clear major differences within the Muslim Brotherhood. This, however, does not just reflect strength. Those who have different views are instead operating as independent Islamists or perhaps even thinking of turning to al-Qa'ida rather than joining the Brotherhood and expressing their positions in its ranks. It should be emphasized that for Syrians to join the Brotherhood today is a questionable decision because they could organize for Islamism far more freely as concealing their ultimate goals. In other words, the Syrian Brotherhood might come to be seen as an outdated organization of a previous generation, a phenomenon that is clearly not happening in Egypt (where the Brotherhood outlasted its younger rivals) or Jordan.

NOTES

1. *Ruz al-Yusuf,* January 28 to February 3, 2006.
2. For a history and analysis of Islamist movements in Egypt, see Barry Rubin, *Islamic Fundamentalism in Egyptian Politics,* 2nd revised edition (New York: Palgrave, 2002).
3. http://www.islah.300.org/vboard/showthread.php? t=120471, January 23, 2005s.
4. Al-Jazeera TV, February 6, 2005. View this statement at http://www.memritv. org/search.asp?ACT=S9&P1=534.
5. *Al-Sharq al-Awsat,* February 10, 2006.
6. Ibid.
7. *Al-Hayat,* January 16, 2001.
8. On the Brotherhood's participation in the debate over elections, see A. Shefa, "Towards the September 7 Presidential Elections in Egypt: Public Debate over the Change in the Electoral System," *Middle East Media Research Institute (MEMRI) Inquiry and Analysis Series,* no. 237, September 2, 2005, http:// memri.org/bin/articles.cgi?Page=archives&Area=ia&ID=IA23705.
9. On this and other issues in the struggle between Islamists and liberals, see Barry Rubin, *The Long War for Freedom: The Arab Struggle for Democracy in the Middle East* (New York: Wiley Press, 2005), pp. 1, 23–24.
10. *Times of London,* January 31, 2006.
11. *Gulf News,* February 11, 2006.
12. *Al-Sharq al-Awsat,* February 10, 2006.
13. For examples, see the documents translated in "The Muslim Brotherhood Movement in Support of Fighting Americans Forces in Iraq," *MEMRI Special Dispatch Series,* no. 776, September 3, 2004.
14. MEMRI TV, June 14, 2006, http://www.memritv.org/search.asp? ACT=S9&P1=1169.
15. See, for example, the interview with Humam Sa'id, assistant controller general of the Jordanian Muslim Brotherhood, in *al-Sharq al-Awsat,* August 7, 2004.

16. On these issues and on the Muslim Brotherhood as a parliamentary party, see Magdi Khalil, "Egypt's Muslim Brotherhood and Political Power: Would Democracy Survive?" *Middle East Review of International Affairs (MERIA) Journal*, vol. 9, no. 2 (June 2006), http://meria.idc.ac.il/journal/2006/issue1/jv10no1a3.html (accessed on December 3, 2009).
17. This point is discussed in Rubin, *Islamic Fundamentalism in Egyptian Politics*.
18. Ibid.
19. Ibid.
20. For a detailed history of this era and group, see Rubin, *The Long War for Freedom*.

2

YUSUF AL-QARADAWI: THE MUSLIM BROTHERS' FAVORITE IDEOLOGICAL GUIDE

Ana Belén Soage

Shaykh Yusuf al-Qaradawi has become a household name following his regular appearances on the religious program *Al-Shari'a wal-Hayat*, broadcast
weekly by satellite TV channel al-Jazeera. However, even before this Qatar-
based TV channel was launched in 1997, al-Qaradawi had been identified as
one of the key figures of Islamism, capable of drawing large crowds, of more
than a quarter million people.[1]

He is not only popular with the masses, but he is also held in high regard
among his peers. Mustafa al-Zarqa, a well-known Islamic scholar in his own
right, considered owning a copy of *Al-Halal wal-Haram fil-Islam* authored
by al-Qaradawi to be "the duty of every Muslim family."[2] Abu-l-Ala
al-Mawdudi described his yet another book *Fiqh al-Zaqa* as "the book of
this century in Islamic jurisprudence."[3] Extraordinarily prolific, al-Qaradawi
has written well over 100 books, has his own website in Arabic, and super-
vises Islam Online (bilingual English/Arabic). The website Qaradawi.net
boasts:

> Every contemporary Muslim has read one of his books, messages, articles or
> rulings [*fatwas*], or listened to one of his lectures, sermons, lessons, discus-
> sions or responses, either in a mosque, at university, in a club, on the radio, on
> television or on cassette.[4]

FROM POOR RURAL BOY TO INTERNATIONAL CELEBRITY

Al-Qaradawi's humble origins did not foreshadow his future renown.[5] He
was born in a small village in the Nile Delta in 1926. His father died when
he was only two, and he was brought up in the household of his paternal
uncle, a poor and pious tenant farmer. Young Yusuf soon proved his intelligence and tenacity and had memorized the Koran when he was nine. When
he finished primary school, his uncle tried to convince him to learn a trade,

but al-Qaradawi eventually persuaded his uncle to allow him to enroll at al-Azhar, which offered the only prospect of an education for boys of poor families. He first attended the Azhari institute in Tanta, the provincial capital, and then went on to Cairo to study at the teaching mosque al-Azhar itself. Diligent and hardworking, he invariably finished top of the class, which brought him modest monetary awards that supplemented his small income.

During Yusuf's first year in Tanta, an event changed the course of al-Qaradawi's life. One of his cousins took him to a lecture by Hasan al-Banna and, he recalls, "it was love 'at first word.' "[6] From then on, he would take every opportunity to listen to al-Banna's speeches and sermons, and he eventually became a member of the Muslim Brothers' Society. Al-Qaradawi paints an extremely idealized image of al-Banna, describing him when he addressed his followers: "He shined, as if his words were the Revelation, or a firebrand from the light of prophecy."[7] He exonerates of all the "mistakes" committed by the Brotherhood, such as the assassinations of Judge Ahmad al-Khazandar and Prime Minister Mahmud al-Nuqrashi; al-Qaradawi blames those attacks on the Society's secret organization, which, he argues, had got out of hand. Al-Qaradawi was caught in the wave of arrests that followed the murder of al-Nuqrashi and spent several months in prison. It was there that he learnt of al-Banna's assassination, on February 12, 1949. He remembers:

> While the Egyptian nation was overwhelmed with grief, people in the West—especially in Europe and the United States—celebrated what they deemed a happy occasion.... They knew more than anybody the worth of the man and his preaching, and the enormity of the danger he represented for them.[8]

Al-Qaradawi would be jailed again twice as member of the Muslim Brothers' Society: in 1954–1956 and in 1962. He was forbidden to preach in 1959. When he came out of prison in 1962, he was sent to Qatar to run al-Azhar University's center there. He established the Department of Islamic Studies at the Teacher Training College and, later, the Faculty of Islamic Law. In 1973, he obtained his doctorate from al-Azhar for his thesis on the role of zakat[9] in the resolution of social problems. He has been instrumental in the development of Islamic banking, now a multimillion dollar industry. He has also made regular appearances in the Qatari media, including al-Jazeera. In addition, he cofounded the European Council for Fatwa and Research (ECFR) in 1997 and the International Association of Muslim Scholars (IAMS) in 2004; he heads both these institutions.

Al-Qaradawi was a member of the Muslim Brothers' Society for several decades but claims to have left the organization because he sees himself as "the property of all Muslims, and not just of the Muslim Brothers."[10] However, his books are almost compulsory reading for the society's members, and, in 2002, he was offered the position of General Guide—an offer that he turned down. He even feels entitled to meddle in the society's internal affairs, as shown by his public support for the young Muslim Brothers who in the mid-1990s tried to set up a political party—Hizb al-Wasat—against the wishes of their leadership. Al-Qaradawi has arguably become the Muslims Brothers' main ideologue, and they guarantee that every work he publishes becomes an instant bestseller.

CONCERNS FOR ISLAM IN THE WEST

The ECFR and the IAMS promote the development of an Islamic jurisprudence adapted to the circumstances of contemporary Muslims to avoid the *Shari'a* (Islamic law) from becoming irrelevant. The fact that these associations are based in Europe reveals the Brotherhood's concerns for Muslim minorities living in the West and also a perception of the potential opportunities these rapidly growing minorities represent. In the launching ceremony of the IAMS in London, al-Qaradawi set the association's objectives as follows (translation provided by Islam Online):

1. Raising the awareness of Muslims about their religion.
2. Alarming [*sic*] the Muslims to the perils surrounding their religion and identity under the guise of carefully tailored terms like globalization and modernity.
3. Creating a generation equipped with unshakable belief to carry the Islamic torch.
4. Being a guiding light for all Muslims and finding optimal solutions to their problems.
5. Unifying the ranks of Muslim scholars when dealing with the nation's [*sic*[11]] major issues.
6. And acting in unison in the face of the nation's enemies by concentrating on common grounds and thrashing out differences.[12]

These objectives reflect a fear that Muslims—especially those living in the West—might gradually forsake their religion. Al-Qaradawi has dealt with this topic on more than one occasion. His first major work, *Al-Halal wal-Haram fil-Islam*, was commissioned by al-Azhar in order to answer the dilemmas confronting Muslims living in the West and has been translated into several languages; its English title is *The Lawful and the Prohibited in Islam*. More recently, the Saudi-financed Muslim World League asked him to write *Fi Fiqh al-Aqalliyat al-Muslima* (*On the Jurisprudence of Muslim Minorities*) for the same purpose.

While radical Islamists traditionally have insisted that it is forbidden for Muslims to live in the "abode of war"—that is, in non-Muslim lands[13]—al-Qaradawi sees it as a positive development. He contends that "that powerful West, which has come to rule the world, should not be left to the influence of the Jews alone." Furthermore, the Muslim presence encourages new conversions to Islam.[14] In fact, the *shaykh* is convinced that the whole of

Europe will eventually convert to Islam because Islam only offers salvation from "materialism" and "promiscuity."[15]

An advocate of *ijtihad*—the *ulama*'s independent reasoning based on the Koran and traditions about Islam's founder—al-Qaradawi insists on the flexibility and leniency of Islam, which dictates that the particular circumstances of the believers should always be borne in mind.

Two of his rulings in relation to Muslims living in the West illustrate this point. In normal circumstances, Muslims are not supposed to deal with Western banks because their operations are based on interest, which is considered usury (*riba*) in Islam. However, owning a house is a necessity, and often the only way to afford buying one is to take a loan from one of those banks. In this case, necessity converts a normally forbidden act into one that is acceptable.[16]

The second example concerns converts. Based on a prophetic tradition (*hadith*), all four orthodox legal schools of Islamic law (*madhahib*, sing. *madh'hab*)[17] dictate that a Muslim cannot inherit from a non-Muslim and vice versa. Nevertheless, al-Qaradawi prefers to rely on the view of scholars who argued that the non-Muslim referred to in that tradition is the adversarial non-Muslim and have consequently ruled that converts can legitimately inherit from their non-Muslim parents.[18]

IS ISLAM "UNDER THREAT"?

The objectives of the IAMS allude to the oft-repeated claim that Islam and its *umma* (the community of believers) face a series of threats. Al-Qaradawi develops that theme in some detail in works like *Ummatu-na Bayna Qarnayn* (*Our Community Between Two Centuries*) and *A'da al-Hall al-Islami* (*The Enemies of the Islamic Solution*),[19] in which he identifies the following challenges: clinging to the *umma*'s Islamic identity in the face of Western pressures[20]; keeping Islam as the main reference and carrying its message to non-Muslims; getting out of the "prison of backwardness" the *umma* is locked into, by overhauling the education system and encouraging creativity; achieving social justice through the distribution of *zakat*[21]; finding the right equilibrium in relation to the status of women, without oppressing them nor giving them free rein "to do as they please"[22]; substituting elected governments for the tyrannies that rule the Muslim world, thus realizing "the spirit of the *shura*" (consultation)[23]; and o above all, "recharging" the *umma*'s faith and morality.[24] As he puts it:

> The umma will not advance thanks to the frivolous, the degenerates, the drunkards, the drug traffickers or the traders in stale and contaminated food-stuffs. Nay, it will advance with the help of the pure of heart who stay in the straight path—and those are the people of the faith.[25]

However, these challenges seem nothing when compared to the three "major threats" that face the *umma*: Zionism, disintegration, and globalization. Zionism is the most dangerous threat, says al-Qaradawi, who claims it pursues a twin strategy of the creation of Greater Israel and the normalization of relations with its Arab neighbors,[26] goals that seem somewhat contradictory.

Regarding disintegration, he urges all the forces of the *umma*—Muslims and Christians; Sunnis and Shi'a; Arab nationalists and Islamists; rich and poor; proprietors and tenants; rulers and subjects—to stand together in the face their common enemies: the Zionists, crusaders, idolaters, communists, and others.[27]

As for the threat of globalization, he asserts that it means "[t]he imposition of American political, economic, cultural and social supremacy over the rest of the world"[28] and contrasts this perceived neocolonial model to Islam's universal message, which, he says, dictates equality between all men on the basis of human dignity and responsibility, "for they all partake in their worship of God."[29]

Al-Qaradawi shares with radical Islamists the conviction that the West fears and hates Islam because it represents a potential threat to the hegemony of the West. During his frequent bouts of populism, he denounces global conspiracies against the Muslim religion.[30] However, the *shaykh* attributes Western hostility to ignorance and is convinced that better knowledge of Islam would lead to admiration of the religion, and even conversion of people to Islamic faith.[31] A firm advocate of interreligious dialogue, he stresses that "the Koran orders us to concentrate on what we share, not on what we differ, striving for understanding, because we all believe in monotheism and in the divine messages revealed by God."[32] In addition, dialogue provides a forum in which to proselytize, which is an obligation for Muslims.[33]

However, yet another reason to talk to people of other faiths is "to form a united front against the enemies of faith, preachers of atheism and licentiousness, supporters of materialism, advocates of nudism, sexual promiscuity, abortion, homosexuality and same-sex marriages."[34] The *shaykh* remembers with fondness the alliance of al-Azhar, the Muslim World League, Iran, and the Vatican during the UN Conferences on Population (Cairo, 1994) and Women (Beijing, 1995).[35]

This leads him to discuss yet another "danger" threatening the Muslim world: secularism. Al-Qaradawi writes that "positive law entered our countries like the Jews entered Palestine: infiltrating on the sly."[36] He argues that although the separation of religion and state might have been necessary in the West, where the church constituted an obstacle to progress, this was never the case in the Muslim world, where the "imposition" of secularism "forces Islam to bear the burden of a history that is not its history, of an *umma* that is not its *umma*, in a land that is not its land, resulting from circumstances it did not live."[37]

He often attacks Muslim secularists, presenting them as an elite rejected by the people for not sharing their creed and values.[38] He denounces that "some Arab and Muslim secularists are following the U.S. government by advocating the kind of reform that will disarm the nation from the elements of strength that are holding our people together,"[39] that is, religious values. In the prologue to *Tarikhu-na al-Muftara Alay-hi* (*Our Slandered History*), he says he wrote the book as a response to "the secularists who oppose the *Shari'a* and want us to import our values, notions, laws and traditions from the West."[40] He describes them as "the enemies of the *umma*...who want to destroy its historical memory...and if they can't destroy [it], they try to distort it."[41]

A final threat to Islam that has already been alluded to is communism. The importance of communism is after the collapse of the Soviet Union, but for decades it was a constant topic in al-Qaradawi's writings. In the early 1970s, he borrowed the concept of the "inevitability of communism" from historical materialism and started a series on the "inevitability of the Islamic solution" (*hatmiyyat al-hall al-islami*). He seeks to expose the contradictions of communism and attacks its materialist conception of existence, moral relativism, and tyranny. He portrays communism as another form of colonialism and another "crusading" trick to influence Muslims to deviate from Islam in order to destroy them.[42]

In his memoirs, he recalls that in the Tur prison, where he was being held, there was a separate wing for the communists. He described their "dry, soulless, hopeless, selfish life," the result of losing "the light of the faith and the soul that believes in God and in the next life."[43] Furthermore, he claims that Islam preceded communism in championing the poor, through the institution of *zakat*.[44] He even speculates that if Marx had had the opportunity to know Islam he might have found in it what he was looking for.[45] He also argues that it was the Jews who introduced communism to the Arab world, for "it is well known that communism is the scion of Judaism,"[46] which leads us to the thorny issue of antisemitism.

The *shaykh's* attitude toward the Jews is rather ambiguous. On the one hand, he insists that the dispute with them is over land, and not religion, and that the Koranic verses that imprecate them should be interpreted in their historical context (i.e., the Jewish tribes' betrayal of Muhammad).[47] He even stresses that Judaism is the closest religion to Islam.[48] However, he also equates Judaism with Zionism, when he exhorts Muslims to think: "If every Jew in the world is mobilized for Israel, why do Muslims not mobilize for Palestine, the al-Aqsa mosque, and all the important questions that demand our unity?"[49]

Elsewhere, he accuses the Jews of destroying the caliphate because it hindered the establishment of Israel[50] and refers to the Jewish state as "the usurper Zionist entity" and "the parasitic intruder."[51] He supports suicide attacks against Israeli civilians—or, rather, he thinks of Israel as a militarized society in which everyone is either a soldier or a reservist[52]—and dubs the terrorist attacks of Hamas and Islamic Jihad "heroic acts of martyrdom."[53]

WHAT ABOUT ISLAMIST TERRORISM?

The reader would have noticed that Islamic terrorism is nowhere to be seen among the challenges identified by al-Qaradawi. He does deal with the topic, by gently chastising those he views as having developed their own interpretations of the sacred texts, comparing them to someone who ventures into the sea without being a good swimmer.[54] He expresses concern for their frequent use of excommunication (*takfir*), which justifies violence against those who do not share their view of Islam.[55] He contends that if someone deserves punishment for their beliefs, that punishment is not for humans but for God to mete out, on the Judgment Day.[56] However, he refers to the radicals as "youth" in need of guidance and justifies their violence as arising out of the failure of the Muslim societies to adhere to Islam. Even intercommunal violence, rife in Egypt in the late 1980s and early 1990s, is attributed to such a failure, as some Muslims blame it on the Coptic minority.[57]

In a work, first published in 1982, and, which by 2001 had already gone through twelve editions, al-Qaradawi wrote:

> We must be brave and recognize that our behavior has contributed to pushing those youths to what we dub "extremism." We pretend to be Muslims but fail to implement Islam. We read the Koran but do not execute its rulings. We profess to love the Prophet but do not follow his example. We write in our constitutions that the state's religion is Islam but do not give it the place it merits in government, legislation and orientation. [...] We should start by reforming ourselves and our society according to God's commands before we demand from our young people serenity, good sense, calm and restraint.[58]

Moreover, al-Qaradawi attacks the critics of the radicals as people who "do not live for Islam, are not concerned by the problems of the *umma*...[and] only care for their own interests." He urges them to come down from the ivory tower to get to know those "youth": "Their huge hopes, their warm feelings, their sincere determination, their noble intentions, and their good actions."[59] He also criticizes the official *ulema* (Islamic scholars) for their submission to the political establishment, which has cost them the respect of the Islamist youth.[60] He accuses "the forces inimical to the triumph of Islam" of using radicalism as an excuse to target the whole of the Islamist movement, instigate clashes between the different Islamist forces, alienate the population from the Islamist project, and discourage the Islamists from continuing their fight.[61]

After the first Word Trade Center bombing in 1993, the massacre at Luxor, Egypt, and also the attacks on the U.S. embassies in Kenya and Tanzania, al-Qaradawi continued to make excuses for Islamic terrorism and seemed reluctant to admit to the size of the problem:

> There are amongst Muslims a few individuals or groups that use violence indiscriminately. Still, they do not represent all Muslims, but are small groups whose importance has been inflated by the Western media—and most of them were pushed to extremism by the West's injustices, aggression and iniquity against Muslims, and its continuous support of Israel.[62]

Al-Qaradawi justifies his reluctance to condemn the Islamist radicals by citing his desire to "build instead of destroying, unite instead of separating."[63]

To that, we could add that he shares many of their objectives. A number of authors have noted that "the frontier between 'radical' and 'moderate' Islamism is often elusive or porous,"[64] and al-Qaradawi himself has been accused of "resorting to the same dualisms as bin Ladin."[65] The *shaykh* indicates a difference in strategy, not in aims, when he reproaches the Islamist youth for not following the example of Muhammad, who, before he fled for Medina, used to pray in a Ka'ba full of idols because the Muslims were still unprepared to confront the polytheists; only when they returned to Mecca triumphantly did he destroy those idols.[66]

THE ISLAMIC AWAKENING

The distinction between moderate and radical Islamists first appeared in the Egypt of the 1970s as one of the consequences of the Islamic awakening (*al-sahwa al-islamiyya*). The Muslim Brothers, after a period in prison or exile that lasted from the mid-1950s to the early 1970s, were allowed to recover their place as the largest civil society organization in the country.[67] A significant number of Brothers who had sought asylum in Saudi Arabia or other Gulf countries returned to Egypt with plenty of petrodollars and a rigorous version of Islam, which, nonetheless, did not challenge the status quo. Instead, they pursued legal means—notably elections and lobbying—to impose a rigid Islamic morality gradually. However, the awakening also led to the proliferation of small groups of radicals—many of them former Muslim Brothers disenchanted with the transformation. These Brothers, mostly young and from a poor background, had no stake in the system and preferred to change it by a variety of means, including violence.

The Islamic awakening is attributed to a general disenchantment with Arab socialism: its despotism, corruption, poor economic performance, and, finally, defeat in the Six Day War. Furthermore, after the death of Nasser, Sadat courted the Islamists to marginalize Nasserists and communists, who were opposed to his realignment with the West. Al-Qaradawi, himself one of the main figures in the awakening, concedes that the abovementioned factors may have contributed to it, but he contends that its most important cause was the *umma*'s divine origin and mission:

> The main feature of our *umma* is to be awakened by Islam and for Islam. [...]
> [T]his *umma* has been hit by serious crises[68] from the beginning of its history
> [...] but [it] has always been able to overcome internal weakness and external
> aggression, to turn defeat into victory and to generate strength out of weakness,
> unity out of division, and a giant body out of scattered limbs.[69]

Al-Qaradawi explains that both the liberal and the socialist alternatives have proven their ineffectiveness and that Muslims have realized that only their faith can save them.[70] To those skeptics who claim that the Islamic awakening has failed because the Muslim world is still overwhelmingly ruled by secular, authoritarian regimes, al-Qaradawi responds by stating that the state is not the sole objective of Islamists and lists the progress the awakening has achieved. In the political domain, *jihad* was revived in Afghanistan and among the Palestinians, and the *Shi'a* in southern Lebanon and also in Chechnya. Two Islamist countries were established: Iran and Sudan.[71] In the social domain, the young, who had previously imitated the West "like monkeys," returned to the religion, and women started to wear the *hijab* (headscarf) again; and in the economic domain, an Islamic sector was set up—although on this point, the *shaykh* admits that there is room for improvement.[72]

The *shaykh* believes that, given the choice, Muslim people would choose the Islamic model[73] and that the main hindrance in the way of Islam is the political establishment.[74] He writes that a rift has occurred between the people, who continue to follow Islam, and the "hypocritical" rulers, who pretend to be Muslims but, in reality, believe in secularism and positive law.[75] He contrasts the fervor of the Muslim people—the youth who go to fight *jihad*, the women who donate their wedding rings to Islamic NGOs, the preachers who pray for their fellow Muslim fighters and curse the Jews, the Serbs, the Hindus, and the Russians—to the indifferent attitude of most Muslim rulers, who yield to foreign pressures in order to serve their own interests.[76] However, this view rather restrained compared to what he was writing back in the 1980s:

> The rulers, whom God has entrusted with responsibility over the Muslim people, walk down a valley that is not the valley of Islam. They form alliances with whoever challenges God and challenge whoever forms alliances with God. They approach those who have walked away from God and walk away from those who have approached God. They promote whoever has degraded Islam and degrade whoever has promoted Islam.... And they only remember Islam during [religions] celebrations, pretending before their peoples, laughing right in their faces![77]

THE ISLAMIC STATE

State power is not the only objective of the Islamists, but it is their final goal, the culmination of a process of gradual Islamization of society (for the moderates) or of armed struggle (for the radicals). They consider an Islamic government necessary to spread the teachings of Islam and implement its law. Surprisingly, al-Qaradawi contends that an Islamic state government is civil, not religious. It is based on elections, homage to the ruler (*bay'a*), and consultation of the *umma* (*shura*), and the ruler cannot do as he pleases but is constrained by *Shari'a*. In addition, he is supervised by the people, to whose advice he must heed to and who may depose him if he deviates from Islam.[78]

The fact that such an ideal regime has never actually existed in Muslim history does not seem to bother the *shaykh*. He urges all believers to play their role in the establishment of the Islamic state if they want to avoid dying a pagan death,[79] like that of the polytheists before the Revelation.

The Islamists aspire to the model of state established by Muhammad and his immediate successors, the "Rightly-Guided Caliphs": Abu Bakr (caliph from 632 to 634 AD), Umar bin al-Khattab (634–644 AD), Uthman bin Affan (644–656 AD), and Ali bin Abi Talib (656–661 AD). Of course, those men were only human, and the account of their rule as peddled by the Islamists has been extremely sanitized.[80] Yet, their example does not provide much guidance: every one of them became a caliph in a different way, so there is no "religious" reason to prefer elections over other options, such as appointment, to choose the leader.

When they asked for advice—which was not very often—they did not necessarily heed to it. The last two Rightly Guided Caliphs were assassinated by fellow Muslims in an atmosphere of civil war, which shows tensions within the *umma* from its very beginning. To sum up, the first Muslim state was not as perfect as the Islamists would lead us to believe—and if it did not even work with Muhammad's revered companions, how could it work now, more than a thousand years later?

Nevertheless, Hasan al-Banna argued that the Islamic model had been "tested by history, when it created the strongest, the most virtuous, the most merciful, the most pious, and the most blessed of *ummas*."[81] Furthermore, he wrote that Muslims had waged humane wars, aimed at civilizing and exalting the truth.[82] Sayyid Qutb, who was the main ideologue of the Muslim Brothers' Society from the early 1950s until his execution in 1966, similarly wrote that the aim of the Muslim conquests had been to eliminate the obstacles in the way of Islam[83]: the territories occupied were "conquered for freedom, light and joy,"[84] and the blessing of the first period of Islam "lasted for a thousand years."[85]

Al-Qaradawi likewise maintains that the objective of the Islamic conquests was to carry the message of Islam to the vanquished, "so they could choose for themselves."[86] He also insists—against historical evidence—that *Shari'a* was the exclusive point of reference for all Muslims, rulers and ruled, for thirteen centuries—until their lands were colonized by the West.[87] Under the influence of the latter, the Muslims abandoned their faith so God abandoned them, and they lost Palestine, just as in the past as they had lost al-Andalus.[88]

One of the most notorious aspects of *Shari'a* is the physical penalties known as the *hudud*—the punishments meted out to those who have overstepped the "limits" set by God: amputation for theft, stoning for adultery, flogging for drinking alcohol, and the like. Al-Qaradawi defends the *hudud*, explaining that the alternative—prison—is a school of crime, and that, in any case, an Islamic society would prevent the temptation to offend by providing everything people might need.[89] He criticizes the Western focus on the *hudud*, which he attributes to a capitalist philosophy that puts the rights of the individual—in this case, the criminal—before those of society.[90] Furthermore, he describes the return to *Shari'a* as "both a religious and a national [*qawmi*] reaffirmation" because it means getting rid of what remains of colonialism in the legislative domain.[91]

However, *Shari'a* is not just the *hudud*; according to the Islamists, *hudud* provides all that is necessary to deal with any situation. Hasan al-Banna's main contribution to Islamism was precisely the conception of Islam as a comprehensive system (*nizam shamil*),[92] and the idea has been frequently reasserted by al-Qaradawi:

> [Islam] is, by himself, a comprehensive school [of thought], a creed, an ideology, and cannot be satisfied but by [completely] controlling society and directing all aspects of life, from how to enter the toilet to the construction of the state and the establishment of the caliphate. No Muslim who believes that Islam is the word of God can conceive that this great religion will ever accept being a mere appendix to socialism or any other ideology.[93]

Or, more recently, in the al-Jazeera program *Al-Shari'a wal-Hayat*:

> We believe in the totality of Islam. Islam is not only spirituality. Islam is religion and world, missionary work and temporal power, creed and law, rectitude and strength. Islam is industry and agriculture. Islam is art. Islam is in everything.[94]

Al-Qaradawi argues that this "totality" of Islam means that it cannot be implemented in a piecemeal fashion. He asserts that if somebody believes in 99 percent of Islam but fails to believe in the remaining 1 percent, he cannot be considered a Muslim.[95] Of course, such a comprehensive system includes politics. In one of his theological works, the *shaykh* explains that the Koran provides the general principles of government, whereas the prophetic Sunna is the commentary of the sacred book and shows how it should be interpreted.[96] As we have seen, al-Qaradawi has identified *itjihad* as the procedure by which Islam can respond to the challenges of the present age. He has also criticized the blind imitation of the rulings of any particular school of jurisprudence.

This stance was controversial, even revolutionary, when first advocated by Jamal al-Din al-Afghani and Muhammad Abduh but has long since become the orthodox position. The principles of *takhayyur* (selection) and *talfiq* (combination), which consist of choosing and combining the rulings better adapted to the modern world regardless of the legal school they hail from, were used in the mid-twentieth century to modernize the juridical systems of the Muslim world—particularly in the field of family law, which remains the province of Shari'a.[97]

By contrast, there is no possibility of "updating" rulings present in the Koran, which al-Qaradawi describes as "the book of all time, of all humanity, of all religion, of all truth"—contrary to the books of the "time-limited religions," such as Judaism and Christianity,[98] whose message was superseded by Islam. He therefore criticizes those for whom certain Koranic precepts are no longer relevant, forcefully stating: "We must vigorously resist those insolent attempts against God that pretend to strip the Koran of its quality of eternal."[99]

AL-QARADAWI, A MODERATE?

In 2003, the RAND Corporation, a U.S. think tank often consulted by the American government, published a report on "Civil Democratic Islam"[100] in which al-Qaradawi was identified as a "reformist traditionalist, who takes a relatively progressive stance on many social issues but is aggressive on the issue of 'Islamic' foreign policy."[101] *Al-Shari'a wal-Hayat* devoted a whole program to the report, during which al-Qaradawi dismissed the label of "reformist traditionalist" as a contradiction in.[102]

For good measure, he has proposed his own classification of the Islamist movement by identifying four trends: the excommunicatory (*tayyat al-takfir*); the inflexible (*tayyar al-jumud wal-tashaddud*); the violent (*tayyar al-unf*); and, finally, the moderate (*tayyar al-wasatiyya*).[103] Needless to say, he belongs to the last of these trends. Nothing more is needed to testify al-Qaradawi's influence in Islamist circles than the fact that since he adopted the term *wasatiyya* as his catchword in the early 1990s, it has almost become a cliché.[104] Even the radicals have sought to claim it for themselves.[105] However, the *shaykh* is the undisputed leader of the *wasatiyya* movement and has been dubbed its "spiritual father."[106]

The term *wasatiyya* comes from the Koran in which it is written that God announced to Muslims: "Thus, we have appointed you a middle community [*ummatan wasatan*], that ye may be witnesses against mankind, and that the messenger may be a witness against you" (Koran 2:143). It has been adopted to refer to a "middle way," a moderate version of Islam. Al-Qaradawi's definition of the term is interesting because it shows how he sees himself:

> [*Wasatiyya*] is the balance between mind and the Revelation, matter and spirit, rights and duties, individualism and collectivism, inspiration and commitment, the Text [i.e. the Koran and the Sunna] and personal interpretation [*ijtihad*], the ideal and reality, the permanent and the transient, relying on the past and looking forward to the future.[107]

That balance—which the Muslim Brothers have incorporated into their discourse—accounts for al-Qaradawi's popularity; it is no coincidence that the young Brothers who sought to establish a party in 1996 called it Hizb al-Wasat, the "middle-way party." The *shaykh* offers conservatism without rigidity and combines pragmatism with idealism. He represents the reassurance of tradition while at the same time helping Muslims to adjust to the demands of the modern world. His conspiracy theories offer a comforting explanation for the sorry state of "the best community that hath been raised up for mankind" (Koran 3:110). His occasionally messianic tone gives hope to a deeply religious people for whom daily life is often a struggle. He is supported by the establishment because he does not seek to "rock the boat" just like the Muslim Brothers that look up to him.

NOTES

1. Raymond W. Baker, "Invidious Comparisons: Realism, Postmodern Globalism, and Centrist Islamic Movements in Egypt," in: John L. Esposito (ed.), *Political Islam: Revolution, Radicalism or Reform?* (Cairo: The American University in Cairo Press, 1997), p. 125.
2. Al-Qaradawi Net, "Al-Sira al-Tafsiliyya lil-Qaradawi," November 24, 2004, http://www.qaradawi.net/site/topics/article.asp? cu_no=2&item_no=1221&version=1&template_id=190&parent_id=189 (accessed January 6, 2008).
3. Ibid.
4. Ibid.
5. The biographical information that follows is available at http://www.qaradawi.net/site/topics/index.asp?cu_no=2&lng=0&template_id=189&temp_type=41&parent_id and http://www.islamonline.net/Arabic/personality/index.shtml (accessed January 9, 2008).
6. Yusuf al-Qaradawi, "Durus Fiqhiyya fil-Qarya: Al-Taysir Mabda'-i Mundhu al-Bawakir," Islam Online, http://www.islamonline.net/Arabic/personality/2001/12/article5.SHTML (accessed January 4, 2008).
7. Ibid.
8. Yusuf al-Qaradawi, "Ightiyal Hasan al-Banna: Araha al-a'da Kathiran wa-alamuna Akthar," Islam Online, http://www.islamonline.net/Arabic/personality/2001/12/article9.SHTML#5 (accessed January 9, 2008). The claim of celebrations in the West following al-Banna's assassination seems to have originated with Sayyid Qutb, who was studying in the United States at the time.
9. The *zakat* is the percentage of their income Muslims should pay to finance charity for the poor or projects of interest to the community (e.g., mosques, orphanages).
10. Yusuf al-Qaradawi, *Al-Ikhwan al-Muslimun: 70 Aman fil-Da'wa wal-Tarbiyya wal-Jihad* (Cairo: Maktabat Wahba, 1999), p. 287; *Nahnu wal-Gharb: As'ila Sha'ika wa-Ajwiba Hasima* (Cairo: Dar al-Tawzi wal-Nashr al-Islamiyya, 2006), p. 206.
11. We assume that the term "nation" here is a translation of the Arabic *umma*, which designates the community of believers.
12. Al-Qaradawi, quoted in Ali al-Halawani and Hany Mohammad, "Scholars Launch pan-Muslim Body in London," Islam Online, July 12, 2004, http://www.islamonline.net/English/News/2004–07/12/article01.shtml (accessed on January 10, 2008). See also "Al-Ittihsd al-Alamī li-Ulama al-Muslimin," *Al-Shari'a wal-Hayat,* Al-Jazeera, July 4, 2004, http://www.aljazeera.net/channel/archive/archive? ArchiveId=95379 (accessed on January 10, 2008)
13. The medieval ulema divided the world into two areas: the territories in Muslim hands were *Dar al-Islam*, "the abode of Islam"; all the rest was *Dar al-Harb*, "the abode of war." Later, some authors introduced a third concept to name those territories with which the Muslim state had signed temporary treaties of nonaggression: *Dar al-Sulh* or *Dar al-Ahd*, "the abode of truce" or "the abode of covenant."

14. Yusuf al-Qaradawi, *Fi Fiqh al-Aqalliyyat al-Muslima: Hayat al-Muslimin Wasat al-Mujtamaat al-Ukhra* (Cairo: Dar al-Shuruq, 2005), pp. 33–34.
15. "Sheik Yousuf al-Qaradhawi: Islam's 'Conquest of Rome' Will Save Europe from its Subjugation to Materialism and Promiscuity," *MEMRI*, July 28, 2007, http://www.memritv.org/clip_transcript/en/1592.htm (accessed January 9, 2008); the author thanks Barry Rubin for pointing out that resource. See also Yusuf al-Qaradawi, *Ayna al-Khalal?* (Cairo: Dar al-Sahwa, 1985), p. 93 and *Hawla Qadaya al-Islam wal-Asr* (Cairo: Makabat al-Wahba, 1992), p. 168, where al-Qaradawi describes the "wretchedness" of people in the West.
16. *Fi Fiqh al-Aqalliyyat al-Muslima*, p. 45.
17. There are four legal schools in Sunni Islam: the *Hanafi*, the *Shafi'i*, the *Maliki*, and the *Hanbali*. The differences between them are minor, and they recognize each other as orthodox.
18. *Fi Fiqh al-Aqalliyyat al-Muslima*, pp. 58–59.
19. Yusuf al-Qaradawi, *Ummatu-na Bayna Qarnayn* (Cairo: Dar al-Shuruq, 2000), pp. 169ff; *A'da al-Hall al-Islami* (Cairo: Maktabat al-Wahba, 2000).
20. For Islamists like al-Qaradawi, Eastern Christians are part of the *umma* because, if for Muslims Islam is creed and law, for Christians living in the abode of Islam, it is culture and civilization; see Yusuf al-Qaradawi, *Kayfa Nata'amil ma al-Qur'an al-Azim* (Cairo: Dar al-Shuruq, 2000), p 125.
21. Al-Qaradawi describes zakat—which is normally fixed at 2.5 percent of annual income—as one of the instruments to redistribute wealth, but he does not mention any other; *Ummatu-na Bayna Qarnayn*, p. 174.
22. Ibid. p. 176; see also *Hawla Qadaya al-Islam wal-Asr*, pp. 166–168. Elsewhere, the *shaykh* insists that the privileges of men have over women in Islam are justified. They should be the head of the household because they are more rational than women, and they should inherit twice as much because they face more financial responsibilities. See *Kayfa Nata'amil ma al-Qur'an al-azim*, p. 64.
23. Following the lead of Islamic modernists like Jamal al-Din al-Afghani and Muhammad Abduh, mainstream Islamists interpret the *shura* as an early version of democracy. See Yusuf al-Qaradawi, *Al-Islam Kama Nu'min bi-hi: Dawabit wa-Malamih* (Giza: Nahdat Misr, 1999), pp. 44–45; *Ummatu-na Bayna Qarnayn*, p. 177.
24. *Ummatu-na Bayna Qarnayn*, p. 177.
25. *Al-Islam Kama Nu'min bi-hi*, p. 178.
26. Ibid. pp. 180ff.
27. Ibid. pp. 199ff; see also Yusuf al-Qaradawi, *Al-Sahwa al-Islamiyya Bayna al-Juhud wal-Tatarruf* (Cairo: Dar al-Shuruq, 2001[1982]), pp. 94–95 (where he writes of "the hellish triangle" formed by Jews, Crusaders, and communists); *Hawla Qadaya al-Islam wal-Asr*, p. 116.
28. *Ummatu-na Bayna Qarnayn*, p. 232.
29. Ibid. pp. 231–32.
30. For example, Yusuf al-Qaradawi, *Al-Thaqafa al-Arabiyya al-Islamiyya Bayna al-Asala wal-Mu'asira* (Cairo: Maktabat Wahba, 1994), pp. 172ff; *Al-Sahwa al-Islamiyya min al-Murahaqa ila al-Rushd* (Cairo: Dar al-Shuruq, 2002), pp. 340–343; *Al-Sahwa al-Islamiyya Bayna al-Juhud wal-Tatarruf*, pp. 91–95; *Hawla Qadaya al-Islam wal-Asr*, pp. 46–47. See also Al-Shari'a wal-Hayat, "Al-Muslimun wal-Unf al-Siyasi," Al-Jazeera, May 23, 2004, http://www.

aljazeera.net/channel/archive/archive?ArchiveId=92972 (accessed January 10, 2008).

31. Al-Qaradawi Net, "Al-Qaradawi: 'Lam Ad'u li-l-'unf wa-Nushaddid ala-l-Ghadb al-Aqil,'" February 11, 2006, http://www.qaradawi.net/site/topics/article. asp?cu_no=2&item_no=4161&version=1&template_id=104&parent_id=15 (accessed January 10, 2008).

32. *Ummatu-na Bayna Qarnayn*, p. 244. See also "Al-Hiwar al-Islami al-Masihi," *Al-Shari'a wal-Hayat*, Al-Jazeera, June 20, 2004, http://www.aljazeera.net/channel/archive/archive?ArchiveId=94477; "Hiwar al-Adyan," Al-Jazeera, November 4, 2001, http://www.aljazeera.net/channel/archive/archive? ArchiveId=90035 (both accessed on January 10, 2008).

33. *Fi Fiqh al-Aqalliyyat al-Muslima*, p. 67.

34. Ibid.

35. Ibid. p. 69; see also *Ummatu-na Bayna Qarnayn*, p. 233 and "Hiwar al-Adyan."

36. Yusuf al-Qaradawi, *Bayyanat al-Hall al-Islami wa-Shubuhat al-Almaniyyin wal-Mutagharribin* (Cairo: Matkabat al-Wahba, 1988), p. 183.

37. *Al-Sahwa al-Islamiyya Bayna al-Juhud wal-Tatarruf*, p. 88; see also *Al-Thaqafa al-Arabiyya al-Islamiyya*, pp. 169–170. Of course, the *ulema* were not always as tolerant of science as the shaykh contends, but their record is without a doubt better than that of the Catholic Church.

38. Yusuf al-Qaradawi, *Taqafatuna Bayna al-Infitah wal-Inghilaq* (Cairo: Dar al-Shuruq, 2000), p. 64.

39. Quoted in "Reform According to Islam," Al-Jazeera Net, December 19, 2004, http://english.aljazeera.net/English/archive/archive?ArchiveId=3779 (accessed on January 12, 2008).

40. Yusuf al-Qaradawi, *Tarikhu-na al-Muftara Alay-hi* (Cairo: Dar al-Shuruq, 2006), p. 8; see also *A'da al-Hall al-Islami*, pp. 164–166.

41. *Tarikhu-na al-Muftara Alay-hi*, p. 9.

42. *A'da al-Hall al-Islami*, pp. 131–133.

43. Yusuf al-Qaradawi, "Dhikrayat al-Mu'taqal," Islam Online, http://www.islamonline.net/Arabic/personality/2001/12/article10.SHTML (accessed on January 10, 2008).

44. *Al-Islam Kama Nu'min bi-hi*, p. 42.

45. *A'da al-Hall al-Islami*, pp. 135–136.

46. Ibid. pp. 109ff, 132. Yusuf al-Qaradawi, "Min al-Tur li-Hightep: Rihla Qasya la Tunsa," Islam Online, http://www.islamonline.net/Arabic/personality/2001/12/article11.SHTML (accessed on January 10, 2008).

47. "Ilaqat al-Muslimin bi-l-Yahud," *Al-Shari'a wal-Hayat*, Al-Jazeera (undated), http://www.islamonline.net/Arabic/personality/2001/12/article11.SHTML (accessed on January 10, 2008).

48. Ibid. Statements such as these have brought him the wrath of more radical Islamists, who consider the Jews enemies of Islam. See "Reading in Qaradawism: Part 1. Loyalty and Disownment," Allahuakbar Net, http://www.allaahuakbar.net/jamaat-e-islaami/Qaradawism/loyalty_and_disownment.htm; "Some mistakes of Yusuf al-Qaradawi," Islamic Web, http://islamicweb.com/beliefs/misguided/qaradawi.htm; G.F. Haddad, "Yusuf al-Qaradawi," *Living Islam*, August 2007, http://www.livingislam.org/k/yq_e.html (all accessed on January 10, 2008).

49. *Ummatu-na Bayna Qarnayn*, p. 216.

50. Yusuf al-Qaradawi, "Filistin. Sina'at al-Mawt," Islam Online, http://www. islamonline.net/Arabic/personality/2001/12/article6.SHTML (accessed on January 10, 2008). The idea that the caliphate was destroyed because Ottoman sultan Abd al-Hamid would not agree to sell Palestine to the Zionists is part of the Muslim Brothers' mythology, as in Mahmud Jami's *Wa-Araftu al-Ikhwan* (Cairo: Dar al-Tawzi wal-Nashr al-Islamiyya, 2004), pp. 34–35.

51. Ibid.; "Al-Intifada al-Filistiniyya wal-Amaliyyat al-Fida'iyya," *Al-Shari'a wal-Hayat*, Al-Jazeera, December 9, 2001, http://www.aljazeera.net/channel/ archive/archive?ArchiveId=90148 (accessed on January 10, 2008); *Al-Sahwa al-Islamiyya Bayna al-Juhud wal-Tatarruf*, p. 92.

52. This idea is often reiterated on *Al-Shari'a wal-Hayat*. See, for example, "Al-Intifada al-Filistiniyya wal-Amaliyyat al-Fida'iyya"; "Wajib al-Muslimin Tujah al-Intifada," Al-Jazeera, April 8, 2001, http://www.aljazeera.net/ Channel/archive/archive?ArchiveId=89585; "Al-Irhab wa-Hamlat al-Karahiyya Didd al-Arab wal-Muslimin," Al-Jazeera, June 19, 2001, http://www. aljazeera.net/Channel/archive/archive?ArchiveId=89901; "Al-Irhab wal-Unf," Al-Jazeera, October 27, 2002, http://www.aljazeera.net/channel/archive/ archive? ArchiveId=91187 (all accessed January 9, 2008).

53. *Ummatu-na Bayna Qarnayn*, p. 114.

54. *Al-Sahwa al-Islamiyya Bayna al-Juhud wal-Tatarruf*, p. 72.

55. Yusuf al-Qaradawi, *Zahirat al-Ghulu fi l-Takfir* (Cairo: Al-Jama'a al-Islamiyya, 1978). See also his comments in "Mafhum al-Usuliyya," *Al-Shari'a wal-Hayat*, Al-Jazeera, October 19, 1997, http://www.aljazeera.net/channel/archive/ archive?ArchiveId=91754; "Ghazwat Badr al-Kubra fil-Sira al-Nabawiyya," Al-Jazeera, December 10, 2000, http://www.aljazeera.net/Channel/archive/ archive?ArchiveId=89413 (both accessed on January 9, 2008).

56. Al-Qaradawi, *Thaqafatu-na Bayna al-Infitah wal-Inghilaq* (Cairo: Dar al-Shuruq, 2000), p. 26. See also *Fi Fiqh al-Aqalliyyt al-Muslima*, p. 71 and *Tarikhu-na al-Muftara Alay-hi*, p. 182.

57. *Bayyanat al-Hall al-Islami*, pp. 245–247. The *shaykh* often insists that in countries with a Muslim majority, it is unfair that the interests and views of the minority prevail; see ibid. p. 246; Yusuf al-Qaradawi, *Al-Hulul al-Mustawrada wa-Kayfa Janat ala Ummatina* (Cairo: Matkabat Wahba, 1977), p. 6; *Al-Ikhwan al-Muslimun*, p. 268; *A'da al-Hall al-Islami*, p. 13. Of course, that fails to take into account the many Muslims who would not wish the implementation of *Shari'a*.

58. *Al-Sahwa al-Islamiyya Bayna al-Juhud wal-Tatarruf*, p. 20.

59. Ibid. pp. 21–22.

60. Ibid. pp. 20–21; 73ff.; *Ayna al-Khalal?*, pp. 24–25. An example of that submission is al-Azhar's fatwas in favor of land reform during the Nasserist period and against it under Sadat. Some commentators agree with the shaykh on this point: According to Tamir Moustafa, "the government's increasing control of religious institutions was also perhaps the single most important factor contributing to the resurgence of radical Islamic groups"; see his "Conflict and Cooperation Between the State and Religious Institutions in Contemporary Egypt," *International Journal of Middle East Studies* 32 (2000), p. 10. Saad Eddin Ibrahim, for his part, has argued that "if well tuned and properly functioning, establishment and Sufi Islam would reduce Islamic activism to political and sociological irrelevance." *Egypt, Islam and Democracy* (Cairo: The American University in Cairo Press, 2002), p. 69.

61. *Al-Sahwa al-Islamiyya Bayna al-Juhud wal-Tatarruf*, pp. 8–9.

62. *Ummatu-na Bayna Qarnayn*, p. 245; see also "Muhawalat Taghyir al-Manahij al-Islamiyya," Al-Jazeera, http://www.aljazeera.net/channel/archive/archive?ArchiveId=90282.

63. *Ummatu-na Bayna Qarnayn*, p. 16.

64. Guilain Denoeux, "The Forgotten Swamp: Navigating Political Islam," *Middle East Policy* vol. 9, no. 2 (2002), p. 75.

65. Raja Ibn Salama, "Al-Hadayan al-Dini al-Usuli: Ba'd al-Madakhil al-Nasfiyya li-l-Dirasa," *Jaridat al-Siyasa*, November 10, 2004, http://www.alarabiya.net/Articles/2004/11/10/7858.htm (accessed January 9, 2008).

66. *Al-Sahwa al-Islamiyya Bayna al-Juhud wal-Tatarruf*, pp. 79–80.

67. Gilles Kepel argues that the Muslim Brothers underwent a significant transformation during the "dark years" and refers to them in their new reincarnation as "néo-Frères Musulmans"; see his *Le prophète et Pharaon* (Paris: Editions du Seuil, 1993), chapter 4.

68. The terms used are *naksat* and *nakbat*, plurals of the words that designate the Arab defeats at the hands of Israel in 1948 (*nakba* or "catastrophe") and in 1967 (euphemistically known as *naksa* or "setback").

69. *Ummatu-na Bayna Qarnayn*, pp. 102–103.

70. *Al-Hulul al-Mustawrada*, *Passim*; "Al-Islam wal-Siyasa," *al-Shari'a wal-Hayat*, Al-Jazeera, May 12, 2002, http://www.aljazeera.net/Channel/archive/archive?ArchiveId=90658 (accessed January 9, 2008).

71. According to al-Qaradawi, Iran's revolution "revived the hopes of victory" of the Islamist movement, and the implementation of Shari'a in Sudan "put an end to the state of disarray and chaos" in that country(!). The shaykh neglects to mention the Taliban, who had been ruling most of Afghanistan for four years by the time this book was published.

72. *Ummatu-na Bayna Qarnayn*, pp. 112–123.

73. Yusuf al-Qaradawi, *Dars al-Nakba al-Thaniyya: Li-Madha Inhazimha wa-Kayfa Nantasir* (Cairo: Maktabat Wahba, 1987), pp. 37ff; *Al-Ikhwan al-Muslimun*, pp. 295–296.

74. *Al-Sahwa al-Islamiyya Bayna al-Juhud wal-Tatarruf*, pp. 86–87; *Dars al-Nakba al-Thaniyya*, pp. 136–137; *A'da al-Hall al-Islami*, pp. 139–153.

75. *A'da al-Hall al-Islami*, pp. 139–142; *Dars al-Nakba al-Thaniyya*, p. 37.

76. *Ummatu-na Bayna Qarnayn*, p. 202.

77. *Al-Sahwa al-Islamiyya Bayna al-Juhud wal-Tatarruf*, pp. 86–87.

78. Al-Qaradawi, *Bayyanat al-Hall al-Islami*, pp. 158–160; see also *Al-Islam Kama Nu'min bi-hi*, pp. 43–45.

79. Al-Qaradawi, *Al-Ikhwan al-Muslimun*, p. 297. Similarly, al-Banna wrote that until an Islamic state was set up, "all Muslims are living in sin"; see "Bayna al-Ams wal-Yawm," p. 154; "Risalat al-Mu'tamar al-Sadis," p. 322; "Nahwa al-Nur," p. 66; all in *Majmu'at Rasa'il al-Imam al-Shahid Hasan al-Banna* (Alexandria, Dar al-Da'wa, 1998).

80. For a warts-and-all account of the history of the caliphate, see Faraj Fawda, *Al-Haqiqa al-Gha'iba* (Cairo: Dar wa-Matabi' al-Mustaqbal and Beirut: Dar al-Ma'arif, 2003).

81. Hasan al-Banna, "Nahwa al-Nur," pp. 66–67.

82. Hasan al-Banna, "Risalat al-Jihad," pp. 276–279; "Ila Ayy Shay Nad'u al-Nas," pp. 39, 55–56; both in *Majmu'at al-Rasa'il*.

83. Sayyid Qutb, *Fi Zilal al-Qur'an* (Beirut, Cairo: Dar al-Shuruq), pp. 294–295; *Ma'alim fi al-Tariq* (Damascus: Dar Dimashq, 1964?), p. 83.

84. Qutb, *Fi Zilal al-Qur'an*, p. 673.
85. Sayyid Qutb, *Khasa'is al-Tasawwur al-Islami wa-Muqawwumati-hi*, p. 46, and *Hadha al-Din*, p. 26. Both available to download at http://www.daawa-info. net/books1.php?author= قطب20% سيد (accessed January 13, 2008).
86. *Fi Fiqh al-Aqalliyyat al-Muslima*, p. 34.
87. *Tarikhu-na al-Muftara Alay-hi*, pp. 25–31. As Noel Coulson has shown, Shari'a was, in fact, so impractical to implement that an alternative system, the *mazalim* jurisdiction, came to effectively marginalize it. See his classic *A History of Islamic Law* (Edinburgh: Edinburgh University Press, 1999), especially chapter 9.
88. Yusuf al-Qaradawi, *Al-Sahwa al-Islamiyya Bayna al-Ikhtilaf al-Mashru wal-Tafarruq al-Madhmum* (Cairo: Dar al-Sahwa, 1990), pp. 48–49; *Dars al-Nakba al-Thaniyya*, p. 34; *Ayna al-Khalal?* p. 21.
89. Al-Qaradawi, *Bayyanat al-Hall al-Islami*, pp. 176ff.
90. Ibid.
91. Ibid.
92. For a discussion of totalitarian influences on Hasan al-Banna, see Ana Belén Soage, "Hasan al-Banna or the Politicisation of Islam," *Totalitarian Movements and Political Religions*, vol. 9, no. 1 (March 2008), pp. 21–42.
93. *Al-Hulul al-Mustawrada*, p. 313. This work was first published in 1971, before Sadat's *infitah*, at a time when establishment *ulema* still spoke of "Islamic socialism" (*ishtirakiyyat al-Islam*).
94. "Al-Muslimun wal-Unf al-Siyasi 1," *Al-Shari'a wal-Hayat*, Al-Jazeera, May 23, 2004, http://www.aljazeera.net/channel/archive/archive?ArchiveId=92972 (accessed January 8, 2008).
95. Yusuf al-Qaradawi, *Madkhal li-Ma'rifat al-Islam: Muqawwamatu-hu. Khasa'isu-hu. Ahdafu-hu. Masadiru-hu* (Cairo: Maktabat al-Wahba, 1996), p. 158.
96. Yusuf al-Qaradawi, *Al-Sunna, Masdar al-Ma'rifa wal-Hadara* (Cairo: Dar al-Shuruq, 2002), p. 200. The same ideas are contained in several of al-Banna's messages to his followers; see "Da'watu-na," p. 19, and "Ila Ayy Shay Nad'u al-Nas," p. 41; both in *Majmu'at al-Rasa'il*.
97. The process is explained in detail in Coulson, *History of Islamic Law*, pp 182–201. In the Arab world, the most important figure of the reform of the civil code, not only in Egypt but also in Iraq, Syria, Jordan, and Lybia, was Abd al-Razzaq al-Sanhuri (1895–1971).
98. *Kayfa Nata'amil ma al-Qur'an al-Azim*, p. 63; see also *Madkhal li-Ma'rifat al-Islam*, pp. 153–157.
99. *Kayfa Nata'amil ma al-Qur'an al-Azim*, pp. 63–64.
100. Cheryl Benard, "Civil Democratic Islam: Partners, Resources and Strategies," RAND Corporation, 2003. Available to download from http://www.rand. org/pubs/monograph_reports/MR1716/ (accessed January 13, 2008).
101. Ibid. p. 30.
102. "Al-Islam al-Dimuqrati al-Madani," *Al-Shari'a wal-Hayat*, Al-Jazeera, December 14, 2004, http://www.aljazeera.net/Channel/archive/archive? ArchiveId=108218 (accessed January 13, 2008).
103. "Al-Wasatiyya fil-Islam," *Al-Shari'a wal-Hayat*, Al-Jazeera, October 26, 1997, http://www.aljazeera.net/channel/archive/archive? ArchiveId=91751 (accessed January 8, 2008).
104. In one of his works, al-Qaradawi affirms that it was the civil war in Algeria **that** pushed him to dedicate his energies to advocating *wasatiyya*. See his prologue

to Umar Abdullah Kamil's *Al-Khawarij al-Judud: Al-Mutatarrifun, Istabahu Dima al-Muslimin wa-Qatalu al-nisa wal-Atfal wal-Musta'minin* (Cairo: Maktabat al-Turath al-Islami, 1998), p. 7.

105. The polemic Wahhabi preacher Muhsin al-Awaji, known for his admiration of bin Ladin and his criticism of "liberal influences" in Saudi Arabia, has **estab**lished the Muntada al-Wasatiyya (The Club of Moderation) and manages the website www.wasatyah.com.

106. Patrick Haenni, "Divisions chez les Frères musulmans. La nouvelle pensée islamique des déçus de l'expérience militante," *La République des idées*, April 2005, http://www.repid.com/article.php3? id_article=341 (accessed January 8, 2008).

107. *Thaqafatu-na Bayna al-Infitah wal-Inghilaq*, p. 30.

3

THE MUSLIM BROTHERS IN EGYPT

Ana Belén Soage and Jorge Fuentelsaz Franganillo

ESTABLISHMENT OF THE SOCIETY AND THE PREREVOLUTIONARY PERIOD

The founder of the Muslim Brothers' Society, Hasan al-Banna, was born in 1906 in Mahmudiyya, a small village near Alexandria.[1] Under the influence of his father, who had some reputation as a religious scholar, young Hasan read Rashid Rida's *al-Manar*[2] and frequented the *hasafiyya* Sufi order. He also participated in associations that promoted Islamic values and counteracted the activities of Christian missionaries. Upon finishing primary school, he was able to persuade his father—who would have wanted him to pursue his studies at the al-Azhar teaching mosque—to let him become a schoolteacher.

In 1923 he traveled to Cairo to complete his education at the teacher-training Dar al-Ulum college and was shocked by "the wave of atheism and licentiousness"[3] that had engulfed the Egyptian capital. In order to combat the situation, he organized a group of students from al-Azhar and his own college to preach not only at mosques but also in the cafés where workers gathered.

Upon graduation, al-Banna's first posting as a schoolteacher was in the Suez Canal town of Ismailiyya. There, he continued his proselytizing in mosques, religious associations, and coffee shops. According to his own account, a group of workers came to him one day looking for his guidance, and it was with them that he launched the Muslim Brothers' Society in the late 1920s.[4] The society's initial aim was to educate its members in gaining a correct understanding of Islam, and its early meetings were not unlike those of Sufi congregations; al-Banna even adopted the Sufi title of *al-murshid al-amm* (general guide). Soon, branches of the society appeared up and down the canal zone.

In 1932 al-Banna was transferred to Cairo, and the capital also became the new headquarters of the Muslim Brothers' society; his organization grew exponentially both inside Egypt and abroad. It also became involved in the agitated political life of the time. Al-Banna was influenced by the totalitarian ideology of the new leaders of Germany and Italy, which was popular in nationalist and anti-British circles; so he developed the concept of Islam as a "total" or "comprehensive" system (*nizam shamil*). During the society's fifth congress, held in 1938 to commemorate the tenth anniversary of its establishment, al-Banna explained:

> It is our conviction that the rulings and precepts of Islam are comprehensive and organize the affairs of this life and the next. Whoever believes that those precepts are only concerned with worship and spirituality is mistaken. Islam is creed and worship, country and nationality, religion and government, action and spirituality, Book [the Koran] and sword.[5]

Throughout the second half of the 1930s, the Muslim Brothers became increasingly politicized and assertive. Their youth organization, the yellow-shirted "rovers," held mass rallies and demonstrations to demand the implementation of *Shari'a* (Islamic law) and challenge other youth groups—notably the Green Shirts of the pseudo-Fascist Young Egypt party and the Blue Shirts of the nationalist Wafd. During the Second World War, al-Banna took part in anti-British, pro-Axis plotting. As a result, he and his advisers were banished from Cairo, briefly jailed, and the society's meetings and publications were temporarily banned. After this first clash with the authorities, al-Banna decided to set up a secret paramilitary group under the innocuous name of "Special Apparatus."

The Muslim Brothers' Society came out of the war stronger than ever. Its ideology was attractive to a profoundly religious Egyptian people who no longer trusted the self-serving political elite. The Brothers' anti-British stance and support for the Palestinian cause were popular among the Egyptian nationalists. The Brotherhood's schools and hospitals offered crucial services to the urban working class, whose living conditions had worsened dramatically as a consequence of wartime inflation and the unemployment that resulted from the withdrawal of the Allied troops. By 1945, the society claimed it is made up of half a million members and as many sympathizers. Its main competitor, the Wafd, had been compromised by its wartime cooperation with the British and was trying to recover its credibility through an alliance with the Communists, whose numbers had increased considerably. The visceral anticommunism of al-Banna, combined with his antagonism toward the Wafd, drew him closer to King Faruq, who granted the Muslim Brothers financial support and wide room for maneuver.

The postwar years were a period of great instability in Egypt, which reflected the profound crisis of its parliamentary system. Street skirmishes between the different groups became commonplace and political assassinations very frequent. The Brothers' Special Apparatus contributed to the mayhem by multiplying its attacks against the British, Egyptian Jews—accused of collusion with Zionism—and Egyptian public personalities. In March 1948, it assassinated Judge Ahmad al-Khazandar, who had passed harsh sentences on some Muslim Brothers. In November, the police found an arms depot in Ismailiyya and, a few days later, documentary proof of the existence of the Special Apparatus in an abandoned jeep. Fearing that al-Banna was preparing a coup, Prime Minister Mahmud al-Nuqrashi ordered ban the Brotherhood whose response was to assassinate him. Al-Banna tried to distance himself from the violence, but in vain: on February 12, 1949, he was shot, probably by the secret police, and left to bleed to death.

The assassination of Hasan al-Banna plunged the society into a period of uncertainty and power struggles continued until the appointment of a compromise candidate, Hasan al-Hudaybi, as general guide. The new leader was a retired judge, uncharismatic but close to the palace, which permitted the Muslim Brothers to resume their activities. However, the following period in Brothers' history would not be marked by its general guide but by the society's new ideologue, Sayyid Qutb, who joined in the early 1950s.

THE BROTHERS AND THE FREE OFFICERS

In July 1952 a group of army officers led a coup against the palace. Informed sources claim that the Muslim Brothers played a significant role in that coup and that Anwar Sadat and, possibly, Gamal Abdel Nasser himself had been members of their Special Apparatus.[6] When all political parties were banned in January 1953, the society was allowed to continue its work as an "organization." However, it soon became clear that the society and Egypt's new leadership had conflicting views of the each other's future task: the former saw in the officers an instrument to realize their vision of an Islamic state, whereas the latter wanted to turn the Brothers into the grassroots they lacked. Qutb was even offered a leadership position in the Liberation Rally, Nasser's first project for a single-party system, but the society refused to grant legitimacy to a regime unwilling to implement *Shari'a*.[7]

Relations between the former allies rapidly deteriorated. Together with the Communists, the Muslim Brothers organized demonstrations against the new regime demanding a return to civilian rule. A crisis came when a young member of the Brotherhood tried to assassinate Nasser in October 1954. The incident, which greatly boosted Nasser's popularity, gave him the chance to move against the society and the revolution's figurehead, Muhammad Naguib, for his alleged complicity in the crime. Tens of thousands of Brothers were arrested, savagely tortured, and placed on trial. Many received lengthy jail sentences with hard labor, and seven, including Hasan al-Hudaybi, were condemned to death, although the general guide's penalty would be later commuted to life imprisonment. However, even during the darkest days of Nasserist persecution, it is estimated that the society had between 250,000 and 300,000 members.[8]

Sayyid Qutb would spend much of the rest of his life in jail, with respite for a few months in 1964–65. From behind prison bars, he wrote the majority of his works, including the most influential *Ma'alim fi'l-Tariq* (*Signposts on the Road*), published in 1964. In the book, he stated that modern Muslim societies cannot really be considered Muslim because they are not ruled the principles set by God. Together with their Western counterparts they are, in reality, *jahili* (barbarian) societies, just like the Arabs before the Revelation. In Qutb's Manichean vision of the world, there is no third alternative:

> Either Islam or *jahiliyya*. There is no intermediate state half-Islam and half-jahiliyya that Islam can accept. Islam clearly indicates that the truth is one, not multiple, that everything that is not truth is perdition, and that the two cannot be mixed. Either God's government or *jahiliyya* government. Either God's *Shari'a* or human caprice [*hawa*].[9]

Qutb added that *jihad* would be necessary to depose the corrupt rulers of the Muslim world, who were an obstacle in the way of the instauration of an Islamic order. When there was a new security clampdown on the Muslim Brothers in August 1965, Qutb's book, *Ma'alim*, was found in virtually every house the police searched, and it was produced as evidence that they were preparing a coup. Qutb was rearrested and, after a show trial, he was executed.

Qutb's writings eventually caused a split within the Islamist movement. In the 1970s, many young Muslim Brothers started to criticize the older generation for their passivity in the face of government aggression. They left the society and set up militant groups inspired by Qutb's ideas. Most of the members, and especially older ones, remained loyal to the moderate strategic line taken by General Guide Hasan al-Hudaybi who, in 1971, published *Du'a la Quda* (*Preachers, Not Judges*), ostensibly against Abu al-Ala al-Mawdudi but, in reality, a criticism of Qutb who had adopted some of the main ideas of the Pakistani author.

The Comeback Under Sadat

In 1967 a coalition of Arab countries suffered a crushing defeat at the hands of Israel in the Six Day War. Egypt lost the Sinai Peninsula; the Suez Canal, which was an important source of revenues, was blocked. Encouraged by the *ulama*, many Muslims interpreted the defeat as God's punishment for the regime's departure from religion and its persecution of the Islamists. Aware of the change in public mood, Nasser sought to carry the favor of his critics by encouraging religious activities to display his Muslim credentials. In 1970 he died a broken man and was replaced by Vice President Anwar al-Sadat. Eager to consolidate his authority and marginalize the Nasserist and leftist opposition, Sadat embraced religion as the main source of his regime's legitimacy. The state-controlled media referred to him by the epithet of *al-ra'is al-mu'min* (the pious president).

As part of his realignment with the West, Sadat also initiated a timid attempt to democratize the regime. In the early 1970s, political prisoners, including the Muslim Brothers, were freed, and from 1976 opposition parties were allowed to operate. In 1973 Umar al-Tilmisani was appointed new general guide of the society after the death of Hasan al-Hudaybi and, under his leadership, the Brothers recovered some of their prominence, especially among students. It was precisely at the universities that a new generation of Brothers was recruited, often among the members of the more radical Gama'at Islamiyya (Islamic Organizations). The new blood injected into the organization made possible the resurgence of the society, which from this point onward has been dubbed the "neo-Muslim Brethren."[10]

With their victory of sorts in the 1973 Yom Kippur War, Egyptians felt that their national honor had been restored. However, Sadat was criticized for his rapprochement with the West, particularly the United States, and for his policy of *infitah* (economic liberalization), which only seemed to benefit a few. In addition, his peace overtures to Israel alienated many ordinary Egyptians, who after decades of propaganda considered the normalization of relations with the "Zionist entity" nothing short of treason. The Muslim Brothers' weekly *al-Da'wa* criticized the negotiations and soon started to attack Sadat's other policies and what they saw as the immorality of Egyptian society. As his popularity was on the slide, the president became increasingly authoritarian. In February 1981, a massive and indiscriminate campaign of arrests targeted not only the Islamists but also the secular opposition. This was the last straw for the Islamist radicals: on October 6, Sadat was assassinated during a military parade held, ironically, to mark the anniversary of the 1973 war.

THE MUBARAK YEARS

Following Sadat's assassination, his successor, Husni Mubarak, vowed to carry on with political and economic liberalization. However, the new president was cautious about change, opting for a "democracy in doses in proportion to our ability to absorb them"[11] and systematically extending the state of emergency that granted him extraordinary powers. The 1980s saw regular—if flawed—multiparty elections, a greater degree of press freedom, and the release of political prisoners, including the Muslim Brothers. Throughout that decade, the society's 1970s generation succeeded in turning the organization into a major player on the Egyptian political scene.

The Takeover of the Professional Unions

In the 1980s, the Islamists assumed control of most student unions and teachers' clubs. On the other hand, the student leaders in the 1970s entered the labor market and continued their political activity through the professional unions, with the full backing of General Guide Umar al-Tilmisani. According to prominent Muslim Brother Abd al-Mun'im Abu al-Futuh, it was al-Tilmisani who convinced the Brothers to rule out the use of violence and become a civil society organization—and that, despite the opposition of the "old guard," especially former members of the Special Apparatus like

Mustafa Mash'hur, Kamal al-Sananiri, and Ahmad Hasanayn.[12] The general guide supported the rising figures of the 1970s generation or "new guard"— people like Hilmi al-Jazzar, Abu al-Ila Madi, Isam al-Aryan, and Abu al-Futuh himself—and they came to occupy leading positions within the unions of their respective professional trade.[13]

There were two dozen professional unions in Egypt. They are important for new graduates, to whom they provide access to the job market and offer benefits such as loans, subsidized goods, and inexpensive health insurance. However, by the time the Muslim Brothers turned their attention to the unions, their members had become disillusioned by a leadership often seen as sleazy, detached from their immediate concerns, and engaged in petty infighting. The Brothers tapped into this dissatisfaction, and their campaigns concentrated on the needs of the members, particularly young professionals. They denounced the mismanagement and corruption and emphasized ethics while underplaying the society's politicoreligious ideology. More significantly, they were able to get out the vote and, as a result, the percentage of professionals taking part in union elections rose considerably throughout the 1980s.[14]

However, the Muslim Brothers were regularly accused of resorting to underhand tactics. It was rumored that they paid the membership fees of their supporters before the elections, thereby making them eligible to vote. They also provided transportation to the polling stations, where it was reported that young Brothers asked voters as they entered: "Are you giving your vote to God?"[15] Nevertheless, there is no denying that they gained the vote of people who would never define themselves as Islamists. Under their leadership, the unions were well managed and had greatly developed social services, increasing the provision of grants and low-interest loans, subsidized health care, even a compensation salary to members during their military service. Unsurprisingly, they soon became the largest—sometimes, the sole—force on the board of all the main unions.

The first union to fall to the Brothers was that of the doctors in April 1984. The engineers' union followed in 1986 and that of the pharmacists in 1988. The Brothers were careful to avoid a confrontation with the regime, leaving the position of union *naqib* (secretary general) to a candidate palatable to it. However, the unions became their platform to participate in the political life of the country. In a way, such participation was a continuation of a long tradition of union involvement in politics; for instance, in the 1970s and 1980s, the lawyers' union had played a prominent role in the opposition to Sadat's *infitah* economic policy and the Camp David Accords. However, the Brothers' use of the unions often failed to take into account the views and interests of the members they were supposed to represent.[16]

Increasingly Prominent Political Role

For Umar al-Tilmisani and the new guard, the Brothers' takeover of the professional unions was a step toward full participation in the political process. Egypt being a working (if quite imperfect) democracy, the priority of all political forces is to get represented at the People's Assembly. However, the general guide's demands for an overturn of the 1954 ban on the society went unheeded, and he also faced the opposition of the old guard, which was still clinging to al-Banna's rejection of the multiparty system.

In the mid-1980s, the 1970s generation tried to establish a political party—ostensibly separate from the society but inspired by its principles—Hizb al-Shura in 1986, Hizb al-Islah on several occasions, and Hizb al-Amal in 1995, but the Parties' Commission turned down their applications.[17] In fact, the commission has turned down 90 percent of the applications to set up political parties, irrespective of the political or religious affiliation of the applicants.

That did not deter the younger Brothers. Given that the electoral laws then in force demanded that all candidates run for the elections on the list of one of the registered political parties, they negotiated a series of alliances. In the 1984 elections for the People's Assembly, they ran on the list of the Wafd. It was a tactical move by both sides: the Brothers had the opportunity to field candidates, whereas the Wafd could raise its share of the vote, thereby reaching the threshold that would secure its presence in parliament. The move was successful, and the alliance obtained just over 15 percent of the vote, or 58 seats, of which eight went to the society's candidates. For the 1987 elections, the Brothers formed a united front with the Labor and Liberal Parties. This coalition with weaker and less ideologically defined partners, which allowed them to impose a common program including the implementation of *Shari'a*, came to be known as the Islamic Alliance. It won 17 percent of the vote, or 56 seats, out of which 36 were occupied by Muslim Brothers.

As in the unions, the society's candidates for parliament are popular because, contrary to "regular" politicians, they are perceived as accessible to the people of their constituency and the the society candidates freely engaged with their local community. Financially self-reliant,[18] they were in a position to provide services such as clinics, schools, and discount grocery shops to a population often living below the poverty line. In addition, their messianic message, embodied in the electoral slogan *al-Islam huwa al-hall* (Islam is the solution), appealed to the Egyptian people, most of whom are very religious and have been disenchanted by the political projects of successive regimes over the years. The Brothers also benefited from the absence of a credible alternative; the other opposition parties have been described as "exclusive clubs where members meet to chat and drink tea."[19]

Despite its strategy to get around the regime's refusal to legalize it, the society was keen on avoiding a direct confrontation. Throughout the 1980s, there was a tacit agreement whereby the Brothers could expand their presence in civil society in exchange for their respect the regime's "red lines." However, by the end of the decade, they had become more assertive. The first direct clash occurred in the run-up to the 1990 parliamentary elections, when the society and Wafd led a boycott to protest against the new electoral law, which gerrymandered districts in favor of the ruling National Democratic Party (NDP). This move undermined the credibility of the elections, the regime in front of the international community. As it turned out, the real victor was abstention: although officially the voter participation was 45 percent, independent estimates put it as low as 20 percent.

The following year provided a new opportunity for the society to flex its political muscles, when Egypt joined the multinational coalition against Saddam Hussein. Predictably, the universities witnessed rowdy student protests, often supported by the teachers' clubs. More significantly, ten professional unions controlled by the Muslim Brothers issued a series of statements against military intervention. The government, in turn, launched a smear campaign against the Islamists, accusing them of "treason." Then, in October 1992, an earthquake hit Cairo, leaving over 500 dead, 10,000 injured, and many more homeless. While the regime's attempts to deal with the disaster were criticized as belated and inadequate, the Muslim Brothers proved themselves capable and efficient. Through their network of urban and rural branches, they were often the first to reach the victims and provide them with emergency shelter, food, clothing, and cash.

The Backlash: Internal Divisions, 1992–2003

By the early 1990s Husni Mubarak had realized that his timid steps toward democracy had not earned him the legitimacy he sought. He felt that an increasingly aggressive opposition had taken advantage of political liberalization in an irresponsible manner; hence President Mubarak decided to start curtailing the limited freedoms he had granted. Symptomatic of this change was the frequent resort to presidential decrees, which seriously undermined the significance of the very institutions the regime had empowered in the previous decade, particularly the People's Assembly. The Muslim Brothers were not the only victims of the government clampdown on civil liberties, but their position as an illegal organization made them especially vulnerable.

Furthermore, a number of events played against the society. Domestically, Islamic radicals were waging a bloody campaign of terror against the security forces, the Coptic minority, secular Muslim intellectuals, and foreign tourists.[20] Outside Egypt, the unexpected victory of the Front Islamique du Salut in the 1992 Algerian elections alarmed the Egyptian regime, already uneasy about the Muslim Brothers' growing role in civil society. In addition, it was revealed that American officials had been secretly meeting the prominent members of the society, which was interpreted as U.S. fears of a repeat of the Iranian scenario in Egypt. The Brothers were thus the victims of both their relative moderation, which made them credible partners for dialogue, and of the often blurry lines between radical and moderate Islamism. As a result, they often became the target of harassment, arbitrary arrest, and detention without charges. From the mid-1990s, their referral to military courts for trial became common.

In 1992 the Egyptian security forces raided the offices of the Salsabil computer company, arresting its two owners—one of whom was Khayrat al-Shatir, a senior member of the society apparatus—and confiscating a large number of documents. The raids revealed the so-called Enablement Project (*mashru al-tamkin*[21]) of the Brothers, a plan to infiltrate government institutions and civil society organizations gradually with a view to a taking over power. They also showed that the Muslim Brothers had re-created the state by setting up sections dealing with all the domains in which they deemed it necessary to have influence: students, professionals, the security services, elections, human rights, and so on. The society claimed that the allegations were untrue, but some leaders of the new guard admitted that the documents seized were authentic, although they tried to minimize their importance and portrayed them as merely reflecting the delusions of a handful of hardline old guards.[22]

Also in 1992, the Muslim Brothers' superb organization skills and a very low level of participation helped them to win the elections to the board of the lawyers' union, a traditional bastion of the nationalists and the left. The regime decided that enough was enough, and it passed the 1993 union law, according to which half of the union members—on the second and third rounds just one-third—had to vote in order for the elections to be considered valid. Otherwise, an administrative board would be appointed to take care of matters until new elections could be held. The government also moved against the student unions. Thousands of Islamist candidates were deleted from the electoral lists, the secular Horus union was supported as an alternative and, eventually, only candidates sanctioned by the university were permitted to run. Tear gas became a regular weapon against student demonstrations, and any function related to politics was banned from the campuses.

The measures taken at the universities achieved their aims: by 1994, the Muslim Brothers controlled only six of the twenty-eight student unions. However, the professional unions' law only had limited success, and the Interior Ministry resorted to stopping the elections from taking place altogether, in the pretext that some of the candidates belonged to an outlawed movement (i.e., the society). From 1995 onwards, the Muslim Brothers' control of the unions was lifted, starting with the lawyers' union. In the hands of the government's cronies, the situation reverted to the bad old days. Within a few years, the unions' money had run out and they were no longer in a position to offer the services provided when the Brothers were at the helm.

The society had not given up its campaign to be legalized. One of its rising stars, Isam al-Aryan, who was a parliamentarian in the 1987 assembly and had opposed the 1990 electoral boycott, wrote in January 1995:

> Allowing the Brothers a legal presence would revitalize the political life of the country because it would correct the flawed motivation of the government and would open the way to the will of the people. It would also represent a challenge to the political parties and push them to renew themselves to stand the competition, as well as forcing the Islamic movement itself to respect competition and renew its ideas.[23]

However, later the same month, a major raid on the society's offices was conducted. Eighty-two Brothers were arrested, including twenty-eight leading members who were attending a meeting of the Shura Council (the society's "parliament"), and were charged with plotting to overthrow the Mubarak regime. In May 1995, Mubarak publicly denounced the society for its politicization of the unions during his Labor Day speech, and, in a June interview, accused it of only pretending to be moderate.

Furthermore, in June of that year, there was an assassination attempt on the Egyptian president while he was in Addis Ababa for a meeting of the Organization of African Unity. Although the society vigorously condemned the attack, it was accused of links to the Sudanese National Front and the Egyptian Jihad and Jama'at Islamiyya groups, which were blamed for the attack. Thousands of Brothers were detained, and dozens were referred to the military courts. In November, fifty-four Brothers received three to five years of hard labor, including some of the society's most prominent figures: Isam al-Aryan, Muhammad Khayrat, Muhammad Habib, and Abd al-Mun'in Abu al-Futuh.

Also, 1995 was an election year, a fact probably not unrelated to the raid. The elections introduced a novelty: independent candidates were allowed to contest. The society fielded 170 candidates. In fact, a great number of independent candidates reflected the weakness and lack of legitimacy of the political parties but also the rising number of businessmen sought to boost their political influence and gain parliamentary immunity. However, the regime had changed its attitude toward an opposition that had "ungratefully" boycotted the previous elections and was determined to avoid its securing one-third of the seats, which would obstruct the nomination of Mubarak for a fourth term in 1999. As a result, the 1995 elections were the most corrupt and violent since Mubarak became president, leaving dozens dead (most killed by police fire) and hundreds injured. The government eventually secured a 94 percent majority[24]; the only Muslim Brother to be elected was later disqualified for belonging to a banned organization.

The Hizb al-Wasat Episode

The third general guide, Umar al-Tilmisani, had been able to bridge the gap between the society's old guard and the 1970s generation, and the latter were the champions of his campaign to raise the Muslim Brothers' profile in the Egyptian society. His death in 1986 permitted the old guard to restore their control over the society and left the new feeling "like orphans."[25] A weak man, Hamid Abu al-Nasr was appointed general guide, with former member of the Special Apparatus Mustafa Mash'hur as his deputy, who many suspected was really in charge of the organization. When Abu al-Nasr passed away in 1996, Mash'hur became general guide with the *bay'at al-maqabir* (the graveyard pledge of loyalty) while his predecessor was being buried. In 2002, when he in turn died, he was succeeded by his own deputy, eighty-three-year old Ma'mun al-Hudaybi, who happened to be the son of second General Guide Hasan al-Hudaybi. Younger Brothers were dismayed.

The conflict within the society was partly a struggle for power; its "young princes" had become increasingly frustrated by the way decisions were taken by a reduced group of old guarders.[26] However, it also had an ideological basis: the 1970s generation is made up of modern men, with modern views on political pluralism, the issue of citizenship, and the status of women in society.[27] In contrast, many of the old guard retain Hasan al-Banna's distrust for party politics, think that the Copts should be happy with the status of *dhimmis*,[28] and are extremely conservative in their attitude to women. Moreover, their common prison experience turned them into a close-knit group wary of outside actors.

Mona el-Ghobashy has minimized the crisis within the society, arguing that it is not dissimilar to the generational conflict witnessed in other Egyptian political parties.[29] However, Sawsan al-Jayyar points to a more fundamental difference between the two groups regarding the source of authority (*marja'iyya*): for the old guard, that source should be *Shari'a*, whereas the new guard believes that it should be the community of believers (*jama'a*)[30]— that is, they advocate popular sovereignty.

At the beginning of 1996, new-guarder Abu al-Ila Madi presented yet another application to register a party under the name of Hizb al-Wasat (the "Middle-way" Party) without the general guide's authorization, which was responsible for him and his supporters leaving the society.[31] The "official version" is that the leadership believed that the time was not right to form a political party, but the truth is that many in the old guard were still intrinsically opposed to the idea and feared losing the society's most dynamic members to the new party.[32]

The security services soon detained Madi and two more founders of Hizb al-Wasat, together with ten Brothers unconnected to the party. They were all charged with belonging to an outlawed organization and were tried by a military tribunal. Six of the detainees were absolved, including the three "Wasatis"; the rest were condemned to between three and seven years in prison. However, the Parties' Commission rejected Madi's application, alleging that the new party would not be adding anything new to the Egyptian political landscape, and most of the "rebels" eventually returned to the society.

The next elections to the People's Assembly took place in the year 2000. On this occasion, there was less government interference because the Supreme Court had ruled that judges should oversee voting as it took place. However, there was another crackdown on the Brotherhood prior to the elections. The ruling NDP managed to secure a 93 percent majority after co-opting the "independent" businessmen. The Brothers did reasonably well considering the circumstances—so many of their strongest, most moderate candidates in prison—and seventeen of their candidates were elected (although one of them would later be removed by the government). In comparison, all the other opposition groupings—Wafdists, Nasserists, Liberals, members of Tagammu, and the like—obtained only sixteen seats despite fielding 352 candidates.

Mahdi Akif: A New Beginning?

In March 2004, Mahdi Akif, who had been appointed general guide after the death of Hasan al-Hudaybi in January of the same year, held a press conference at the journalists' union to present a manifesto to the Egyptian and international media. The document marked the beginning of a new chapter in the history of the Muslim Brothers' Society. It showed that despite belonging to the old guard generation, the new leader intended to further the organization's political dimension, almost forgotten since the arrests and trials of the mid-1990s. The initiative brought together the two main tendencies within the society: the old guard, which has traditionally prioritized proselytizing, and the new guard, more interested in politics. The text dealt with religious, social, political, economic, and cultural reforms; the relationship with the Copts; and the situation of women. In addition, it explicitly condoned the parliamentary system, criticized the Egyptian regime for the slow pace of reforms and rejected foreign interference, notably the Bush administration's Greater Middle East Initiative.

The manifesto offers Islam as a solution to the moral crisis provoked by the neglect of traditional values and Western influence. It lists thirteen areas of reform: the individual, who should be made to adhere to Islamic morality and rites; politics, with the Brothers vowing their support for democracy and popular sovereignty; a fully independent judicial system that ensures that all legislation is compatible with *Shari'a*; electoral reform; the economy, to set up a kind of protectionist capitalism; education, to inculcate religious and patriotic values; the independence of al-Azhar; the fight against poverty; social life, which should be based on an "integral Islamic system"; the situation of women, who can access any position except that of president but should pursue a particular program of studies "that responds to their nature, role and needs"; the reaffirmation of national unity and equality between Copts and Muslims; a cultural life built on Islamic values; and, finally, a foreign policy reminiscent of Nasser's theory of the three circles: the Arab, the African, and the Islamic.

In 2005 there were two elections: the first to the presidency in September and the second to the People's Assembly during November and December. With the United States pressing its Arab allies to democratize, the presidential election was not the usual plebiscite but a multicandidate race. Ten candidates came forward, although only Husni Mubarak, Ayman Nur of the Future Party, and Nu'man Gom'a of the New Wafd could boast any popular support. The voter turnout was low and irregularities widespread. According to official figures, Mubarak obtained almost 90 percent of the vote, followed by Nur, with just over 7 percent (13 percent, according to independent observers); Go'ma got less than 3 percent. Nur thus emerged as the only credible opposition candidate and a potential rival to Gamal Mubarak, widely expected to take over from his father in the future. Immediately after the election Nur was accused of fraud in the registration of his party and condemned to five years in prison.

As for the elections to the People's Assembly, its first round was relatively clean, but the regime became nervous about the society's good results. The second and third rounds were characterized by fraud, violence, and intimidation on the part of the security services, which blocked the electoral colleges in which the Muslim Brothers were expected to win. Despite those measures, the society was the only political grouping whose presence in parliament actually increased: out of the 161 candidates it fielded, it obtained eighty-eight seats out of the 444 up for grabs, compared to only seventeen seats in the previous elections. The ruling NDP obtained 145 seats, but a large number of "independent" candidates joined its ranks, finally giving them 311 seats—a loss of ninety-three seats compared with the previous election. The other parties obtained less than ten seats. These results confirmed the lack of popular support for the secular parties and the expanding popular base of the Muslim Brothers' Society.

After the elections, government harassment continued, especially after several dozen students belonging to the society, all dressed in black and covered with hoods, held a martial arts show at al-Azhar University in December 2006 reminiscent of events organized by Hamas or Hizballah. The society claimed that the students had acted on their own accord, but hundreds of its members were arrested, including prominent figures such as Muhammad Ali Bashar, Khayrat Shatir, Mahmud Azzat, and Isam al-Aryan. Several publishing houses belonging to the society were closed, together with its newspaper *Afaq Arabiyya* and its headquarters in Alexandria. In addition, the government-controlled media started a full-blown campaign against the Brothers, and parliamentary president Fathi Surur, Interior Minister Habib Adli, Mubarak's son Gamal and, finally, Mubarak himself publicly denounced the danger they represent.

In May 2007, the People's Assembly approved a series of constitutional reforms that included an explicit ban on the political use of Islam and the possibility of excluding independent candidates from running in elections, which could lead to the present parliament being declared illegal. The regime decided to extend the state of emergency that was in place since Sadat's assassination for another two years—in effect suspending the Constitution. In the two elections since the constitutional reform—the renewal of a third of the Upper House of Parliament, the Shura Council in June 2007, and the local elections of April 2008—the Muslim Brothers were effectively prevented from taking part in either of them. Also in April 2008, a military tribunal condemned twenty-five of them to between three and ten years in prison; Muhammad Ali Bashar and Khayrat Shatir, both members of the society's ruling body, got seven years for the financing of an illegal organization.

The Muslim Brothers reacted to the political, judicial, and media campaign against them following the al-Azhar incident by announcing the drafting of a political program aimed at assuaging the concerns of certain sectors of Egyptian society, particularly the Coptic community and the secular intelligentsia. However, the plan backfired when the draft of the program, which was sent to a numerous intellectuals, politicians, and *ulama* in the summer of 2007, was the object of fierce criticism. In the document, the Brothers insisted on their commitment to parliamentary democracy but made a series of proposals that could hardly be described as compatible with democratic values. The most polemic were the banning of women and Copts from becoming head of state and the creation of a body of *ulema* to advise parliament on the Islamic validity of its legislation. Following the negative reception of the draft, the society postponed sine die the publication of its program, alleging that the political climate was not conducive for its implementation.

The program fiasco reopened the rift between the Muslim Brothers' old guard and the younger Brothers, which the new leadership had worked to heal. Rumors of a possible split, strenuously denied by the society, was nevertheless rife. The program was openly criticized by the Syrian branch of the Muslim Brothers, thereby revealing the ideological divide between the different branches of the organization set up by Hasan al-Banna; their leader, Ali Sadr al-Din al-Bayanuni, asserted during its presentation in London that some of its proposals were incompatible with the concept of "civil society." Finally, it revived the debate about the society's real commitment to democracy, since it seemed to confirm the argument that so-called moderate Islamists accept the democratic voting procedure but do not subscribe to democratic values such as pluralism, gender equality, and the ability to make laws that do not coincide with its own interpretation of Islam.

As this book was going to press, two important developments were making news in the Egyptian media. The first was Mahdi Akif's announcement that he intends to step down from his position as general guide next January, instead of running for another six-year mandate—a first in the history of the society. The second development, no doubt related to Akif's departure and consequent wish to leave a legacy, is his resolve to present a slightly modified version of the Brothers' political program, toning down its most controversial points[33]. Just as the issue of the program, the search for a new leader will demand extensive negotiations between the different groups that constitute the society and is likely to exacerbate tensions within the movement.

NOTES

1. For an overview of al-Banna's life and ideology, see Ana Belén Soage, "Hasan al-Bannā or the Politicization of Islam," *Totalitarian Movements and Political Religions*, 9(1) (March 2008) 21–42.

2. *Al-Manar*, edited by Rashid Rida, was probably the most influential Islamic publication of the first half of the twentieth century. For a study of Rida's influence on the Islamist movement, see Ana Belén Soage, "Rashid Rida's Legacy," *The Muslim World*, 98(1) (January 2008) 1–23.

3. Hasan al-Banna, *Mudhakkirat al-Da'wa wal-Da'iya* (Cairo: Dar al-Shihab, 1966), p. 53.

4. The exact date is not known because al-Banna would later relate that the Society was established in Dhu al-Qi'da 1347/March 1928, whereas the hegira date corresponds to the period April–May 1929.

5. "Risalat al-Mu'tamar al-Khamis," in *Majmu'at Rasa'il al-Imam al-Shahid Hasan al-Banna* (Alexandria: Dar al-Da'wa), p. 167.

6. Su'ud Mawla, *Min Hasan al-Banna ila Hizb al-Wasat : Al-Haraka al-Islamiyya wa-Qadaya al-Irhab wal-Ta'ifiyya* (Beirut: Al-Ula, 2000), pp. 34, 45–47; Mahmud Jami, *Wa-'arafna al-Ikhwan* (Cairo: Dar al-Tawzi' wal-Nashr al-Islamiyya, 2004), pp. 26, 89ff.

7. However, three prominent Muslim Brothers—Muhammad al-Ghazali, Salah Ashmawi, and Hasan al-Baquri—agreed to participate in the government and, as a result, were expelled from the society.

8. Elie Kedourie, *Islam in the Modern World and Other Studies* (London: Mansell, 1980), p. 58. Kedourie continues: "The figure seems by no means an exaggeration, for the Brethren appealed to that Islamic solidarity which is perhaps the most profound instinct of the people" (ibid.).

9. Sayyid Qutb, *Ma'alim fi'l-Tariq* (Damascus: Dar Dimashq,?), p. 201.

10. The term is Gilles Kepel's. See his *Le prophète et Pharaon* (Paris: Editions du Seuil, 1993), chapter 4.

11. Quoted in Maye Kassem, *Egyptian Politics: The Dynamics of Authoritarian Rule* (Boulder, CO and London: Lynne Rienner, 2004), p. 55.

12. According to Abu al-Futuh, until the early 1980s the only difference between the Brothers and members of the radical Islamist organizations was about when, not if, to resort to violence. Declarations to Abd al-Rahim Ali, in the latter's *Al-Ikhwan al-Muslimun: Azmat Tayyar al-Tajdid* (Cairo: Markaz al-Mahrusa, 2004), pp. 81–82.

13. Since the "new guard" of the 1970s, there have been two more generations, with ages of the Brothers now ranging from their twenties to their fifties. These new generations, especially the younger one, have been very vocal about feeling marginalized and ignored within the society. See Khalil al-Anani, "Makhad Ya'tasir al-Jama'a wa-Yubriz Tanaqudat Bayna Arba'at Ajyal: Shabab al-Ikhwan al-Muslimin fi Misr Yukassirun al-Mahzurat wal-Shuyukh la Yaktarithun," *al-Hayat*, November 23, 2007.

14. For instance, the level of participation in the elections for the doctors' union rose from 7 percent in 1980 to 35 percent in 1988 and 45 percent in 1990. See Ali, *Al-Ikhwan al-Muslimun*, p. 88.

15. Ibid., p. 93.

16. According to an internal report, the society not only made use of the unions' facilities as if they were its own, but it also pursued its own political agenda irrespective of the consequences for the relationship between the unions and the state, on which the former ultimately depended. See Hesham al-Awadi, *In Pursuit of Legitimacy: The Muslim Brothers and Mubarak, 1982–2000* (London: I. B. Tauris, 2004), pp. 151–152, 181–183.

17. The *shura* (literally, consultation) is an institution of tribal, pre-Islamic Arabia alluded to in the Koran, if only twice, and rather vaguely (Koran 3:159 and 42:38). It has been identified with the modern parliamentary system. Hizb al-Islah and Hizb al-Amal mean the Party of Reform and the Party of Hope, respectively.

18. Muslim Brothers are expected to pay a monthly fee, and the society also relies on donations made to the network of mosques it controls. However, most of its funding is suspected to come from abroad, mainly from the Gulf countries.

19. Antoine Basbous, *L'islamisme, une révolution avortée?* (Paris: Hachette, 2000), p. 232.

20. The violence peaked in 1993, when over a thousand people were killed, most of them in the governorates of Upper Egypt.

21. A reference to the life of Muhammad, who while he was in Mecca was in the phase of "weakness" (*iftid'af*), but after his *hegira* to Medina entered the phase of "strength" (*tamakkun* or *tamkin*).

22. Ali, *Al-Ikhwan al-Muslimun*, pp. 99–100. However, Husam Tamam asserts that it was the new generation that drafted the Enablement Project; see his *Tahawwulat al-Ikhwan al-Muslimun: Tafakkuk al-Idilujiya wa-Nihayat al-Tanzim* (Cairo: Maktabat Madbuli, 2006), p. 9.

23. Quoted by Sawsan al-Jayyar, *Hum...wal-Ikhwan* (Giza: Hala, 2007), p. 36.

24. The ruling NDP initially obtained 317 seats out of the Assembly's 444 elected members, but only after 100 independents subsequently joined its ranks.

25. Ali, *Al-Ikhwan al-Muslimun*, p. 121.

26. The term "young princes" is Joshua A. Stacher's; see his "Post-Islamist Rumblings in Egypt: The Emergence of the Wasat Party," *The Middle East Journal*, 56(3) (Summer 2002) 418–419.

27. Stacher has remarked on the influence of Islamic intellectuals belonging to what he calls "the Wasatiyya (Centrist) stream of thought:" Yusuf al-Qaradawi, Tariq al-Bishri, Muhammad Imara, Muhammad Salim al-Awwa, etc. Ibid. pp. 417–418.

28. The term *dhimmi* refers non-Muslims living in an Islamic state. Although they were tolerated, they had to pay a capitulation tax known as *jizya* and were often the victims of discrimination. An example of the old guard's attitude to non-Muslims is an interview in 1997 in the course of which Mustafa Mash'hur said that the Copts should be barred from top army posts and pay the *jizya*; quoted in Mona El-Ghobashy, "The Metamorphosis of the Egyptian Muslim Brothers," *International Journal of Middle East Studies*, 37 (2005) 386, 394, n. 57.

29. Ibid. p. 387.

30. Al-Jayyar, *Hum...wal-Ikhwan*, p. 53.

31. According to current deputy leader Muhammad Habib, the founders of Hizb al-Wasat were not expelled from the society but chose to leave it. Interview with the authors, May 5, 2008.
32. Ibid.
33. However, deputy leader Muhammad Habīb considers the launch of a new version of the program unlikely in the near future. Interview with the authors, June 6, 2009.

4

THE CROSSROADS OF MUSLIM BROTHERS IN JORDAN

Juan José Escobar Stemmann

Manifestations of Islamic activism are abundant in Jordan. The country's Islamist movement has played a key role in political life almost since independence. As traditional allies of the monarchy, the Muslim Brothers have participated in politics when the regime has engaged in political openness. However, their moderation in domestic politics has been accompanied by a growing radicalization on foreign policy issues of their refusal to accept the Israel-Jordan peace treaty and their staunch opposition to the Western military intervention in Iraq.

Hamas's victory in the Palestinian elections followed by its seizure of the Gaza Strip along with the growing presence of Palestinian militants in the Jordanian organization have prompted a change of attitude on the part of the government, which has restricted the Brotherhood's social activities and lessen its capacity for mobilization.

FROM COOPERATION TO CRISIS

The Jordanian branch of the Muslim Brothers was created in 1945 by Abd al-Atif Abu Qura, a wealthy businessman from Salta who came into contact with the Egyptian Muslim Brothers during a visit to Palestine in the late 1930s. In 1944, impressed by Hasan al-Banna's call for *jihad* against colonialism and Zionism, Qura contacted the Egyptian leader and asked him to help establish a wing of the Brotherhood in Jordan. The following year, al-Banna sent two members of the organization to assist Abu Qura in setting up the association in Jordan. During the early years, the organization focused on education and on the struggle in Palestine. In 1947, Abu Qura sent a battalion of 100 members to fight alongside the Palestinians against the Jewish forces there.[1]

With the patronage of King Abdullah, the Brotherhood acquired legal status as a charitable association in January 1945. The king had a number of reasons for supporting the Muslim Brothers. By legalizing Muslim Brotherhood, he hoped to prevent them from becoming radical. Moreover, support for the organization bolstered his own Islamic legitimacy, while the growth of the Islamists would help him counter the pan-Arab nationalist forces that had become a threat to monarchies in the region.[2] Following the 1948 war and the mass arrival of Palestinian refugees in Jordan, the Brotherhood's position changed considerably. From being merely an association dedicated to fostering the teaching of Islam, it became a political organization capable of competing with nationalist and left-wing parties. A new class of professionals, representing the Jordanian middle class, gained control of the organization. Under this new leadership, the Brotherhood maintained its policy of cooperation with the regime although its program took on more political overtones in calling for the installation of an Islamic state governed by *Shari'a*.

The overthrow of the Egyptian monarchy in 1952, Nasser taking over power, and the repression suffered by the Muslim Brothers in Egypt facilitated an alliance between Jordan's monarchy and the country's Islamists, who joined forces to combat the left-wing and nationalist forces that, backed by Syria, Iraq, and Egypt, posed a serious challenge to King Hussein. As a result, the Muslim Brothers were permitted to field candidates in the first Jordanian parliamentary elections held in 1956, in which they gained four seats. The following year they supported the regime in its battle against the nationalist forces, which led to the ban on political parties in Jordan. As a charitable association, the Brotherhood evaded the ban and capitalized on its status as the only nongovernmental civil organization to widen its activities. In 1963, it set up the Islamic Center Charity Society (ICCS), an institution that was to bring together under one name the majority of the organizations through which the Brotherhood carried out its educational and community work. However, the Brotherhood's relations with the regime were not always easy. Indeed, they were characterized by highs and lows, and even periods of crisis. In 1956, the riots against the British presence in Jordan threatened the participation of the Islamists in the 1956 elections. In 1958, the Brotherhood's criticism of the Baghdad Pact prompted the arrest of the general guide.[3]

The Brothers also backed the Jordanian regime during the civil war of 1970–71, which resulted in the PLO leadership being expelled to Lebanon. Although they participated actively in Palestinian militia training camps in Jordan, they did not support the Palestinian resistance groups in their confrontation with the Jordanian army. The fact that they stayed out of the conflict allowed them to consolidate their relations with the monarchy. The Brothers' support was rewarded with the appointment of a prominent Brotherhood member, Ishaq Farhan, as education minister, a post he held from 1970 to 1974. Furthermore, they were allowed to occupy the political and social space left by the Palestinian resistance in the refugee camps and residential areas of the capital. This circumstance, combined with the rise in Islamist movements across the Middle East, facilitated the expansion of the Brotherhood movement in universities, professional associations, and charitable societies in Jordan.[4] The process of political openness initiated by the

Jordanian regime in 1989 brought the Islamists their best ever electoral success; they gained twenty-two of the eighty contested seats in the elections to the National Assembly. A short time later, the Brotherhood joined the government of Mudar Badran, securing five ministries (education, health, justice, social development, and Islamic affairs). This was the golden age of relations between the country's regime and its Islamists, who left a significant imprint on education.[5]

The year 1991 was a key year for Jordan. The regime's support for Iraq following the invasion of Kuwait left it isolated. The Middle East peace conference in Madrid afforded the country a new opportunity to rebuild its ties with the West and pursue peace with Israel. In turn, this led to a structural change in the Jordanian regime's relations with the Muslim Brothers. The Badran government was dissolved, and no Islamist has held a government post since then in Jordan.[6] The problems soon commenced for the Brotherhood. A new electoral law reduced the Islamist presence in the National Assembly in the 1993 elections, in which the Islamic Action Front (IAF)—the political party created in 1992 by the Brotherhood to comply with the requirements of the new legislation—contested for the first time.[7] The law was accompanied by a series of other measures against the Islamists, such as exclusion from government contracts and the curtailment of their university activities. The signing of the Wadi Araba peace treaty with Israel in 1994 and the Jordanian government's refusal to amend the electoral law resulted in the deterioration of Brotherhood's relations with the regime, and led to the Islamists' decision to boycott the 1997 elections, in which they were joined by the nationalist and left-wing parties.[8]

The ascension to the throne of King Abdullah II in 1999 heralded a new era in relations between the Jordanian regime and the country's Islamists. The expulsion of Hamas leaders that year demonstrated that Jordan did not seek a strategic role in the future of the West Bank, preferring to focus on domestic matters and maintaining good relations with the Palestinian Authority. Following the outbreak of the *intifada* (uprising) in the occupied territories, the economic crisis in Jordan, and the growing instability in the aftermath of terrorist strikes on the United States in 2001, the new king postponed the elections initially scheduled for 2001 by two years. The elections to the Lower House were held in June 2003. Muslim Brothers, who were aware that their absence from parliament had diminished their influence, even though they had been the broadest and best-organized political force, changed their strategy toward authorities, opted to contest the elections, and won of the 110 seats. A prior agreement between the regime and the Islamists resulted in fewer candidates contesting and limited electorate support for the IAF. In return, the king allowed a substantial number of the Islamist members of parliament (MPs) to be of Palestinian origin, a step that was interpreted as indicating support for the integration of the Palestinian sector in Jordanian society.[9]

However, the return of the Islamists to parliament did not prevent their relations with the government from deteriorating further due to the change in the balance of forces within the organization and the growing radicalization of Islamist rhetoric on foreign policy. The Iraqi crisis added a new element of tension to a relationship that had already been placed under strain by the process of normalization of Jordan's relations with Israel. Following the publication of a series of government measures in response to the increasingly radical Islamist stance on the conflicts in the Middle East, several Brotherhood imams were arrested in October 2004 for failing to heed the instructions issued by the Preaching and Guidance Council on the Iraqi conflict. Mosque pulpits had become vehicles for incendiary statements designed to stir up the *jihad* against American soldiers in Iraq. The imams arrested included Ibrahim Zaid Kilani, a former government minister and president of the Shura Council. The situation soon returned to normal when the Brotherhood bowed to the government's power.

A series of events that took place in 2006 radically altered the Jordanian government's attitude toward the Islamists. The victory of Hamas in the Palestinian elections in January triggered major fears among most Middle East countries, causing them to step back from the process of political openness set in motion in the region. Soon after, the Jordanian Islamists won a clear-cut victory in the elections to the professional associations. In May 2006, the Muslim Brothers appointed a new IAF secretary general, Zaki Bani Irshad, a Jordanian of Palestinian origin; this decision was interpreted by the regime as further evidence that Hamas had managed to penetrate the organization. The condolences expressed in June by two prominent IAF leaders (Ahmad Sukkar and Muhammad Abu Faris, both MPs) to the family of Abu Mus'ab al-Zarqawi, the al-Qa'ida leader killed in Iraq, was considered by the Jordanian authorities the point of no return in the radicalization process. Maruf Bakhit's government arrested and prosecuted the two IAF MPs, who spent several months in solitary confinement in prison before eventually receiving a pardon from the king.[10]

Despite the increasingly strained relations with the government, the Muslim Brotherhood prepared their political apparatus carefully for the two elections to be held in 2007 (municipal and parliamentary). However, although the Islamists were the favorites to win the local elections in July, withdrew from contention on election day, accusing the government of electoral fraud. The Brotherhood stepped up the ferocity of its criticism and insisted that the organization would cross the red line if the regime did. The government refused to back track, and the Jordanian prime minister launched unprecedented attacks on the Brotherhood. The king himself stepped in to defuse the tension a few days later, with a declaration guaranteeing that the parliamentary elections would be free and fair, which was interpreted by the Islamists as a royal assurance that they could t. A meeting between the prime minister and the more moderate wing of the Muslim Brothers eventually defused the crisis.[11]

The decision not to contest the local elections saw the Islamists excluded from power at the municipal level and the scenario was capitalized on by the

Jordanian government. At a time when Hamas was growing stronger in Gaza, the Jordanian regime ordered a series of measures designed to curb the influence of the Brotherhood. The ICCS was closed down, and its institutions were removed from Islamist control. Steps were taken to control the participation of Islamist students in state-run universities, and lecturers belonging to the Brotherhood were from the universities. The *zakat* system was amended, and Islamists were dismissed from the committees; the Society for the Protection of the Koran was closed down; and the administration of Zarqa University was taken away from the Islamists. These blows to Brotherhood support structures were aimed at reducing the influence of the Jordanian Islamists and limiting their scope for community action.[12] Shortly afterwards, the government forced the moderate wing of the Brotherhood to exclude members of the Palestinian sector from the list of candidates for the parliamentary elections in November. Sidelining the leaders of the IAF, the Shura Council agreed to field a limited list of "acceptable candidates" for the elections that were held on November 20, 2007. The decision merely compounded the debacle of Jordan's main Islamist party, which won just seven seats (compared to seventeen in 2003), plunging official Islamism into an identity and leadership crisis from which it has still not recovered.

INTERNAL RIFTS

The internal elections held in recent years show that the Muslim Brothers are divided into four main currents or sectors.[13] During the early years, their political rhetoric was restricted to a small number of issues: support for the Palestinian cause and condemnation of the Soviet camp. The spread of Sayyid Qutb's ideas across the Middle East at the end of the 1960s triggered debate within the organization, with some advocating the creation of a clandestine wing and armed action against the regime's policy of repression, while others were anxious to avoid the errors committed in Egypt and called for channels of communication to be opened with the government and for an emphasis on social actions. This division lies at the root of the split between hawks and doves in the organization. Two schools of thought have since then vied with each other to define the Brotherhood's political discourse in Jordan.[14]

The most radical or hawkish sector is drawn mainly from the generation of Trans-Jordanian Islamists who gave unwavering support to the Jordanian regime during the conflict with the Palestinians in the 1970s. The discourse of this sector is radical in its ideology, including open calls for an Islamic state to be installed and references to concepts such as divine sovereignty. Its members are closer to the radical rhetoric of Qutb than to the liberalizing discourse. They are also the most nationalistic and defend the need to ensure the preeminence of the Trans-Jordanian component on the political scene. This sector controlled the Brotherhood during the 1980s but is now a minority in an organization currently dominated by the Palestinian faction. Its main representatives are Shura Council members Ahmad Kafawin and

Ahmad Zarqa. Other prominent members include Muhammad Abu Faris, one of the leading exponents of scholarly Salafism in the Brotherhood.[15]

With the resumption of parliamentary life in 1989, the doves—led by Hamza Mansur and the former speaker of the National Assembly, Abd al-Atif Arabiyat—regained control of the organization. The Muslim Brothers participated actively in the drafting of the National Charter in the early 1990s showing a readiness to work with other groups of Islamists. An outcome of this was the creation of the IAF in 1992, thus consolidating the incorporation of the Islamists into the political scene.

The peace process with Israel had an impact on the internal debate in the Brotherhood and led to the emergence of a third current, called *wasat* (center), midway between the hawks and the doves. This was a younger generation that cut its teeth on the struggle in the universities and in professional associations. Its emergence coincided with the appointment of Abd al-Magid Zunaybat as the general guide in place of Abd al-Rahman Khalifa, which marked the end of charismatic figures at the helm of the organization and heralded a more limited role for its leader—to the benefit of the Brotherhood's structure, in which centrists held the majority. The centrists gained power after the 1994 elections when Salam al-Falahat, the general supervisor, and other young members such as Imad Abu Diyya and Jamil Abu Baker joined the executive council. In 1997 they secured virtually all the top council positions. In principle, their ideas coincide with the vision of the moderate sector with respect to the political process, although they refuse to be identified with the state. They also believe that Jordan's Islamists should set their own agenda rather than subordinate their political actions to the needs of Hamas. It was this third current or sector that successfully called for an end to the election boycott in the late 1990s and spearheaded the changes to the Muslim Brothers' political program.[16]

The control exerted by the centrists was gradually eroded by the emergence of a fourth current, which was the product of the special relationship between the Muslim Brotherhood and Hamas. The expulsion of Hamas leaders from Jordan in 1999 triggered an internal dispute within the Brotherhood. Some leaders were accused of colluding with the regime in the expulsion. The dispute led to the emergence of the reformist sector, which is today the biggest current of the Muslim Brotherhood in Jordan, although not necessarily the one most represented among the organization's leadership. The term reformist can be misleading given that the sector fully supports the objectives of Hamas, the Palestinian Islamist group. The sector comprises Jordanian Islamists of Palestinian origin and they have gradually taken over the organization's power bases.

The movement has capitalized on the popularity of Hamas among Islamist militants in Jordan. Today, its members control virtually all the professional associations, whose main political goal is to oppose normalization of relations with Israel. They also control the main Islamist newspaper, *al-Sabil*. A characteristic of this sector of the Brotherhood is that it contains supporters of the radical Qutb discourse as well as more moderate reformists who have embraced the reformist rhetoric because they realize that the policies of openness initiated by Arab regimes should be of benefit. Both groups are united, however, by their radical opposition to the normalization of ties with Israel and by their defense of the right to resist using every possible means.

The internal elections of 2002 saw the reformist sector, in an alliance with the hawks, obtain a majority on the executive council. This period coincided with the Brotherhood's resumption of its parliamentary activity. Most of the seventeen Islamist MPs elected in the 2003 elections belonged to the reformist sector. The return of the Hamas leadership to Jordan became one of the main demands of the new council. Since then, centrists and reformists have to share the leadership of the organization. In the 2006 internal elections, Salam al-Falahat was appointed the new general guide while Zaki Bani Irshad, a Jordanian of Palestinian origin, was elected head of the IAF after being chosen by the outgoing (reformist-controlled) executive council.

The main point of friction between the centrists and reformists concerns the extent of the Muslim Brotherhood's political participation, especially in light of Hamas's victory in the Palestinian territories. The Brotherhood's traditional position had been outlined in a book written in 1994 by Abdalah al-Akaylah, *Islamists Participation in the State*, in which the author acknowledged the limitations of the role played by the Muslim Brothers in Jordan. The country's difficult situation, weakness, and external dependence made the establishment of a truly Islamic state difficult. The Brotherhood was conscious of this context and hence did not seek to replace the regime with an Islamic state. Its strategy was to renounce violence and advocate gradual, progressive, and peaceful change.[17] The success of Hamas in the 2006 elections served to boost the reformist sector. Azzam al-Hunaydi, the Islamists' spokesman in the parliament elected in 2003, declared shortly afterwards that the Muslim Brothers were ready to govern in Jordan. The reformists, led by Zaki Bani Irshad, wanted to change the status quo and turn the Brotherhood into a genuine partner in the political decision-making process. This change of strategy was not well received by the regime, which was suspicious of the intentions of the Jordanian Islamists, especially after Hamas took power by force in Gaza.[18]

The poor election results for Muslim Brothers in 2007 have inevitably affected the organization. The centrists and doves, pressured by the Jordanian government, drew up the list of candidates but excluded personalities belonging to the reformist sector, such as Ali al-Utum. The list drew criticism from the reformists on account of the exclusion of candidates sympathetic to Hamas and also from the hawks, who accused the moderate sector of allying itself with the government to eliminate them. The IAF secretary general boycotted the election preparation meetings. The crisis eventually led to the severing of formal and organizational ties between Hamas and the Muslim Brotherhood in Jordan. Although the decision was not accepted by the executive council, Hamas decided to become independent and appoint a new general guide. One of the implications of this decision was that Muslim

Brotherhood militants in the refugee camps in Syria and Lebanon opted to join the Palestinian organization.[19]

The Reformist Discourse

In 2005, following the lead of their Egyptian and Syrian counterparts, the Jordanian Muslim Brothers published a new political program reflecting the evolution of their political doctrine over the past decade. The document drawn up by the IAF, entitled *The Islamic Movement's Vision on Reform in Jordan*, came at a time when a spring of democracy appeared to be emerging after the military intervention in Iraq. The Islamists hoped to capitalize on the situation and position themselves as fundamental players in the processes of political openness under way in the region. Realizing that they had little choice but to take part in political life, the country's Islamists have fully embraced the rhetoric of political reform. Declarations that democracy was anathema to Islam and calls for an Islamic state ruled solely by Shari'a are a thing of the past.[20]

The following concepts feature in the program of the Brothers: of popular sovereignty (before, only the sovereignty of God—*hakimiyya*—existed); the holding of free and fair elections; freedom of worship; the right of assembly and demonstration; freedom to create political parties; an independent judiciary; and the establishment of a truly parliamentary monarchy. Democratic methods are applied stringently within the organization, and every four years, elections are held to choose the Shura Council, which, in turn, elects the secretary general of the IAF as well as the general guide of the Brotherhood, a post that—unlike in Egypt—is not held for life.

Politically, Jordan's Islamists appear to partly follow the doctrinal evolution promoted by parties such as Justice and Development Party in Turkey and Morocco and Wasat in Egypt. However, some analysts see their ideology as being closer to the anti-liberal, conservative, and anti-Western leanings of the founder of the Muslim Brothers, Hasan al-Banna, than to the new tenets of the Justice and Development Party in Turkey or Wasat in Egypt. They also consider that the country's Islamists have adopted the rhetoric of political liberalization for purely practical reasons, not because of any deep-seated evolution in their doctrine. A case in point is the economic chapter of the new political program, which stresses that the solution to the major economic problems faced by the country's economy is to apply *Shari'a*. The Islamists counter this argument by emphasizing the internal democracy practiced by the organization. The argument is partly true given that they only recognize this right for those who share their political, ideological, and cultural outlook. The experience of Islamist movements in power leads to a degree of skepticism. The examples of Iraq and Hamas in Gaza show that, once in power, Islamists tend to show scant regard for political pluralism.[21]

Still, the reformist platform of the Muslim Brothers represents a new ideological development in the movement's political discourse. The recognition of democratic values, pluralism, and the free transfer of power have become new paradigms for the Islamists. However, it should be stressed that there are still many gray areas in their new political thinking. The process is full of ambiguities and is far from consolidated. Moderate Islamist thinking is evolving slowly toward pluralism, not liberalism, and the Muslim Brothers are no exception in this regard: they remain extremely conservative on social issues, and the recognition afforded to civil liberties is conditioned by considerations of public order and social decorum.[22]

ORGANIZATIONAL NETWORK AND SUPPORT ACTIVITIES

The highs and lows experienced in their relations with the government have not prevented the Muslim Brothers from setting up organizations in various fields and putting in place an extensive network across the country. Nursery schools, hospitals, cultural centers, youth centers, and charity associations together form an institutional network that is used by the Brotherhood to consolidate its influence in Jordanian society. Most of the community actions undertaken by the Muslim Brothers are carried out through the ICCS, which was set up in 1963. The society has four regional centers—in Zarqa, Mafraq, Irbid, and Ramtha—and thirty-two committees. It is run by a nine-man executive committee appointed by the Brotherhood. Until 2007, the society managed forty-one educational centers, from nurseries to schools. They included Dar al-Arqum and Dar al-Aqsa (with over twenty establishments across the country). These private schools, aimed at the middle and upper classes, combine the national curriculum with religious instruction. The society also runs Zarqa University and Islamic Community College. The ICCS also runs two hospitals and fifteen medical centers. Its flagship is the Islamic Hospital in Amman, which opened in 1982 and employs over 1,100 people. The ICCS has six centers that manage training and income generation projects, as well as thirty-three centers dedicated to funding orphanages and poor families. Also part of the Muslim Brotherhood's institutional network in Jordan are the Association of Islamic Studies and Research and the Society for the Preservation of the Koran, which has over 100 centers throughout the country.[23]

The institutions affiliated with the ICCS aim to recruit the middle classes by offering them employment and services. They guarantee employment for Brotherhood members and create a social fabric that attracts new followers and mobilizes support for Islamist causes. The institutions have become symbols of the Islamist alternative to the state. The Jordanian government is fully aware of the importance of the support network and for that reason decided to close down the ICCS in 2007. Since then, the capacity of the Brotherhood to undertake community work has been severely curtailed, and revenue has declined sharply. Some analysts consider the closure of the ICCS to be one of the causes underlying the poor results obtained by the Islamists in the last elections.[24]

The political activism of Brotherhood members has seen them engage extensively in the running of professional associations, which, given the negligible presence of trade unions, are the main vehicles for collective representation in the country. Islamists currently control the professional associations for engineers, architects, and lawyers and are the main opposition group in the associations of doctors, civil servants, and nurses. Moreover, the peculiar makeup of Jordan's political system and the coincidence of views on issues such as political reform or the Israeli–Palestinian conflict have facilitated dialogue between the Islamists and other political forces in the country. The initiation of this dialogue can be traced to the opposition of virtually all the political forces to the 1993 electoral law, which led the opposition parties to set up a coordination council comprising thirteen parties in total (communists, Ba'athists, nationalists, socialists, and so on), including the IAF. The entire council supported the boycott of the 1997 elections. Although its importance has diminished due to the fact that many members are not represented in parliament, it continues to table proposals and issue joint statements on a range of issues of common interest (electoral reform, quotas for women, and so on). The council is a source of pride for the IAF and is held up as a model for other Arab countries. In the National Assembly the IAF has had few problems allying itself with other political forces and has voted with them on many occasions.[25]

THE IDEOLOGIZATION OF FOREIGN POLICY

Like their brethren in the Middle East and North Africa, Jordan's Islamists have taken on the role of heirs of Arab nationalism and have adopted the anti-Western and anti-imperialist discourse that characterized the latter for many years. In recent times, their doctrinal evolution and moderation on issues of political reform have been accompanied by a radicalization of their discourse on foreign policy questions. The main bone of contention remains the Palestinian issue, on which they maintain their maximalist position. In their electoral programs they reiterate repeatedly that it is the religious obligation of all Islamists to liberate the whole of Palestine. They reject an Israeli state and consider that *jihad* is the only way to restore the rights of Muslims in Palestine. They also consider that the Arab-Israeli conflict is part of a much older historic process. In their view, the conflict with the Jews began not in 1948 but when Muhammad emigrated to Medina and reached agreements with Jewish tribes, only for them to be broken later.[26]

The peace treaty with Israel in 1994 marked the beginning of a series of clashes between the Islamists and the Jordanian government. The creation of highly active committees in professional associations to fight the normalization of relations with Israel, as well as the campaigns to boycott individuals, firms, and institutions with Israeli ties, further strained relations with the government. The Islamists have expressed their opposition to initiatives such as the roadmap, which they describe as a road to surrender, and have openly supported suicide attacks, which they consider to be "martyrdom operations" and the only weapons to resist an enemy that is militarily vastly superior. Like their Palestinian counterparts, Jordanian Islamists believe that Israel was forced to withdraw from Gaza by the military pressure exerted by Palestinian resistance. The current crisis within the organization has also had consequences for the position of the Islamists with regard to the situation in Gaza, where Hamas's seizure of power has generated considerable confusion in the Brotherhood. While the reformist sector defends the measure, the moderates prefer to ignore the incident and call for Palestinian unity.[27]

U.S. military intervention in Iraq is another factor contributing to the hardening of the tone of Islamist criticism, which has reached unaccustomed heights. Not only has the Jordanian government come under fire for allying itself with the United States in the Iraq war, Arab governments have also been denounced for their failure to act. Moreover, support has been expressed openly for resistance and *jihad* against American occupation. In some cases, the Jordanian government has been accused of apostasy, and the legitimacy of the monarchy has even been called into question. The government clamped down hard on the criticism, which was unprecedented in its ferocity, as attested by the editorials of the main mouthpiece, *al-Sabil*. This newspaper has also regularly published articles by authors praising Osama bin Ladin and the Iraqi resistance. Although openly critical of the methods employed by people such as al-Zarqawi (beheadings, killings of Iraqi civilians), the authors defend the use of violence by the resistance and confer martyr status on those who give their lives for the cause. Their rhetoric on the right to resist foreign occupation clearly reflects the radicalization of the positions of the more moderate Islamists with respect to foreign policy.

From a geostrategic perspective, the interests of the Muslim Brothers in the Middle East are tied to those of Hamas. Although opposed to Iran's policy in Iraq and Afghanistan, they applaud Iranian support for Hizballah and for the Palestinian Islamist organization. They also defend the position of the Syrian authorities and denounce the campaign orchestrated by the United States to pressure the regime in Damascus. The Brotherhood's interests lead it to ally itself with Iran, Syria, and Hizballah and distance itself from its counterparts in other countries. In Iraq, there is a clear conflict between the Jordanian Muslim Brothers and the Islamic Party of Iraq, which plays an active part in the political process designed by the United States. The Jordanian Islamists oppose occupation and support resistance and have thus moved closer to the Association of Muslim Scholars led by Hareth al-Dari, an advocate of armed struggle against American occupation. Their position differs also to that of the Muslim Brothers in Lebanon, who have aligned themselves with the March 14 forces against Hizballah, and to that of their Syrian Brothers, who are part of the Salvation Front opposition movement.[28]

The Islamists are also highly critical of the West, whom they accuse of double standards and see as the cause of a large proportion of the problems

suffered by the *umma* (community of believers). The United States bears the
brunt of the criticism on account of its support for Israel and its military
intervention in Iraq. For these reasons, the Islamists refuse to have any contact with official U.S. government representatives. Criticism is leveled at
Europe too for its failure to act and inability to take a more balanced approach
to the Israeli–Palestinian conflict. However, the Islamists stress the need for
good relations with the European Union due—among other reasons—to its
sizeable Muslim community. They underline the importance of organizations sympathetic to the Muslim Brotherhood in many European countries,
which have become the main representatives of the Muslim communities.
Consequently, their reaction to the crisis triggered by the publication of the
cartoons against Muhammad was more muted, and they called for dialogue
with the European authorities to avoid a repetition of such acts. The Islamists
have a negative opinion of the Barcelona process, criticizing in particular the
economic basket because of the neoliberal vision of economic relations it
imposes, which benefits Europeans only.[29]

Some critics within the Brotherhood have begun to challenge the organization's strict and maximalist positions on foreign policy issues. Ruhayl
al-Gharayba, a leading member of the IAF and former director of its policy
department, recently published an Islamic legal opinion in which he called
for international reality to be interpreted using a different paradigm. He
argues that it is necessary to move on from the classic Koranic notion that
splits the world into two opposing camps, and he advocates that the positions adopted by the Muslim Brothers on international affairs should be
based on political considerations, not on the ideological dogma of Islamist
movements.[30]

Opposing Agendas

The Islamists' poor showing in the 2007 elections was the logical outcome of the change in attitude on the part of the Jordanian regime toward
the Muslim Brothers, a change caused by the exceptional circumstances in the
region since 2006. Hamas's triumph in the Palestinian elections, the second
Lebanon war, and the alliance between Hizballah, Iran, and Syria sent alarm
bells ringing in the Jordanian government, which looked on anxiously as the
Hamas-linked reformist sector gained control of the IAF. In the eyes of the
government, the Islamists had changed. No longer content with the political
role they had traditionally played in Jordan, they wanted to be influential
players in the political decision-making process and also sought to increase
their power and influence by accepting external support from countries with
which Jordan does not have good relations. For the Jordanian regime, the
Muslim Brothers today represent a threat as a result of the transformations
undergone by the organization. Their discourse of opposition to the state
has become more radical, and Hamas has managed to position its sympathizers among the leadership of the country's Islamists. The measures taken by
the government, particularly the takeover of the ICCS, have restricted the

Brotherhood's capacity to carry out its community work and have cut its revenue drastically. The government view is that once the Islamists cease to work for the general interests of the country, they should no longer retain the benefits they enjoyed, as compared to other political groupings.

Although the IAF was at pains to attribute the loss of electoral support to the government's campaign in favor of certain candidates and its vote-purchasing act, the 2007 parliamentary election results also evidence the internal crisis suffered by the organization.[31] In April 2008, the decision by the Brotherhood's executive council to suspend IAF Secretary General Zaki Bani Irshad and the leader of the hawkish sector, Muhammad Abu Faris, for one year did not prevent a leading hawk, Haman al-Said, from being elected general guide of the Brotherhood, nor did temporary suspension prevent Bani Irshad from remaining as head of the IAF. Two opposing agendas coexist in the organization at present. One is focused on Jordan's national and internal issues and the other seeks to increase involvement in Palestinian matters, allying itself with the Hamas policy. Pressure from the authorities and the current split among the Jordanian Islamists could turn the Muslim Brothers into an organization with negligible political clout in Jordan.

NOTES

1. Janine A. Clark, *The Islamic Center Charity Society in Jordan: The Benefits to the Middle Class* (Bloomington, IN: Indiana University Press, 2004), p. 84.
2. Marion Boulby, *The Muslim Brotherhood and the Kings of Jordan, 1945–1993* (Atlanta: Scholars Press, 1999), pp. 45–47.
3. Mohamed Abu Rumman, *Islamic Politics in Jordan* (Amman: Friedrich-Ebert Stiftung, 2007), p. 8.
4. Ibrahim Gharayba, *The Muslim Brotherhood in Jordan, 1946–1996* (Amman: 1997), pp. 59–74.
5. Various factors influenced the results obtained by the Muslim Brothers in 1989. Having been the only organization allowed to engage in social activities for decades, it had the organization, skill, and contacts with the population that other candidates lacked. Moreover, the Brothers capitalized on the vote of refugee camps, which had no representation following the departure of the PLO in 1971. See Quintan Wiktorowicz, *The Management of Islamic Activism* (New York: State University of New York Press, 2001), p. 87.
6. Beverly Milton-Edwards, "A Temporary Alliance With the Crown: The Islamic Response In Jordan," in James Piscatori (ed.), *Islamic Fundamentalism and the Gulf Crisis* (Chicago, IL: The American Academy of Arts and Sciences, 1991), p. 106.
7. Sabah El-Said, "Between Pragmatism and Ideology," *The Washington Institute Policy Papers*, N. 39 (1995), p. 2.
8. Vid Ziad Abu-Amr, "La monarchie jordanienne et les Frères musulmans ou les modalités d'endiguement d'une opposition loyalist," *Les états Arabes face à la contestation Islamiste* (IFRI, 1996), pp. 125–144.
9. Abu Rumman, *Islamic Politics in Jordan*, p. 25.
10. Nathan J. Brown, "Jordan and Its Islamic Movement: The Limits of Inclusion," *Carnegie Papers*, No. 74 (November 2006), p. 16.

11. Abu Rumman, *Islamic Politics in Jordan*, p. 28.

12. Ibid., p. 77.

13. Interview by the author with Mohamed Abu Rumman, journalist at *al-Ghad* newspaper, February 5, 2006.

14. Gharayba, *The Muslim Brotherhood in Jordan*, p. 35.

15. In a book entitled *Participation in the Government of the Yahiliyya*, Muhammad Abu Faris issued a *fatwa* rejecting the arguments used by the doves to justify joining the Badran government. The doves used the arguments set out by Umar al-Ashkar in his *Right to Participate in Government and Local Councils* to counter the *fatwa* by Abu Faris. Curiously, al-Ashkar acknowledged the very arguments used by Abu Faris to promote nonparticipation, although he recommended participation to serve the organization's long-term interests. See Abu Rumman, *Islamic Politics in Jordan*, p. 36.

16. Ibid., p. 36.

17. See Abdalah al-Akaylah, "The Experience of the Islamic Movement in Jordan," in Azzam al-Tamimi, *Islamist Participation in Power* (London: Liberty Organization, 1994).

18. Abu Rumman, *Islamic Politics in Jordan*, p. 43.

19. Ibid., p. 58.

20. Ruhayel Graraibeh, *Islamists and the Political Development in Jordan* (Amman: Konrad Adenauer Stiftung, 2004), pp. 79–97.

21. There are important differences in the positions of the various Middle East groups that follow the ideas of the Muslim Brothers. Whereas Egyptian Islamists rule out any possibility that minority religions or women might accede to the highest positions in the state and advocate the setting up of a "committee of the wise" on religious matters to verify if civil laws conform to Shari'a, in Jordan the former general guide Abd al-Magid Zunaybat wrote an article in *al-Ghad* in 2007 in which he accepted that women or Christians might occupy the position of head of state. He also considered that a committee of the wise was unnecessary, given that the aim is to build a modern civil state, not the Islamic state derived from the Caliphate. See Abu Rumman, *Islamic Politics in Jordan*, pp. 45–48.

22. See Nathan Brown, Amr Hamzawy, and Marina Ottaway, "Islamic Movements and the Democratic Process in the Arab World: Exploring the Grey Areas," *Carnegie Papers*, 67 (March 2006); Juan José Escobar Stemmann, "Islamists and Democracy: Imposible debate?" *Política Exterior*, No. 116 (March 2007– April 2007).

23. Clark, *The Islamic Center Charity Society in Jordan*, pp. 92–93.

24. Abu Rummann, *Islamic Politics in Jordan*, p. 70.

25. Russell E. Lucas, "Deliberalization in Jordan," in Larry Diamond, Marc F. Plattner, and Daniel Brumberg (eds.), *Islam and Democracy in the Middle East* (2003), pp. 99–106.

26. Sabah al-Said, "Between Pragmatism and Ideology," p.13.

27. Abu Rumman, *Islamic Politics in Jordan*, p. 49.

28. Ibid., p. 52.

29. Author interview with Abd al-Magid Zunaybat, former general supervisor of the Muslim Brothers, December 18, 2004. The Jordanian Brothers and their Egyptian counterparts agree as regards the need to draw a clear distinction between the European Union and the United States. This explains why the Islamists have promoted dialogue with officials of European countries but not with the Americans.

30. Abu Rumman, *Islamic Politics in Jordan,* p. 55.
31. The Muslim Brothers won only six seats in the 2007 elections, gaining just 100,000 of the 2 million votes cast. Some observers note that the decline in popularity of the movement, particularly among Jordanians of Palestinian origin, is due, among other reasons, to the criticism that followed Hamas's taking power in Gaza. Events in Gaza have triggered suspicion and doubts as to the political ambitions and the plans of the Palestinian Islamists.

5

THE SYRIAN MUSLIM BROTHERHOOD

Robert G. Rabil

In contrast to its sister organization in Egypt, the Muslim Brotherhood in Syria began by engaging in the politics of parliamentary democracy at the time of the country's independence in 1946. This policy compelled the Brotherhood to forego its Islamist agenda and pursue more or less a pragmatic policy. Syrian Ikhwan members contested in parliamentary elections, served in cabinets, and engaged in realpolitik. However, the ascension to power of the secular and Alawi-dominated Ba'th party posed a significant threat to the ideology and practice of the Brotherhood, which had already been affected by the political trend set by secular, socialist, and nationalist parties. In 1964, a Muslim Brotherhood insurgency erupted in Hama, which was swiftly put down by the incumbent regime. Yet, the regime failed to pay attention to the organization's growing underground activity.

The insurgency restarted in a disorganized manner in 1976 but soon turned into full-scale urban warfare against the regime and its supporters. The decisive and final showdown took place in Hama in 1982, which was quelled by the regime using tremendous force.

Since then the regime has pursued a consistent policy toward the outlawed Muslim Brotherhood, aimed at fragmenting the Brotherhood by attempting to neutralize its radical elements and co-opt its moderate members. Forced exile also took a toll on the Ikhwan leadership, whose voice was clearly absent from the brief revival of the civil society reform movement at the turn of the century.

Partly in response to their crisis of irrelevance, the Brotherhood leadership initiated a process aimed at transforming the organization into one by saying that it espouses pluralism and liberal values. As a result, it was able to forge a working relationship with parties and movements of different ideological stripes within the ranks of the Syrian opposition. However, the alliance with former vice president Abd al-Halim Khaddam has undermined its efforts to spearhead an all-encompassing oppositional force.

Meanwhile, the regime has clamped down on the opposition, including those calling for reform from a nationalist standpoint. Growing isolation and international pressure on the regime only deepened its commitment to maintain power at the expense of making what George Alan described as neither bread nor freedom. More recent overtures to Syria from international actors have not changed its policy of repression, carried out in the name of stability and protecting Syria's national interest. Consequently, the regime would most likely continue to proscribe organized activity by the Brotherhood, even at the cost of taking the lead by itself in a relative Islamification of Syrian society to preempt the Brotherhood.

IDEOLOGY VERSUS PARLIAMENTARY POLITICS: 1947–1963

The first signs of Muslim activism were visible during the French mandate over Syria in the 1930s. In the latter part of the decade, groups of Muslim activists emerged in several Syrian cities to resist the French rule. Ironically, it was the French who helped these isolated groups to merge so that they could be involved as a single organization, as the French insisted, to address the contentious issue of Islamic teaching in schools.[1] Out of this organized activity, a movement by the name of Shabab Muhammad (Young Men of Muhammad) was born.

Meanwhile, a young Syrian student, Mustafa al-Siba'i, studying in Cairo returned home to Damascus. During his stay in Cairo, Siba'i became influenced by the Muslim Brotherhood and its founder Hasan al-Banna. The Muslim Brotherhood, or the Ikhwan, dedicated itself to "liberating the Islamic nation from foreign rule" and "establishing a free Islamic state."[2] Inspired by the Egyptian Muslim Brotherhood, Siba'i, leading Shabab Muhammad, founded a branch of the Muslim Brotherhood in Syria, which went on to become a political force in the country.

Following Syria's independence from France in 1946, the Ikhwan became active in the country's inchoate parliamentary democracy. It participated in the country's first postindependence parliamentary elections in July 1947. Though it did not present its own nationwide list, Ikhwan members Mahmud al-Shaqafa, Muhammad Mubarak, and Ma'ruf al-Dawalibi won the elections, respectively, in Hama, Damascus, and Aleppo.[3]

Around this time, the Palestinian issue had become important to Syria's political forces. In fact, in September 1947, the Syrian Ikhwan issued a National Charter declaring their support for the establishment of an Arab state in Palestine.[4] According to the Information Center of the Muslim Brotherhood in Syria, they participated in the 1948 war and their forces were led by al-Siba'i.[5]

Before long, the reverberations of the Arab defeat in Palestine and the polarization of Syrian politics led Colonel Husni al-Za'im to mount a coup d'etat in March 1949 and suspend party politics. The Muslim Brotherhood, along with Syria's other political parties, was outlawed.[6] However, Za'im's rule did not last long, for he was removed by another officer, Colonel Sami Hinnawi, in August 1949. The Syrian Ikhwan resumed their political activity shortly after the coup. They prepared themselves to run for the

November elections and participate in drafting of the constitution. On November 11 the same year, they established the Islamic Socialist Front (ISF), which presented a full list only in Damascus. The November elections for the 143-member parliament resulted in the ISF winning three seats in Damascus, electing Siba'i, Mubarak, and Arif al-Taraqji. One of its supporters, Dawalibi, who was also a member of the People's Party, won in Aleppo. The secular nationalist Ba'th party, which would later rule Syria, also won only three seats.[7]

Leading the ISF, al-Siba'i opposed the proposal to merge with Iraq led by Hinnawi and his supporters in the People's Party. As the idea for a union with Iraq gathered momentum, Colonel Adib al-Shishakli, supported by opponents of the union, mounted a bloodless coup in December 1949. Later that month, the army gave the go-ahead to Khalid al-Azm, an independent, to form a cabinet, which included Dawalibi and Mubarak.[8]

The Brotherhood shifted its attention to a campaign to make Islam the state religion in the constitutional draft, a matter that raised significant opposition in Syria, especially from the Ba'th party, whose supporters clashed with Ikhwan members. Following a tense debate in September 1950, the Syrian Assembly accepted the wording that the religion of the head of state must be Islam. No less significantly, the constitution included the provision that Islamic law (*fiqh*) was the main source (*al-masdar al-ra'isi*) for legislation.[9] Commenting on the Ikhwan's tactful handling of the issue, Joshua Tietelbaum perceptively wrote:

> The Ikhwan seemed quite pleased with how things turned out, a sign that they were content with the final draft.... The Brotherhood knew from the start that to get more of one's desires fulfilled, one often starts out asking for everything. Even religious fanatics can learn to be tactically patient and skilful.[10]

However, this pragmatism exhibited by the Ikhwan did not shield them from the tribulations of Syrian politics, which were affected by the Cold War and the Arab-Israeli conflict. By the early 1950s, Syria had become a battlefield for the cold war. The Western camp devised defense plans to contain Soviet expansion in the Middle East. In October 1950, the United States, Britain, France, and Turkey formally proposed to Egypt the formation of a Middle East Defense Organization (MEDO). Significantly, Britain made the evacuation of its troops from Egypt conditional on Cairo's acceptance of MEDO. But Egypt rejected MEDO. In solidarity with Egypt, the ISF, along with the Ba'th party, denounced MEDO as an imperialist plot. The Ikhwan and the Ba'th party had called for a policy of neutrality between the two cold war camps.[11]

Meanwhile, Shishakli, egged on by secularist parties and figures—the Syrian Social Nationalist Party (SSNP) and Akram Hawrani—moved against al-Ikhwan in the pretext of removing religion from politics. In January 1952, Ikhwan branches were closed, the organization's newspaper banned, and its youth organization dissolved. In addition, some Ikhwan leaders were arrested. Subsequently, the Ikhwan leadership decided to refrain from all overt public activity and concentrate on social and religious activities.[12] The Ikhwan boycotted the October 1953 elections, in which only independents, the SSNP, and Shishakli's Arab Liberation Movement participated. Opposition to Shishakli intensified, and he was removed by a military coup in December, whereupon a caretaker government, with military backing, was formed until elections were held.

Concomitantly, the Western camp devised another defense plan, the Baghdad Pact of 1955. Not only would the pact serve as a bulwark against Soviet expansion in the Middle East but also as a means to protect Iraq as the last bastion of British influence in the region. Because Iraq accepted the pact and Egypt opposed it, Syria became the focal point for opponents and proponents. The Ba'th party and the Communists sided with Egypt's president Gamal Abdel Nasser, who led Arab opposition to the pact.[13] The Syrian Ikhwan, though in principle opposed to the pact, had reservations about fully supporting Nasser.

Nasser had by this time launched a campaign to crush the Egyptian Ikhwan, which reportedly attempted to assassinate him in October 1954. In addition to arresting many Ikhwan members, including their leader Hasan al-Hudaybi, Egyptian authorities executed six members in December. This led to an uproar within the circles of the Syrian Ikhwan, which organized demonstrations in support of their Egyptian colleagues. In turn, the attitude of the Syrian Ikhwan provoked tensions between the Egyptian and Syrian governments. All of this posed a dilemma to the Syrian Ikhwan. How to reconcile their opposition to "imperialist" plans with support for Nasser, whose popularity had surged within the ranks of the Ba'th and the Communist parties in Syria?

At the same time, the Syrian Ikhwan was also facing significant competition from the Ba'th and Communists, whose secular, nationalist, and socialist political discourse appealed to the Syrian masses. The Ikhwan and the Ba'th engaged in recurrent clashes in several Syrian cities, and the Ba'th's increase in political strength was reflected in the 1954 elections in which the party won twenty-two seats. The combination of Nasser's growing popularity in Syria and the strong appeal of secular, nationalist, socialist parties exacerbated Ikhwan's dilemma. It was this dilemma that partly explains the Ikhwan's decision to opt out of the 1954 elections.[14]

As the message of the Syrian Ikhwan appeared to be out of sync with Syria's political trends, the political fortunes of the Ikhwan sank to a new low in the late 1950s. Supported by the Ba'th, Syria entered into a union with Egypt in 1958, establishing the United Arab Republic (UAR). However, this republic came at a great political price for Damascus, as Nasser conditioned his consent to the union on dissolving all political parties and activities in Syria. As long the UAR lasted, from 1958 to 1961, the Syrian Ikhwan beat a political retreat while remaining socially and religiously active.

In 1961, Damascene officers disgruntled with Nasser's exclusive hold on power mounted a coup, and Syria seceded from the union, causing a rift among the country's parties. The secessionist regime held elections in the same year, in which the Ikhwan won ten seats. However, for the next two years, Syria was tormented by conflicts and clashes among Ba'thists, SSNP, Communists, Nasserists, and the Muslim Brotherhood.

THE IKHWAN AND THE BA'TH: REBELLION AND DEFEAT

The breakup of the union had a deep impact on the ideology of the Ba'th party, which advocated Arab unity. It concluded that the parliamentary system was no longer a basis for political action, and a vanguard party (the Ba'th) was needed to lead and transform the society.[15] Hence in March 1963, the Ba'th party seized power in Syria, suspending parliamentary democracy.

The Ikhwan was furious with the Ba'th's seizure of power. According to their literature, the Ikhwan's opposition to the Ba'th grew from several factors; chief among them were that it represented a minority ruling the country, antireligious secularism, and emergency rule, which banned all political activities.[16] Ikhwan militants went underground in Aleppo and Hama, two conservative Sunni bastions, to organize armed resistance. In 1964, agitated by anti-Ba'th conservative *ulama* and prayer leaders, street riots broke out in different cities. However, it was in Hama that the rioting took on a *jihad*-like dimension.

Ba'thist authorities were able to contain the riots and subdue the insurgents in Hama, killing and capturing dozens of them. Among those detained for a few months was Marwan Hadid, who had studied in Cairo where he came under the spell of the Egyptian Ikhwan's radical ideologue Sayyid Qutb. Upon his release, Hadid continued his underground activities, preparing for the next showdown with the Ba'thist regime.

Preoccupied with internal discord and the Arab–Israeli conflict, the Ba'thist regime did not pay significant attention to the growing underground activities of the Syrian Ikhwan. Following defeat in the 1967 war and the loss of the Golan Heights to Israel, the Ikhwan waged a propaganda campaign against the Ba'thist regime. Nevertheless, the regime was able to weather the repercussions of the defeat, and from 1970 onwards, when Hafiz al-Asad seized power, the regime softened its socialist policies by opening up the system to the Damascene merchant bourgeoisie. This rapprochement with the Damascene merchant class helped save the regime during the Ikhwan's rebellion (1976–1982).

Asad's policies, under the rubric of the Corrective Movement, which brought a certain degree of stability and economic prosperity, were more or less made possible by large-scale Arab aid following the 1973 spike in oil revenues and remittances from Syrian expatriates. However, beginning in 1976, the economy slowed down, and inflation and high unemployment took a toll on Syrians, who resented the newly amassed fortunes of senior Ba'thi figures. No less significant, the Syrian Ikhwan resented Asad's involvement in Lebanon's civil war in summer 2006 against the National Movement and its Palestinians allies.

It was just around this time that a random campaign to assassinate prominent figures of the regime and those associated with it began in earnest.
Hadid was arrested in 1976, and this campaign intensified following his
death in prison in June of that year. The Ikhwan regarded his death as an act
of martyrdom. Yet, it was not until 1979 that the Ikhwan waged full-scale
urban warfare against the regime and its supporters.

On June 16, 1979, Ikhwan militants associated with Hadid's Fighting
Vanguard stormed the Aleppo Artillery Academy and murdered dozens of
Alawi officers. According to the Syrian Ikhwan, the organization had no
prior knowledge of the act, nor did it plan or participate in any assassination
scheme against the regime's figures. They asserted that among the major
causes that led to the rebellion was the regime's decree accusing the Muslim
Brotherhood of the Academy massacre and other murders as well as the campaign to detain and execute Ikhwan members.[18]

The Syrian Ikhwan, apparently working now in concert, expanded their
offensive by staging urban uprisings and shutting down the country's main
business quarters. At this critical juncture, Damascus, due to the efforts of
Badr al-Din al-Shallah, head of the chamber of commerce there, kept its
business quarter open. According to Seale, this act turned the tide in favor
of the regime.[19]

The wrath of the regime peaked when Asad narrowly escaped an assassination attempt in June 1980. The regime was able to quell the Ikhwan's
rebellion in most parts of Syria. At the same time, the regime issued Law
49 that made membership in the Muslim Brotherhood punishable by death.
However, with its strong religious roots and historical defiance, Hama
remained a bastion of opposition. Meanwhile, on September 11, 1980,
the Brotherhood released a document titled *Declaration and Program of
the Islamic Revolution in Syria*.[20] It accused the regime of sectarianism and
blamed Asad for the 1967 defeat. They contended that the true battle of the
"Islamic Revolution" was with the Zionists and that the struggle against the
sectarian regime was but a prelude to that decisive fight.[21]

After five years of battling the Ikhwan, the regime had failed to stamp
out its underground activity, now centered in Hama, a testimony to its
entrenched power. When Hama rebelled in February 1982, the regime knew
that its survival depended on totally crushing the insurrection. The battle
for Hama raged for over a month. The regime used scorched-earth tactics,
employing indiscriminate force that left thousands dead. They then bull-
dozed almost a quarter of the city to rubble.[22]

The regime won the day. It reduced Ikhwan in Syria, but it did not completely vanquish the group. The Syrian Ikhwan continued to be active in
the Arab world, particularly in Amman and later in Europe, particularly
in London. Throughout the mid- and late 1980s, the Ikhwan intensified
their propaganda campaign against the regime. Through the organization's
mouthpiece, *al-Nadhir*, it charged that Asad's regime was not only sectarian
but also accused it of collaborating with Zionist forces. Moreover, they continued to be vocal in expressing their objective of dislodging the regime.[23]

In 1990, Ali Sadr al-Din al-Bayanuni, then deputy superintendent general of the Brotherhood, confirmed the movement's position on overthrowing the regime, using all means available.[24]

The regime, for its part, attempted to frustrate the Syrian Ikhwan into exile by assassinating some of its leaders and their families.[25]

WEARING THE GARB OF ISLAM AND RECONCILIATION

The regime was very much aware that while its severe suppression of the Muslim Brotherhood's rebellion had weakened the group, the destruction and loss of life might alienate the majority Sunni community in Syria. Asad had always taken this factor into account. While his regime remained secularist, he personally had tried to appear as a good Muslim and had firmly positioned his Alawi community, which was arguably non-Muslim, as part of mainstream *Shi'a* Islam.

Now he stepped up such efforts to make the government both acceptable to pious Muslims and appear to be the guardian of moderate Islam. Regime figures increased their attendance of Friday prayer services and festivals in mosques and tried to show they were following a Muslim way of life. The regime supported the building of some 80,000 mosques, more than twenty-two higher education institutions for teaching Islam, and also many regional *Shari'a* schools and study circles. It even supported the establishment of the Shaykha Munira Qubaysi women's school in Damascus, in which 25,000 girls were enrolled.[26]

At the same time, it strengthened its relationship with clerics supporting the regime and enhanced their position. This group included two particularly important clerics: the former grand mufti of Syria, Ahmad Kaftaru (who died in 2004) and Muhammad Said al-Buti.[27] In addition, it opened up the political system for men of religion, encouraging moderate clerics to run as independents for the elections of the People's Assembly.[28]

Simultaneously, the regime pursued a two-pronged (though contradictory) policy aimed at taking the wind out of the Syrian Ikhwan's sails. Gathering momentum in the 1990s during the regime's peace negotiations with Israel, this policy supported foreign Islamist movements such as Islamic Jihad, Hizballah, and Hamas, providing them with headquarters in Damascus. The government also launched conciliatory efforts with moderate Ikhwan members. Apparently, the objective of this policy was to co-opt them so as to isolate the radical elements of the Ikhwan, further fragmenting the organization and preventing it from exploiting Syria's peace negotiations with Israel.

In a series of presidential amnesties, the regime released Ikhwan members arrested during the Ikhwan's rebellion. In 1991, 1992, 1993, 1995, 1998, and 2000, the number of prisoners released was 2,864, 600, 554, 1,200, 250, and 600, respectively.[29] No less important, in 1995, Asad allowed the return from exile of the former superintendent general of the Ikhwan, Abd al-Fatah Abu Ghudda. In 1996, Abu Ghudda left Syria for Saudi Arabia, where he died. Upon learning of his death, Asad sent his condolences to his bereaved family and in a symbolic gesture offered to repatriate his body for burial.[30]

The regime's overture to the Ikhwan, however, was tactical and did not reflect any change in its basic position. Abu Ghudda was allowed to return because he was considered a moderate. However, despite his cooperation with the authorities, he left Syria allegedly on account of the regime's tight security, which hindered his movement. Of greater significance were the regime's conditions for the Brotherhood's return. It demanded that the organization issue a declaration condemning its past mistaken behavior and commending the state's correct policy. In addition, the regime insisted that members of the Brotherhood return as individual citizens and not as party members, meaning that they were prohibited from engaging in political activity.[31] As expected, these stringent conditions were rejected by the Ikhwan, which had considered some form of reconciliation with the regime.

THE DAMASCUS SPRING AND WINTER

On June 10, 2000, after three decades in power, Asad passed away. His son Bashar assumed power, hinting broadly at a new era of modernity and reform. In his presidential inaugural speech, he spoke about repairing his country's ailing economy, modernizing the bureaucracy, and enhancing democracy.[32] His statements and initial actions, such as permitting the publishing of independent newspapers and releasing political prisoners, fostered an atmosphere of change to which many reformers, activists, and members of the opposition quickly responded.

In September 2000, a group of ninety-nine Syrian intellectuals issued a statement calling for political reforms, including ending the state of emergency and establishing a rule of law recognizing the freedom of speech, expression, and assembly.[33] In January 2001, this initial petition ballooned into another statement signed by 1,000 Syrians from all walks of life.

In addition to repeating the demands of the first statement, this new petition emphasized holding democratic elections at all levels and, importantly, reconsidering the principle of the vanguard party, in reference to the Ba'th ruling party, which is constitutionally billed as the "vanguard party in society and state."[34] Meanwhile, public forums addressing reform and revitalization of civil society, hitherto banned, mushroomed in Syria, ushering in what came to be known as the Damascus Spring.

Either alarmed by the swiftness and the boldness of the civil society movement or having wished merely to smoke out dissidents, the regime embarked on a gradual and systematic campaign to reduce the movement to insignificance. In the pretext of maintaining stability, the regime arrested many of the civil society movement's leaders. Prominent state officials, such as then Vice President Abd al-Halim Khaddam, charged the activists with abandoning the struggle for Arab rights since they did not address the Arab–Israeli conflict.[35] The Damascus Spring had slowly but steadily turned into winter.

Initially, the Ikhwan expressed its readiness to turn over a new leaf with the new ruler in Damascus. Bashar, keeping to the pattern established by his father, released 600 prisoners in November 2000, of whom 380 were Ikhwan members.[36] He also allowed the return of Abu Fatah al-Bayanuni, the brother of the Brotherhood's leader. At the same time, the regime reasserted its objection to any form of organized political activity by the Brotherhood.

Yet it was the Brotherhood's lack of involvement in the civil society movement that reflected its disenfranchisement from the political scene in Syria. Banned in Syria, frustrated by internal divisions, looked upon warily by reformers, and operating overseas, the Ikhwan leaders, as Eyal Zisser perceptively observed, had become irrelevant in present-day Syrian realities.[37] This partly explains the urgency with which the leadership of the Ikhwan, led by Bayanuni, wanted to reestablish its presence in Syria and participate in the activities of the now-harassed civil society movement.

On May 3, 2001, the Ikhwan published the draft of the Covenant of National Honor for Political Action. The draft stated that it contained preliminary ideas for "dialogue to formulate a covenant of national honor that would regulate the course of political action." The draft underscored the Ikhwan's principles and general objectives. The principles emphasized the following: Islam is a unifier for all Syrians; Syria belongs to the Arab world; and the confrontation between Islam and Arabism (Arab nationalism) is a bygone historical period. The main objective is to build a modern, pluralist state, in which the rule of law is supreme.[38] Significantly, the draft made no mention of the Ikhwan's long-standing demand for the application of *Shari'a* law.

The Ikhwan's embrace of pluralism and supremacy of law was bushed aside by the regime as a political ruse. In an interview conducted with *Sha'ban* Abud for *al-Nahar*, a senior security official explained:

> The matter of the Brotherhood's situation, according to our understanding and analysis, is but an actual crisis the Brotherhood has been experiencing for several years. The Covenant is but an attempt to exit the crisis and make belief that a profound change has taken place, something we doubt.[39]

Going ahead with it plan to discuss and formulate a National Charter, the Ikhwan convened a meeting in London, which included about 50 nationalists, leftists, independents, and Islamists, in August 2002. Issued on August 25, the National Charter closely echoed the May 2001 covenant, although, as Alan George noted, it gave a greater prominence to the role for Islam, which "constituted a civilizational authority and distinct identity for the sons and daughters of our nation."[40]

Meanwhile, though the civil society movement had been harassed by the regime in one way or another, some activists remained steadfast in calling for reform at the peril of being imprisoned. Their efforts, however, increased following the U.S. invasion and occupation of Iraq in April 2003. Taking a nationalist stand, their mantra became couched in the urgency of reform so that Syria could weather the storm of perilous changes sweeping in the region.[41]

However, it was not until the spring of 2005 that the opposition felt a palpable possibility for change in Syria. The assassination of former Lebanese prime minister Rafiq Hariri on February 14, 2005 sparked mass demonstrations—the so called Cedar Revolution—that compelled Syria to withdraw its troops after three decades from Lebanon. Many Lebanese pointed an accusatory finger at Syrian authorities for the assassination, and the UN Secretary-General established an international tribunal to investigate Hariri's murder. Syria's growing international isolation and humiliating withdrawal from Lebanon breathed new life into the opposition, which, for the first time in decades, had seriously begun to seek an alternative to the regime.

Efforts to unite the ranks of the opposition flourished, and the Committee for the Revival of Civil Society, Syria's largest civil society organization, issued a statement calling for the "opening of channels of dialogue" with all segments of Syrian society, including the Muslim Brotherhood. That was the first time in decades that an opposition group inside Syria had called for dialogue with the Ikhwan. This paved the way for a broader oppositional coalition, which crystallized with the release of the Damascus Declaration for Democratic National Change on October 18, 2005.

The Damascus Declaration recommended the establishment of a democratic national regime as a basic approach to the plan for change and political reform, which must be peaceful, gradual, founded on accord, and based on dialogue of the other, and also the adoption of democracy as a modern system that has universal values, based on the principles of liberty, sovereignty of the people, a state of institutions, and the transfer of power through free and periodic elections.[42]

The declaration went on to call for a "just democratic solution to the Kurdish issue in Syria," "suspending the emergency law" and abolishing "martial law and extraordinary courts, and all relevant laws, including Law 49 for the year 1980." Significantly, the declaration, in language similar to that of the National Charter, gave prominence to the role of Islam in society. It stated that "Islam—which is the religion and ideology of the majority, with its lofty intentions, higher values, and tolerant canon law—is the more prominent cultural component in the life of the nation and the people."[43]

Some in the opposition were not happy to ally with the Muslim Brotherhood. They feared that if they did, it would result in the whole opposition incurring the wrath of the regime. Their fears were soon confirmed as the regime intensified its clampdown on the opposition. In May 2005, Syrian authorities arrested Ali al-Abdallah, a human rights activist, for reading a letter written by the exiled Ikhwan leader Bayanuni, during a meeting held by the Atasi Forum which, unlike others, had not been closed by the regime. A week later, on May 24, the authorities arrested the members of the Forum.[44]

This was followed by the murder of Shaykh Muhammad al-Khaznawi, a Kurd and a prominent religious leader who had been critical of the regime and had spoken up for Kurdish political rights. It is believed that the regime ordered the murder of al-Khaznawi because he met with leaders of the Ikhwan in Brussels in February, signaling a possible collusion between the Kurds and the Islamists. The regime frowned upon such a possibility because the Kurds, in the aftermath of the U.S. occupation of Iraq, had been agitating for political and civil rights (including the demand to teach the Kurdish language and acquiring Syrian citizenship). In fact, following widespread riots in March 2004 in Kurdish areas (Qamishli, Hasaka, Dirik, Amuda, and Ras al-Ayn), Syrian authorities swept through the troubled areas, reportedly killing over two dozens protestors and arresting hundreds of Kurds, many of whom were released once quiet was restored.[45]

It was against this background that President Asad convened the Ba'th Party's Tenth Regional Congress in early June. In a show of strength and defiance, he affirmed the dominant role of the Ba'th party, highlighting its pan-Arab credentials.[46] The underlying message was that the Ba'th remained the vanguard party in the society as well as the protector of Arab nationalism. The congress was disappointing to many activists, for they entertained the slim hope that it would discuss a new law for political parties as part of a process to redefine the role of the Ba'th. The Muslim Brotherhood issued a statement in the wake of the congress asserting the "necessity of total and fundamental change" in Syria and that "the Syrian regime in its current structure is unable to reform."[47]

THE NATIONAL SALVATION FRONT

The regime's attempt at reining in the opposition was temporarily shaken in late December 2005. Appearing on al-Arabiyya news network on December 30, 2005, then Vice President Khaddam lashed out at and implicated the Syrian regime in the assassination of Hariri, whereupon he defected to Paris. Khaddam reached out to the opposition, including the Muslim Brotherhood. Khaddam's defection posed a threat to the regime because he was familiar with the structural levers of power and possessed enough capital and political contacts to potentially mobilize the opposition. The reaction of the opposition was mixed. Some opposition members refused to work with Khaddam, for they considered him a symbol of the regime's oppression; after all, he had very recently been involved in the regime's clampdown on the civil society movement. Others expressed a readiness to work with him and welcome other defectors in the interest of bringing change to Syria.

The Muslim Brotherhood's initial reaction mirrored that of the opposition. However, after some hesitation, Bayanuni decided to work with Khaddam. In an interview with the *Financial Times,* he explained that "his movement was willing to work for political transition in Syria with former

regime officials who are ready to commit themselves to democratic change."
He added: "Khaddam...still had to explain his change of heart and past
role, but that he could nevertheless 'contribute to change in Syria.' "[48]

Though no apology from Khaddam to the Brotherhood was forthcoming,
the two men met a couple of times before they convened a conference in
Brussels in March 2006, which concluded with the announcement of a new
opposition coalition, the National Salvation Front (NSF). It largely mim-
icked the liberal values declared by the Damascus Declaration. However,
it failed to attract a significant following, especially within Syria.

Unfazed by the mixed reaction it received from the opposition, the NSF
set about seeking partners hostile to the regime. Significantly, it cultivated
a warm relationship with anti-Syrian forces in Lebanon, raising the specter
for the Syrian regime that Lebanon might become a beachhead for opposition forces. In early May 2006, an NSF delegation, led by Bayanuni, met
with Syria's archenemy in Lebanon, Druze leader Walid Jumbalat, who had
become a vocal enthusiast for a regime change in Syria. Asked about the
meeting, Jumbalat responded:

> I don't conceal my relationship with the Syrian opposition. I tell the opposi-
> tion, if it sees that I can serve its objectives in order to establish a democratic
> state in Syria, I am ready, if they want me to help.[49]

Meanwhile, on May 12, 2006, 300 Syrian and Lebanese intellectuals
signed the Beirut–Damascus Declaration, calling for normalization of relations between Lebanon and Syria. For all intents and purposes, this declaration, coming on the heels of the NSF's meetings with anti-Syrian forces
in Lebanon, confirmed the fears of the regime. Accusing the opposition of
joining in an evil attack with the Bush administration against Syria, the Ba'th
regime immediately responded by arresting activists of all hues. They even
arrested Michel Kilo, an author of the declaration, who is considered the
"godfather of nationalist" reformers in Syria. In addition, they have enforced
their policy of outlawing contact between Syrian dissidents and foreign governments and organizations.[50]

WITHSTANDING INTERNATIONAL PRESSURE

Parallel to these developments, hostilities erupted between Hizballah and
Israel in June 2006. Hizballah's ability to withstand Israel's offensive and
declare a "divine" victory strengthened the hand of the pro-Syrian opposition in Lebanon and reflected well on the Syrian regime, which had
supported the Islamist party since its inception. Two years later, taking
into account the political and sporadically violent pressure, along with the
sense of being abandoned by U.S. and French policy, pro-government,
anti-Syrian forces yielded to the Hizballah-led opposition and included
them in a national unity government in which they had veto power.
Subsequently, the political impasse over electing a Lebanese president was

settled by the election of the commander of the army, General Michel Sulayman.[51]

These developments helped weaken the international efforts to isolate Syria, for it was blamed for impeding Lebanon's presidential elections. Israel held indirect talks with Syria, brokered by Turkey. France invited President Asad to Paris, and a flurry of lobbying activities circulated efforts in Washington's corridors of power. All of this increased the confidence of the Syrian regime.

In contrast to the Syrian regime, the Muslim Brotherhood supported the anti-Syrian forces in Lebanon during the 2006 summer war and criticized Hizballah for turning "from a resistance organization into a party involved in the internal Lebanese conflicts on sectarian grounds."[52] However, Hizballah's popularity in Syria made it difficult to imagine that the Ikhwan had struck a cord with the Syrian public at large.

On the other hand, brushing aside calls by the international community to release members of the opposition, President Asad, in an interview with al-Jazeera on July 16, 2008, asserted that Syria would not allow the international community to meddle in Syria's internal affairs and claimed that Syrian authorities detained only those working against the national interest of the country—a warped charge for those calling for freedom but serious enough to keep them muzzled in prison cells.

PATTERNS AND EXPECTATIONS

The Muslim Brotherhood has transformed itself into a political party that espouses pluralism and liberal values. No longer does the organization publicly promote the application of Islamic law, though it attests to the prominent role of Islam in Syrian society. This transformation grew from and was a response to the crisis of irrelevance the leadership of the Ikhwan suffered after years of forced exile, especially at a time of fluid change in Syria and the region.

Despite a deeply entrenched wariness by the opposition inside Syria about working with the Ikhwan, the organization has managed to become a key player in Syria's all-embracing movement for reform, the Damascus Declaration. By partnering with former vice president Khaddam, whose association with the regime's oppression is still fresh in the collective consciousness of the opposition, the Muslim Brotherhood has reopened chronic fissures in the ranks of the opposition. Nonetheless, the sheer fact that the Muslim Brotherhood has found common ground on principles of democracy with the Syrian opposition is an achievement by itself.

The regime through repression has prevented the crystallization of a liberal alternative for Ba'thist rule. Conversely, the regime's adoption of Islam as a "client" cause has left the average Syrian with the option of either identifying with Islam or with the bankrupt Ba'thist ideology. It is no surprise that many Syrians have chosen Islam. This political preference is manifested by a growing religious revival in society, symbolized by high attendance of

Friday prayer services, high enrollment in religious schools, and widespread wear of the veil.

Though this religious revival may reflect growing Islamic sentiment, it should not be equated with growing support for the Muslim Brotherhood as a specific organization. It is extremely difficult to gauge the extent to which Syrian society supports the Ikhwan. Skeptical of pluralism on account of the Iraqi experience, concerned about the threat of radical Islam on the country's stability,[53] and thrilled by Hizballah's claim of victory over Israel, the average Syrian may find acceptance of the existing regime as the easiest and safest way to live.

Unless radical changes or events overtake Syria, the Muslim Brotherhood has little, if any, hope of operating as a political party there, let alone dislodging the regime. Even if a Sunni Islamist movement were to emerge in Syria, it is likely to be in a different organizational framework than the traditional Brotherhood group.

Notes

1. Patrick Seale, *Asad of Syria: The Struggle for the Middle East* (Berkeley, CA: University of California Press, 1988), p. 322.
2. For details on the Muslim Brotherhood's doctrine and objectives, see The Information Center of the Muslim Brotherhood in Syria, "Introducing the Muslim Brotherhood, Part One and Two," January 29, 2007 and February 7, 2007, respectively, available at http://www.ikhwansyria.com/index. php?option=com_content&task=view&id=19&Itemid=114; http://www. ikhwansyria.com/index.php? option=com_content&task=view&id=218&Itemi d=114.
3. See Joshua Tietelbaum, "The Muslim Brotherhood and the 'Struggle for Syria,' 1947–1958: Between Accommodation and Ideology," *Middle Eastern Studies*, 40(3) (May 2004); see also Patrick Seale, *The Struggle for Syria: A Study of Post-War Arab Politics, 1945–1958* (London: Oxford University Press, 1965), p. 31.
4. For an English translation of the text, see Umar F. Abd Allah, *The Islamic Struggle in Syria* (Berkeley, CA: Mizan Press, 1983), p. 174, first quoted in Tietelbaum, "The Muslim Brotherhood."
5. The Information Center of the Muslim Brotherhood in Syria, "Introducing the Muslim Brotherhood, Part Three," February 20, 2007, available at http://www. ikhwansyria.com/index.php?option=com_content&task=view&id=413&Itemi d=114.
6. For excellent details on Syria's internal politics see Seale, *The Struggle for Syria.*
7. See Gordon H. Torrey, *Syrian Politics and the Military, 1945–1958* (Columbus, OH: Ohio State University Press, 1964), p. 53.
8. Seale, *The Struggle for Syria*, p. 92.
9. Tietelbaum, "The Muslim Brotherhood."
10. Ibid.
11. On this episode see Nadav Safran, *From War to War: The Arab-Israeli Confrontation, 1948–1967* (Indianapolis, IN: The Bobbs-Merrill Company, Inc., Publishers, 1965), p. 103 and Seale, *The Struggle for Syria*, pp. 103–112.
12. Tietelbaum, "The Muslim Brotherhood."
13. Seale, *The Struggle for Syria*, pp. 217–218.

14. For excellent insights into and perspectives on this episode see Tietelbaum, "The Muslim Brotherhood."

15. For the text articulating the new formulation of the Ba'th doctrine, see *Documents of the Arab Ba'th Socialist Party, Nidal al-Ba'th* [The Struggle of the Ba'th], vol. 6 (Beirut: Dar al-Tali'a, 1963), pp. 232–291.

16. The Information Center of the Muslim Brotherhood in Syria, "Introducing the Muslim Brotherhood, Part Five," March 5, 2007, available at http://www. ikhwansyria.com/index.php? option=com_content&task=view&id=1127&Ite mid=114.

17. See Seale, *Asad of Syria: The Struggle for the Middle East,* pp. 92–93.

18. The Information Center of the Muslim Brotherhood in Syria, "Introducing the Muslim Brotherhood, Part Five." According to Hanna Batatu, the organization had dissensions within its ranks. Its members were torn between three groups that held discordant views: the Fighting Vanguard, which attracted the younger members of the Brotherhood, mainly in Hama; the more cautious Damascus faction guided by Isam al-Attar; and the wing of the movement identified with Shaykh Abd al-Fatah Abu Ghudda of Aleppo. See Hanna Batatu, *Syria's Peasantry, the Descendants of Its Lesser Rural Notables, and Their Politics* (Princeton: Princeton University Press, 1999), p. 262.

19. Seale, *Asad of Syria,* p. 326.

20. Higher Command of the Islamic Revolution in Syria, *Declaration and Program of the Islamic Revolution in Syria* (Damascus: n.p., 1980).

21. Ibid.

22. For details, see Middle East Watch, *Syria Unmasked: The Suppression of Human Rights by the Asad Regime* (New Haven, CT: Yale University Press, 1991), pp. 8–21.

23. *Al-Nadhir,* No. 117 (September 1989), pp. 3–4, 8.

24. *Al-Nadhir,* No. 122 (April 1990), p. 7.

25. See Batatu, *Syria's Peasantry,* pp. 275–278.

26. Ibrahim Hamidi, "Can Syria Keep its Islamist Genie in the Bottle," *Daily Star,* August 11, 2005.

27. For example, the regime supports Kaftaru's religious center, which is the largest in Syria, boasting of 5,000 students from many countries. It is run now by Kaftaru's son, Salah al-Din.

28. Currently, cleric Muhammad Habash is a deputy in the People's Assembly.

29. Eyal Zisser, "Syria, the Ba'th Regime and the Islamic Movement: Stepping on a New Path?" *Muslim World,* 95, 1 (January 2005); see also *Tishrin,* December 12, 1995; *al-Hayat,* November 28, 1995; and *al-Hayat,* November 2, 2000, first quoted by Zisser.

30. See Ibrahim Hamidi, "Al-Awda Tashuk al-Ikhwan," [The Return Splits the Brethren], *al-Wasat,* February 24, 1997, pp. 24–25; and Riad Alam al-Din, "Dimashq: Khutat al-Ikhwan al-Muslimin li-Tasi'd Dud Nizam [Damascus: The Plan of the Muslim Brethren to Escalate against the Regime], *al-Watan al-Arabi,* February 13, 1998, pp. 18–19.

31. Ibid (both sources).

32. See the entire inaugural speech in *Tishrin al-Usbu'i* , July 18, 2000.

33. See text of Statement 99 in *al-Hayat,* September 27, 2000.

34. See text of Statement 1000 in *al-Hayat,* January 12, 2001.

35. See Khaddam's statement in *al-Hayat,* February 19, 2001. For details on the civil society movement see Alan George, *Syria: Neither Bread Nor Butter* (London: Zed Books, 2003).

36. Amnesty International, Index MDE 24/044/2001, November 26, 2001.

37. Zisser, "Syria, the Ba'th Regime and the Islamic Movement."

38. See text of the draft in Muhammad Jamal Barut and Shams al-Din Kilani, *Suria Bayn Ahdayn: Qadaya al-Marhala al-Intiqaliya- Bayanat wa- Watha'iq, Hiwarat wa-Sijalat, Maqalat* [Syria Between Two Eras: Transitional Matters-Statements and Documents, Dialogues and Deliberations, Articles] (Amman: Dar Sindbad Press, 2003), pp. 167–173. See also text in *al-Nahar,* May 8, 2001.

39. See text of interview in ibid., 185–186; and in *al-Nahar,* June 20, 2001.

40. George, *Syria: Neither Bread Nor Freedom,* pp. 92–93.

41. See for example the petition signed by 287 Syrians and mailed to President Asad, as published in *al-Safir,* June 3, 2003.

42. See full text of the Damascus Declaration in *YALIBNAN,* November 14, 2005, available at http://yalibnan.com/site/archives/2005/11/syria_full_text.php.

43. Ibid.

44. See *al-Sharq al-Awsat,* May 25, 2005 and *al-Safir,* May 25, 2005.

45. See Robert G. Rabil, *Syria, the United States and the War on Terror in the Middle East* (Westport: Praeger Security International, 2006), pp. 150–151.

46. See President Asad's speech at Syrian Arab News Agency (SANA), June 8, 2005.

47. See Muslim Brotherhood's statement in *al-Safir,* August 6, 2005. For more details on the Congress see Rabil, *Syria, the United States and the War on Terror in the Middle East,* pp. 189–192.

48. See al-Bayanuni's interview with *Financial Times,* "Muslim Brotherhood Leader Supports Syrian Defector, Khaddam," January 7, 2006.

49. See Jumbalat's statements in *al-Sharq al-Awsat,* "Jumbalat Yu'aked En al-Cha'n al-Dakhili al-Suri Ya'ud ela al-Mu'arada 'Dakhel aw Kharej al-Bilad,' " [Jumbalat Confirmed that the Internal Condition in Syria Goes to the Opposition Inside or Outside the Country] May 5, 2006.

50. For example, Kamal Labwani, a human rights activist, was arrested in November 2005 upon his return from a visit to United States, where he met with White House officials. In May 2007, a Syrian court sentenced Labwani to twelve years in prison on charges of contacting a foreign country and "encouraging attack against Syria." See "Syrian Dissident Kamal Labwani Sentenced to 12 Years," *International Herald Tribune,* May 10, 2007.

51. For details see Robert G. Rabil, "Has Hizballah's Rise Come at Syria's Expense?" *Middle East Quarterly,* vol. 14, no. 4 (Fall 2007).

52. See al-Bayanuni's interview on al-Arabiyya, May 2, 2008. Translated excerpts of the interview were published by MEMRI, *Special Dispatch Series,* no. 1923, May 12, 2008.

53. Since 2004 a spate of clashes between radical Muslims and Syrian authorities racked the capital. In April 2004, an attack on an UN building led to a shootout with Syrian authorities in the residential Mezzeh neighborhood. In July 2005, clashes erupted between armed militants and the police on Mount Qassium, which overlooks the capital. Syrian authorities claimed that the militants were members of the radical group Jund al-Sham, which is linked through its leadership to al-Qa'ida. In June 2006, security forces clashed with a group of masked gunmen apparently preparing to stage an attack on Umayyad square in downtown Damascus. For details see Sami Moubayad, "Islamic Revival in Syria," *Mideast Monitor* vol. 1, no. 3 (September 2006–October 2006).

6

HAMAS: THE PALESTINIAN MUSLIM BROTHERHOOD

Hillel Frisch

Palestinian Islamic politics have been dominated in the past three decades by the Muslim Brotherhood, later known as the Hamas. With its seizure of the Gaza Strip, Hamas came to be a virtual government, competing for leadership of all Palestinians on a near-equal basis with Fatah and its Palestinian Authority (PA) regime. Thus, Hamas can be said to be the only Muslim Brotherhood group in the world that also forms a government and rules over large numbers of people.

HAMAS: HISTORY AND BACKGROUND

No other movement in the Arabic-speaking world has succeeded politically like Hamas since it was formally established in 1987. At first a marginal political player in the Palestinian arena, the Hamas has become the major organized force in Palestinian politics, having won a decisive victory in the March 2006 Palestinian Legislative Council elections; it then seized control of the Gaza Strip in a military coup. All the more startling, these successes came despite the assassination of its founder, Ahmad Yasin, in March 2004 and of his successor Abd al-Aziz Rantisi, a month later.

Its origins were humble. The Muslim Brotherhood, established in 1946 in Gaza, was a quiescent force under Egyptian rule, mainly oriented to propagating religious instruction and preaching. So politically quiescent was the movement at the time that at least two of its members, Salah Khalaf (Abu Iyad) and Khalil al-Wazir (Abu Jihad), left it in search of a more active organization and went on to become two of the main leaders of Fatah and the Palestinian Liberation Organization (PLO).

The Brotherhood abstained from military activity even though the movement had some opportunity, despite Egypt's surveillance over its activity, to take a more active role in the guerrilla activities organized in large part by the Egyptian state against Israel in the early 1950s. Nor did the Muslim Brotherhood play any significant role in resistance to Israel when it occupied the area during the 1956 Sinai war.

This same quiescence characterized the Brotherhood after the 1967 war. The Muslim Brotherhood played almost no role when the area became the scene of persistent terrorism against Israeli forces, while movements such as the Palestinian Front for the Liberation of Palestine and Fatah participated in violent opposition to Israeli rule. The wave of violence began in early 1969 and reached its peak in 1970 and early 1971, until it was virtually stamped out by Israeli forces.

There could be no better proof of such acquiescence than both the timing and character of al-Mujama, the major organization within Brotherhood ranks to emerge at the time. It was established in Gaza by Ahmad Yasin in 1973 as a welfare charity association that ran clinics, kindergartens, and education facilities. The Israeli civil administration granted the association its registered charity status in 1978. Funding came from local *zakat* collections, Islamic organizations in Saudi Arabia and the Gulf States, and expatriate Palestinians residing there. Jordan was the major conduit of such funds.

This was also the period in which the Brotherhood, through al-Mujama, became more political. The Brotherhood's radical transformation took place in the newly formed universities and colleges. The focus of such politicization was the power struggle waged around the newly established Islamic University of Gaza, founded after Egyptian President Anwar al-Sadat closed Egyptian universities to Gaza students in retaliation for demonstrations they held against the Camp David negotiations. The al-Mujama political student movements and the victories they scored on many campuses in the West Bank, especially at the new al-Najah National University in Nablus and at Hebron University, propagated the movement in that area as well.

By that time, Gaza University had eclipsed al-Mujama as the most important institution of the growingly politicized Brotherhood. Fortunately for al-Mujama, which had been trying to take total control of the university, in February 1981, the Israeli authorities dismissed the Fatah-oriented president and senior administration as part of their struggle against the PLO-backed National Steering Committee fighting the Camp David Accords.

This move paved the way for Muhammad Siyyam's appointment as the university's president. Siyyam was a veteran member of the Brotherhood and active in al-Mujama. The university quickly took an Islamist turn, imposed an injunction on both the female staff and students to wear the *hijab* and robe, created separate entrances for men and women, and enforced strict gender separation in classes.

Islamization from above was reinforced by the al-Mujama student group from below. The bloc quickly came to dominate the student body and enforced these codes through violence and intimidation of dissenters. By the mid-1980s, it was the largest university in the territories with a student body of 4,500, the only one where the Fatah Shabiba movement (founded at Gaza University by Muhammad Dahlan) was a marginal force.

The importance of this institution as a front organization for the Brotherhood and later Hamas cannot be underestimated. Almost every key leader, subsequently, in Hamas—Abd al-Aziz al-Rantisi, Mahmud

Zahar, Ibrahim al-Yazuri, and Salah Shahada—found employment in the institution.

Part and parcel of al-Mujama and the increasingly political stance of student blocs was a growing rivalry with "nationalist" institutions they regarded as secular. Tension with the PLO climaxed in January 1980 when Islamist activists attacked Red Crescent Society offices and attempted to march on the home of its director, Haydar Abd al-Shafi.

The violence was directed inward throughout the 1980s against social institutions such as cinemas, places selling or serving alcohol, and casinos, which the movement considered un-Islamic. Abd al-Aziz Rantisi, an activist in Khan Yunis, who was to later assume briefly the leadership of Hamas, was the first to become involved in the smuggling of weapons in 1984, with major implications on how the Israeli authorities viewed Brotherhood's activities. If, until then, Israel by and large turned a blind eye to its activities, at this juncture the authorities arrested thirteen members including Rantisi and Yasin, and an arms cache was seized. Ibrahim al-Yazuri temporarily took over the leadership.

THE *INTIFADA* AND THE ESTABLISHMENT OF HAMAS

However, it took the massive popular and unorganized uprising of December 1987 that came to be known as the *intifida* to transform the loose network of Brotherhood institutions into Hamas. The organization was founded in January 1988 and focused primarily on resistance to Israeli rule. Hamas is an acronym for Harakat al-Muqawama al-Islamiyya (The Islamic Resistance Movement), which forms the word zeal. Its founding leaders, Ahmad Yasin, Abd al-Fatah Dukhan, Muhammad Shama, Ibrahim al-Yazuri, Issa al-Najjar, Salah Shahada (from Bayt Hanun), Abd al-Aziz Rantisi, Mahmud Zahar, and others reflected its strong Gaza base—a characteristic that dominates the organization and its leadership to this day.

Resistance to Israeli rule soon came to mean the eradication of Israel altogether.

In August 1988, Hamas, in reaction to a draft "declaration of independence" by PLO leaders, disseminated a charter of its own declaring that all of Palestine was an Islamic trust land, which could never be surrendered to non-Muslims, and was an inalienable part of the Muslim world. The forged *Protocols of the Elders of Zion* is cited as a legitimate document. Needless to say, the charter declared negotiations with Israel and international conferences in pursuit of peace as useless and illegitimate.

Hamas created three separate wings: a political wing, staffed by Yasin's closest allies (Shanab, Yazuri, Rantisi, and Zahhar), produced leaflets, raised funds—especially in Gulf, recruited members, and co-opted mosques. An intelligence apparatus, known as al-Majd (glory) under Yihyah Sanwar and Ruhi Mushtaha was responsible for internal policing and the killing of those accused of collaboration with Israel. Yet, by far the most important organization it formed was its military wing, the Izz al-Din al-Qassam brigades.

Violence characterized by stone-throwing and the use of incendiary bombs gave way to increasing terrorist activity by a professional salaried hardcore. In 1989, the Izz al-Din al-Qassam brigades in Gaza kidnapped and killed two Israeli soldiers. From that point on, Israel came to regard Hamas as Israel's most serious terrorist threat, culminating in the expulsion of nearly 413 Hamas and al-Jihad al-Islami activists to Lebanon in December 1992.

Their expulsion and, even more so, their subsequent repatriation, was an egregious mistake on Israel's part. In Lebanon, they perfected their skills to use explosives under the Hizballah's guidance, leading to the introduction of suicide bombing, a new and more lethal mode of terrorism. The first suicide bombing, by a member of al-Jihad al-Islami, took place in April 1993 in the Jordan valley.

The turn to violence also helped Hamas politically in attracting refugees, white-collar workers, and professionals, especially since it was accompanied by the Brotherhood's increasing conciliation with nationalism. However, success also came at the price of increasing tensions with the PLO and the nationalist camp. Even though in the first two years of the *intifada* it refused to be part of the Unified National Command (an informal structure composed of all the factions within the PLO that led the *intifada*), Hamas agreed to coordinate with the PLO's leadership abroad.

However, these negotiations held primarily with the PLO "outside" failed to dissolve local tensions. From 1989 onward, relations between Hamas and the PLO, particularly Fatah, were fraught with tension. Unlike Arafat, Hamas did not support Saddam Hussein in the first Gulf War, when Iraq invaded Kuwait. Instead, the movement called for both Iraqi and U.S. withdrawal. Consequently, the Gulf states and Saudi Arabia retaliated against the PLO by allocating more funding to Hamas, particularly after Yasin's visit to the area between February and April 1988. With such funds, Hamas was able for the first time to compete with the PLO's welfare infrastructure, particularly since Hamas' institutions were considered more efficient.

Armed confrontations with Fatah broke out in 1990–1991 though relations improved after Israel's expulsion of Hamas leaders in December 1992. In the meeting at Khartoum between Hamas and the PLO in January 1993, both sides promised increased coordination and pledges of mutual nonviolence, and the PLO stalled talks with Israel until the deported activists were returned.

Relations soured once again when Hamas rejected the Oslo peace process and the Declaration of Principles signed on the White House lawn on September 13, 1993. Hamas joined forces with the rejectionists within the PLO and managed to gain considerable support. The first Hamas suicide bombing in Hadera in April 1994 seemed designed as an attempt to sabotage a deal to create the Palestinian Authority, eventually signed on May 4, 1994. Just as Israel began realizing that Hamas was its major terrorist nemesis in the Palestinian arena, Fatah began realizing that Hamas was beginning its bid for ultimate power by attempting to overpower the nationalist camp in the domestic Palestinian arena.

HAMAS AND THE PALESTINIAN AUTHORITY

When the Palestinian Authority (PA) was created in 1994 as part of the Oslo process, Fatah nevertheless remained clearly the leading political and military force, even in Gaza. For a brief period in Palestinian politics between the establishment of the PA in July 1994 and the entry of the PA into the six major towns of the West Bank in January 1996, Gaza, the Hamas stronghold, was the center of the new regime as Arafat set up headquarters in the city of Gaza.

Even after most of the Tunis-based Palestinian politicians and organizations moved to a capital in Ramallah following the agreement of September 25, 1995, giving the PA control of the main West Bank towns, Arafat, realizing the popularity of Hamas in Gaza, spent much of his time there to assure his control in the area.

Gaza became a major source of Hamas opposition to the PA and Fatah. In November 1994, PA security forces gunned down twelve, mostly Hamas, activists in a demonstration outside a Gaza City mosque. The protest was against the PA for arresting and harassing Hamas members.

While Hamas carried out a large number of attacks on Israelis during this period, the peak was a wave of suicide bombings between late February and early March 1996 in retaliation for the killing of a Hamas commander who had organized many of them, the engineer Yahya Ayyash. This offensive was planned, organized, and carried from Gaza by Hamas. The same source launched a boycott of the first Palestinian Legislative Council elections held in January 1996.

Israel reacted to the suicide bombing and political boycott by curtailing work permits and targeting Hamas and Islamic Jihad terrorists. The PA responded to this challenge of its authority with massive arrests of movement leaders, including Rantisi.

Reeling from blows directed both from Israel and the PA, Hamas found respite from an unexpected twist of events. In October 1997, the Mossad tried a failed assassination attempt in Jordan against Khalid Mashal, the head of Hamas's "outside" political bureau. To stave off the embarrassment of having infringed on the sovereignty of Jordan with which Israel concluded peace only three years before, Prime Minister Benjamin Netanyahu released Yasin, imprisoned in Israel since 1989, expelled him to Jordan, and subsequently allowed him to return to Gaza in October 1997.

Two years later, it was Jordan's turn to expel the "outside" Hamas political bureau. Mashal first visited Iran and then moved to Damascus. This symbolized Hamas's clearly growing orientation toward the Iran–Syria axis, which would henceforth supply it with much of its financing along with some of its training and arms.

In retrospect, Hamas's stature at the end of the 1990s was little different from what it had been in the beginning of the decade. Palestinian polling institutes consistently reported that only one-fifth of the respondents in the territories called Hamas the movement they most identified with. Failure to participate in the elections and function as a legitimate opposition was often cited as one of the major reasons for its relative failure to forge ahead in Palestinian public opinion.

Economic reasons also played a role in keeping support for Hamas relatively stagnant. Hamas's terrorism imposed a heavy toll not only on Israel but on Palestinians as well. An increase in terrorism meant greater restrictions on access to the coveted Israeli labor market, particularly for inhabitants from Gaza. The economic dividends of such access involving 100,000 workers in both the West Bank and Gaza easily outweighed the welfare benefits they derived from the social services Hamas provided them. These salaries accounted for one-fifth of the gross domestic product, and through their multiplier effects, perhaps double that.

Yet, Hamas was stymied most by the sheer political, military, and economic resources at the disposal of the PA. If after the Gulf War the PLO and Fatah were strapped for cash and Hamas became the major beneficiary, the Oslo peace process and, to a lesser extent, the slump in the Gulf states' oil revenues turned the tide in the PLO's favor.

This was the decade in which Arafat enjoyed more direct access to the president of the United States than most leaders of states. The PA enjoyed a budget of over $1 billion, at least five times larger than the maximum estimate of Hamas's budget. In addition, the PA employed nearly 150,000 workers, of which over one-third were security personnel. Militarily, Hamas was no match for the PA's dozen or so security forces, especially after Arafat reactivated the Fatah Tanzim, the grassroots militia, in 1996, both as a counterweight to his own security forces and to deter Hamas at the popular level.

Hamas clearly realized where the power lay. Despite massive detentions, particularly in 1996–1997, and more occasional PA security cooperation with Israel against the movement, the Hamas refrained from retaliating against the PLO. It almost always limited its opposition throughout this period to protest demonstrations.

HAMAS AND THE ISRAELI–PALESTINIAN CONFLICT, 2000–2005

All this changed with the outbreak of the PA's low-intensity war with Israel in September 2000. Economically, the trade-off between economic welfare and terrorism disappeared as Israel, in the face of unprecedented high levels of terrorism, reduced to a trickle the number of Palestinian workers allowed into its labor market. Gone was the carrot in the form of access to the Israeli labor market that created popular pressure on Hamas to refrain from violence. Hamas could now revel in the glory of "the resistance" against Israel without being blamed for the social costs it was imposing on the Palestinian society.

With the negotiating process over, after Arafat's rejection of a negotiated solution, the political front became unimportant. The PA and Legislative

Council institutions—and Hamas's refusal to participate in them—were also marginalized. Thus, Hamas's negative effect on the economic side and its boycott of the political side no longer stood as barriers to its position.

Above all, Hamas gained much support from playing a lead role in fighting Israel by outstripping Fatah in its number of acts of violence, principally suicide bombings, and damage inflicted on Israel. According to the Israeli General Security Services, Hamas was responsible for 40 percent of the 142 suicide acts during the fighting between September 2000 and March 2005, compared with 27 percent of the acts carried out by al-Jihad al-Islami and only 23 per cent by Fatah. Hamas was also responsible for the most deadly single attack, a suicide bombing on a Passover religious ceremony in a hotel dining room that left twenty-nine civilians dead.

Some of the movement's growing popularity could also be attributed to deeper religious currents among Palestinians. A poll conducted in March 2000 showed that an overwhelming percentage of the respondents (85.8 percent) felt that the PA should be more religious. Ironically, Hamas's rising stature was reflected in the external symbols—albeit shallow ones—adopted by Fatah. To compete with Hamas's religiously, Fatah created a new fighting arm called the Martyrs of al-Aqsa Brigades, using a logo of the al-Aqsa mosque combined with a verse from the Koran. Video clips of Fatah suicide bombers featured would-be martyrs with a gun in one hand and the Koran in the other. Many of Fatah's announcements were now deeply imbued with religious symbols and Koran verses.

So powerful had Hamas become that, by early 2003, Egypt felt it had to negotiate with all the factions to assure both domestic peace and a peace plan. For the first time, Hamas was elevated to equality with Fatah, the PLO, and the PA. Arafat's illness and subsequent death signaled further that the removal of the PLO and Fatah's charismatic leader from the scene lifted another barrier to Hamas's successful challenge.

Israel gradually achieved success against the insurgency. Successful suicide bombing attempts had risen from four in 2000 to thirty-five in 2001 and sixty in 2002, but now fell by 75 percent over the next two years to only fifteen in 2004, and declined to a far lower level thereafter. Nevertheless, the blow of Israeli counterinsurgency was far softer on Hamas than on Fatah/PA, its major rival.

One major reason was geographical. A turn of the tide in terms of the effectiveness of Palestinian violence was registered mainly after the two Israeli offensives conducted in March (Shield) and June 2002 (Determined Path) in areas "A," during which the major West Bank towns under the jurisdiction of the PA were temporarily reoccupied and then continuously penetrated and policed. Palestinian fighters in those areas lost any temporary sanctuary they formerly enjoyed as Israeli troops pursued them without respite.

A comparison between violent attacks in the West Bank and Gaza offers an even more striking confirmation of the importance of Israeli offensive and preemptive measures of denying Palestinians a sanctuary. In the West Bank, where Palestinians were denied a sanctuary, terrorist attacks more than halved from 2,089 in 2002 to 1,025 in 2003. The number of attacks dropped to 841 in 2004: just over one-third of the attacks that took place two years previously. By contrast, in Gaza, where Palestinians enjoyed a continuous but porous sanctuary, there was almost no decline in the number of attacks from 2002 to 2004 (2,906 in 2002 as compared to 2,771 in 2004).

Comparing Israeli fatalities in the West Bank to those in Gaza between 2002 and 2004 demonstrates in even starker relief the importance of offensive moves and the denial of sanctuary. Whereas Israeli fatalities in the West Bank during this period declined by over 90 percent—from 196 to 18—in Gaza it was a different story. There, Israeli losses actually increased from 25 to 38. It was Hamas's fortune to be strongest politically and militarily in Gaza where no major sustained offensives took place. Hamas's rivals, Fatah and al-Jihad al-Islami, by contrast, were strongest in the Jenin-Nablus areas, which suffered the brunt of Israeli penetration.

Hamas also maintained discipline within movement ranks as factionalism within the PLO, Fatah, and the PA security agencies increased. During the low-intensity conflict between Israel and the Palestinians since September 2000, these tensions often degenerated into open battles. Its high point occurred in the summer of 2004 when Yasir Arafat placed Musa Arafat as head of security in Gaza, giving him control of the main forces there. The nomination came in the wake of a series of armed kidnappings. Thousands protested Arafat's choice, torching the military intelligence building in the Gaza Strip town of Khan Yunis, where forces loyal to the newly appointed PA security chief were stationed. These internal rivalries were far more intense than the confrontations between Hamas and Fatah or the PA.

Finally, despite Hamas's diminishing ability to continue fighting the Israel Defense Forces, Hamas, because of its prominent role in Gaza against the Israeli forces compared with the West Bank, seemed to have been given the credit for the "victory," signified by the dismantlement of all Israel's settlements in Gaza and the subsequent complete military withdrawal on September 12, 2005.

HAMAS'S ELECTORAL VICTORY

Showing political acumen, the movement, after less than a year of attempts to avenge the assassination of its two leaders, began to realize its military limitations and capitalize on its political successes by both accepting unilaterally the lull in fighting and, when Arafat died, pressing for legislative elections.

Accepting the lull was not an easy decision in the face of Israel's escalating antiinsurgency attacks against the Palestinian factions and against Hamas in particular. If from 2003 to 2004 Israeli fatalities from Palestinian terror declined by 36 percent, the number of those killed as a result of targeted killing of Hamas leaders involved in terrorism remained at the same level (fifty-seven in 2003 compared to fifty-five in 2004). By accepting the lull, Hamas avoided the mistake that many organizations make as they try to demonstrate their resolve and satiate feelings of vengeance rather than lay low and renew capabilities for fighting in the future.

Once Hamas, along with the other factions, accepted the lull, it more or less abided by it. The organization was implicated in only one suicide bombing—in August 2005, with an attack on the same bus station in Beersheba as in the previous year.

It was the lull that enabled Hamas to give up its boycott of participation in the political structures of the PA and enter the political fray in full force by adopting a very critical stand against the new Palestinian leadership. To try consolidating his power, Arafat's successor, Mahmud Abbas adopted a two-stage strategy by divorcing the presidential elections from elections to the legislative council. His goal was to centralize power before legislative elections. By contrast, Hamas insisted that the presidential and legislative elections take place simultaneously, as they had in 1996. Since the movement claimed that the presidential elections were illegitimate, it naturally refrained from presenting a candidate to the presidency in the January 2006 elections.

Though miffed by Abbas's decision to hold the presidential election, Hamas nevertheless eagerly plunged into the campaign for elections to the legislative council. One of the most important issues was the electoral system to be used in deciding the then eighty-eight seats, subsequently expanded to 132. In a meeting between Palestinian factions in February 2005 in Cairo brokered by the Egyptians, Fatah committed itself, by the urging of Hamas and other factions, to the compromise position when it agreed to a system in which half of the seats would be contested according to the old system (the multiple member district system that operated in the 1996 elections) and half in which lists would contest elections as a single constituency.

Even then, it took another four months of wrangling—sufficient to postpone the elections from a stipulated date in the summer of 2005 to January 2006—to turn the bill into law finally on June 18, 2005. To cut their probable losses, the incumbents voted in the law only after they enlarged the legislative council considerably from eight-eight to 132 members, half of whom were to be elected according to the multiple-member district system. Ironically, Hamas's subsequent electoral victory would have been far greater under the old system due to the rivalry between official and nonofficial Fatah candidates, which divided the nationalist vote.

As the election process unfolded, it became increasingly apparent that while Fatah possessed quantity Hamas made up for it in quality. Sharp, often overlapping ideological, geographical, generational, and professional divisions between bureaucrats and militiamen hampered Fatah's ability to portray itself as a unified party or to mobilize and campaign successfully.

The fragmented Fatah military wing complicated matters even more. The abundance of armed groups, many heavily armed, increased the probability that political rivalries over attaining a slot on the list or candidacy in a particular district would be settled by force rather than by any civil procedure.

It was hardly surprising under these circumstances that irregularities in drawing up membership lists prompted acts of violence during the Fatah primaries in December 2005. Mahmud Abbas, presiding over the Fatah Central Committee, acknowledged that "cheating was massive." Armed Fatah groups subsequently broke into the Central Elections Commission regional offices to protest the nomination process, threatening to prevent elections altogether. Their violence was directed against Hamas as well.

While Fatah with every passing day was looking like a lawless militia, Hamas tried to project an image of political civility by creating a nominally independent party, the List for Change and Reform, whose title significantly made no allusion to religion or to the movement behind it, and nominated many professionals that appealed to the voters rather than merely to Hamas members. The composition of the countrywide list of sixty-two candidates clearly reflected a technocratic thrust as well as the desire to be broadly representative. There were thirty-four candidates with a professional or academic title (teacher, PhD, MD, engineer, and lawyer) preceding their names. Ten candidates (some of them professionals) were women.

Hamas's campaign for legislative council seemed to have been heavily influenced by the campaign for the four rounds of local elections during the course of 2005 in which its lists emphasized local concerns, professional integrity, expertise, and a willingness to work with members of other lists after the elections.

Yet, however much Hamas downplayed either its religious or guerrilla character in composing its list or in its political rhetoric, it nevertheless retained its basic identity. The list included at least twelve candidates with the title of *shaykh* or with an affiliation to religious institutions and the Waqf (religious endowment) administration, along with several Hamas deportees and prisoners. Politically, it continued to be loyal to its basic objective. Thus, Mahmud al-Zahar, in an election rally in a town in Gaza on the eve of the fourth round of municipal elections, claimed that one of Hamas's objectives was "to protect the resistance project with the goal of completing the liberation of the occupied Palestinian lands."

Though there were expectations that Hamas was gaining ground during the campaign due to the lawlessness of groups linked to Fatah, Hamas's decisive electoral victory on January 25, 2006 surprised most analysts, including Palestinians. Hamas's Change and Reform List won seventy-four seats, with Fatah trailing with only forty-five.

However, the victory must also be placed in proper perspective. Rather than being a landslide, in the unified national list it was a very close race, with Hamas securing 440,409 of the votes and twenty-nine seats against Fatah, which drew 410,554 of the votes and twenty-eight seats. In the districts, by contrast, Fatah's performance was disastrous, with forty-five seats going to Hamas against only seventeen for Fatah.

The gap between the close race in the proportional list vote and the decisive victory in the district lists shows that that the victory for Hamas was just as much of Fatah's making as it was due to the movement's own efforts.

In such constituencies small differences in the number of votes cast to any particular candidate often determines who wins the seat. Many Fatah candidates contested even though they were not officially approved, thus splitting the vote in their camp and ensuring the election of Hamas candidates.

CIVIL WAR AND HAMAS TRIUMPH IN GAZA

Domestically, the newly emergent Hamas government had to face the reality of a split regime: a parliamentary majority and cabinet headed by a Hamas prime minister versus an incumbent president who enjoyed the support of the security forces, of which over 75 percent voted for Fatah in the legislative elections. The tension was aptly captured by an editor of a Palestinian daily who wrote about the prospects of "Algerianization" of the situation, a reference to the Algerian military regime's abrogation of the second round of elections in 1992 after the Islamist FIS won conclusively in the first balloting. This coup set off a bloody Islamist insurgency against the Algerian regime.

For Hamas, it was critical to bring the security forces under the control of its government, and more specifically, under the jurisdiction of the Hamas-controlled Ministry of Interior. The new Hamas government argued plausibly that placing the bulk of the security forces under the government's wing was in accord with the modifications in the PA Basic Law, which ironically Abbas had introduced when he was prime minister during his struggle with Arafat.

To counter Fatah's forces, the Hamas government set up its own Executive Force a month into office. Abbas quickly ruled it illegal and ordered its dissolution. In a meeting of the PLO Executive Council, he claimed that the attempt to transform Hamas's military arm into an official PA security force could begin a round of internal strife that had to be avoided at all costs. Instead of trying to assuage PA fears regarding the emergence of a 3,000-man force, the Syrian-based Hamas leader Khalid Mashal charged that "what is happening in Palestine is a policy carried out by a parallel government, a counter-government which deprives us of our prerogatives and the people of their rights. It is a plot." The die of civil war was cast.

Within five months of the election, the Executive Force was involved in violent confrontations with both rival security forces and Fatah. The conflict took an international dimension after the United States, worried about the empowerment of the Hamas government and its strong links with Iran, began to train the new Special Presidential Guard in August 2006. The goal was to expand the force from 3,500 to 6,000 by the end of the year and deploy most of them in Gaza's sensitive border crossings with Israel and Egypt. Regional power politics soon conflated with growing civil strife when one of the border crossings, Rafah, became the scene of the most serious confrontation to date in December 2006. The violence was sparked by an attempted assassination of a senior PA officer suspected of arresting and torturing Islamist opposition members. In the attack on his car, three of his children, their driver, and a bystander were killed instead, setting off a heavy round of violence between the PA's security forces and Hamas.

To deal with the crisis, the Hamas prime minister, Ismail Haniyeh, decided to cut short a month-long trip to Iran and Arab capitals. The United States, perturbed by Haniyeh's visit to Iran where he was apparently provided with the $36 million he was suspected of carrying with him, pressed Israel to close the Rafah crossing. Israel readily complied, and Haniyeh and his escort were detained on the Egyptian side. The Egyptians stepped in and succeeded in reaching a compromise.

Meanwhile, hundreds of Hamas and Executive Force members descended on the Rafah border crossing site, where scuffles broke out between the Presidential Guard guarding the crossing and Hamas opponents. The melee turned into fierce firefights after unknown assailants attacked the prime minister and his entourage at the border crossing, killing Haniyeh's bodyguard and wounding his son and a senior aide. Senior Hamas officials accused the Presidential Guard of instigating an assassination attempt. The Hamas government announced that, in retaliation, it would double the Executive Force from 6,000 to 12,000 personnel.

It took one more round of massive violence in January 2007 to reflect a shift in the balance of power in Gaza in Hamas's favor. On January 4, Hamas and the Executive Force laid siege in a refugee camp to the home of Colonel Muhammad Ghurrayib, head of one of the main security services in northern Gaza. Neither repeated attempts by Fatah fighters to reach his home in order to break the siege nor his own desperate appeal on Palestinian TV for help prevented subsequent waves of attacks, which resulted in the death of Ghurrayib and six others, including his brother and two daughters. It took two more rounds of fighting in May and June for Hamas to rout the president's security forces and the Fatah militia and take over Gaza completely. In effect, while Hamas had won the election, it then used the subsequent situation to stage a coup, wiping out the opposition party.

Hamas's military takeover of Gaza, palpably demonstrated through the conquest of all key institutions associated with the presidency and the brutal public killings of senior members of the security forces and of Fatah, led to the effective emergence of two political entities: the Hamas-dominated Gaza, in which the elected government of Haniyeh prevailed, and a West Bank PA under Abbas. The latter, in a flurry of presidential decrees, dissolved Haniyeh's government, established an emergency government under former finance minister Salam Fayyad, outlawed Hamas as a political faction and militia, and declared the Executive Force illegal. Haniyeh and Hamas responded by adamantly rejecting the constitutionality and legality of the decrees, principally the one dissolving the elected government of the PA.

A persistent campaign to uproot the respective opposition by each of the governments followed. As of November 2008, over 500 Hamas activists were jailed, and Hamas fund-raising institutions were closed. Similarly, in Gaza, Fatah activists have been suppressed and the group's activities outlawed.

While the Ramallah government is responsible for destroying Hamas-affiliated nongovernmental organizations and the clerics in the mosques, Israeli forces specialize in uncovering cells and arresting their members. It is safe to say that though Hamas has gained total control in Gaza, it paid dearly for that victory in the West Bank. As long as Israel and the West support Abbas's government, there is little likelihood of Hamas replicating its success in the other Palestinian-ruled area. Similarly, the successful repression of Fatah in Gaza means that there is little likelihood that Hamas control will be uprooted by domestic forces or by outside Fatah military formations.

HAMAS AND THE MUSLIM BROTHERHOOD

Other forces and factors, however, might lead to the weakening of Hamas control. It is in this context that Hamas's relationship to the Muslim Brotherhood should be discussed. Despite the stress in the Hamas constitution, distributed in the summer of 1988, that the movement was a branch of the larger overarching Muslim Brotherhood, Hamas has downplayed this relationship in recent years.

Important geostrategic reasons dictate that Hamas distance itself from the Muslim Brotherhood as a whole. Hamas's assumption of government through relatively fair elections made most Arab states, which have authoritarian governments, feel threatened by such a possibility of change from below. That the change involved a radical Islamic movement paralleling the Muslim Brotherhood movements that form the major domestic opposition groups in Egypt, Jordan, and Syria made further crackdowns seem to be a good idea to their rulers.

The most threatened of all these states is Egypt, particularly after the success of Muslim Brotherhood candidates in Egypt's parliamentary elections following Hamas's electoral victory. Since Egypt controls the only crossing at Rafah that connects Gaza to the Muslim and Arab worlds, Cairo has used this power to try to weaken Hamas and reduce the attractiveness of its model for its own citizens.

While this situation gives Muslim Brotherhoods problems with too open a connection with Hamas, the Palestinian group's relationship to Iran—distrusted by the Brotherhood's as a Shi'a and non-Arab state—reinforces their interest in maintaining some public distance. Equally, Hamas's own relationship with Iran as an ally or patron does not encourage it to broadcast its alliance with anti-Iran forces. The fact that Iran's other allies—Shi'a Hizballah in Lebanon and Shi'a insurgents in Iraq—are also seen as enemies by many Sunni Islamists—makes the other Brotherhoods feel the disapproval more. The Syrian Muslim Brotherhood is repressed by that country's government—the same regime that is a sponsor of Hamas and host to its headquarters.

So far Hamas's claim to be a revolutionary group only on the anti-Israel front has done little to dispel the fears of Arab states, especially those of Egypt, which is bent on containing the Hamas government, if not bringing its downfall. While in 2008 Egypt proposed reconciliation plans for Fatah and Hamas, its activities clearly favored Fatah, as Hamas leaders have complained.

Saudi Arabia, strongly opposed to any extension of Iranian and Syrian influence, has cooperated with Egypt by allocating permits to participate in the pilgrimage to Mecca to West Bankers only. The aim is to show that Hamas cannot facilitate one of the most important rites for Muslims.

Nevertheless, the Muslim Brotherhood, especially in Egypt, does have a visible relationship with Hamas. The Muslim Brotherhood has organized widely publicized bus trips by its leading figures and other supporters from Cairo to Rafah in the hope of "breaking the blockade," which participants realize is as much an Egyptian effort as it is an Israeli undertaking. Hamas officials have encouraged attacks on Egyptian soldiers guarding the border on more than one occasion.

FUTURE PROSPECTS

Though "Hamastan" in Gaza covers a small area, continuing Hamas rule over the area is widely perceived as having far-reaching regional and even global implications. One of the major questions concerns the struggle between Arab nationalist-ruled states and opposition radical Islamist groups. The Hamas takeover has been linked to an Islamist revolutionary wave that includes Hizballah's successful challenge to the Lebanese government and the Islamist insurgencies in Eritrea and Somalia, where the rebels have also gained control of considerable territory.

Will Hamas become a safe haven for extending Islamist insurgent activities, a base for Iran and Syria, a model for Islamist groups in Arab states? Hamas and its Gaza regime have become part of a wider struggle between an Iran-led coalition and the United States, a two-bloc conflict that has drawn Arab states to some extent into the latter camp.

The constellation of forces pivoted against Hamas is formidable and the geographic locus of the movement, Gaza, is vulnerable in its dependence on supplies furnished mostly by its foes. Nevertheless, if Iran becomes a nuclear power, if political Islam grows to threaten Arab states and replicate the Hamas experience, and U.S. hegemony is considerably eroded, Hamas could become more powerful and gain hegemony over the Palestinians, as well as serve as a model for other Brotherhoods to become more militant and violent.

2

Europe and the West

7

The Muslim Brotherhood in Europe

Lorenzo Vidino

Since its humble origins in rural northern Egypt in the 1920s, the Muslim Brotherhood has achieved incommensurable successes.[1] A significant, yet often overlooked, part of this history has taken place in Europe, where small, scattered groups of Brothers from Egypt and other Middle Eastern countries have been concentrating since the early 1950s.

A handful of these pioneers were hardened Brotherhood members who sought refuge in the West after fleeing persecution in their native countries. The majority were students, members of the educated community, and urban middle classes of the Middle East who had already joined or flirted with the idea of joining the Brotherhood in their home countries.[2] They initially represented a small, dispersed contingent of militants whose move did not relate to any centralized plan but rather was due to personal decisions that fortuitously brought some Brotherhood figures to spend some years or the rest of their lives in the West. The Brotherhood, at the time barely able to withhold the Egyptian regime's pressure, had no plan of establishing an organic presence in the Europe and hardly kept tabs on what its affiliates where doing there.

Despite isolation from the mother group in the Middle East, the first Brotherhood members and sympathizers who settled in Europe became immediately active. Most of them were university students and, loyal to Hasan al-Banna's focus on developing extensive networks of organizations, they formed Europe's first Muslim student organizations. Most European cities lacked mosques, and these organizations often became the first to open small places of worship, generally little more than garages or small meeting rooms on university campuses. The continent's freedoms allowed the Brothers to freely conduct the activities for which they had been persecuted in their home countries. With little funds but plenty of enthusiasm, they published magazines, organized lectures, meetings, and all sorts of activities through which they could spread their ideology. Their activism soon attracted other Muslim students and small numbers of Muslim immigrant laborers who had not had contact with the Brotherhood in their home countries.

Despite this activism, most of the pioneers' hearts were still in their native countries, interpreting their sojourn in Europe only as a temporary exile before returning home as victors and often comparing their experience to the time Muhammad had spent in exile in Medina after being persecuted in his native Mecca. Yet, while never ceasing to dream of returning home, by the 1970s, a handful of Brothers began to recognize the potential benefits that operating in Europe could have for the Islamic revivalist movement worldwide.[3] They understood that the West did not just constitute the ideal sanctuary but was also a place where the Brothers could come to control the local Muslim population. With scant competition from other Islamic currents and with local governments reluctant to interfere in religious affairs, Europe presented opportunities that the Brothers could not enjoy in any Muslim country.

If the arrival of the first Brothers in Europe was hardly the first phase of a concerted plot by the Muslim Brotherhood to Islamize the West, the interaction of these charismatic refugees with many enthusiastic new sympathizers bore unforeseeable fruits. The small organizations they spontaneously formed soon developed beyond their most optimistic expectations and outgrew their status of student groupings. By the late 1970s the founders of such outfits who had decided to stay in the West understood the necessity of creating new organizations that fulfilled the needs of the growing Muslim population of Europe and not just students. They steadily founded scores of organizations that mirrored Banna's model from the 1930s, establishing youth and women's branches, magazines and propaganda committees, schools, and think tanks.

This adulthood phase of the "European Brotherhood" coincided with epochal events worldwide. In the Middle East, Arab nationalism, having suffered a humiliating defeat at the 1967 war against Israel, had largely lost its appeal, to the benefit of its Islamist rival. Anwar Sadat's new policy of gradual reconciliation had also allowed the accommodationist wing of the Brotherhood, the so-called New Brothers led by Omar Tilmisani, to reorganize themselves.[4] Finally, continuing immigration and family reunifications had made the numbers of the once-invisible Muslim communities, living in Europe, soar.[5] These new populations increasingly needed to fulfill their spiritual needs, seeking places of worship, Islamic literature, and all sorts of guidance to their status of Muslim minorities in non-Muslim countries.

The combination of these factors led the European Brothers to acquire a new outlook and confidence. In various seminars held throughout Europe, top Brotherhood scholars started to redefine some centuries-old religious definitions by stating that the traditional distinction between Dar al-Islam (land of Islam) and Dar al-Harb (land of war) did not reflect the current reality. While the West could not be considered Dar al-Islam because *Shari'a* was not enforced there, it could not be considered Dar al-Harb either, because Muslims were allowed to practice Islam freely and were not persecuted. The scholars decided, therefore, that it was possible for them to create a new legal category. They concluded that the West should be considered Dar al-Da'wa (land of preaching)—a territory where Muslims live as a minority are respected and have the duty to spread their religion peacefully.[6]

The implications of this decision go far beyond the merely theological aspect. By redefining the nature of the Muslim presence in the West, the Brothers also changed the nature of their own role in it. While establishing an Islamic state in the Muslim world was still an important aspect of their agenda, they began to focus more on Europe's growing Muslim population. The Brothers soon understood that their organizational superiority could gain them a position of prominence among European Muslims and immediately embarked on an ambitious attempt to monopolize Muslim life in Europe. Moreover, it was at the time that the Brothers conceived the idea of becoming the official or de facto representatives of European Muslims, aiming at being the sole interlocutors of European governments, media, and intellectual elites on all issues pertaining to Islam.

THE SECRETS TO THE WESTERN BROTHERS' SUCCESS

Over the last thirty years, once they decided to focus their attention on Europe, the European Brothers have become one of the continent's most influential Muslim movements. This evolution has taken place in virtually all European countries where the Brotherhood has established a presence. Today, organizations created by the Brotherhood as its European offshoots, such as the Union of Islamic Organizations of France (UOIF) or the Islamic Society of Germany (IGD) have gained positions of prominence within their countries' Muslim communities. Even though their conservative and politicized interpretation of Islam is generally not shared by the majority of Muslims residing in Europe, Brotherhood-linked organizations have often managed to overshadow most other Muslim organizations, becoming the only movement that has been able to create stable organizations in virtually all European countries and the only truly pan-European Islamic movement.

The Brothers' position of disproportionate influence is unquestionably the consequence of the fragmentation of the Muslim community and the poor organization of competing movements.[7] Nevertheless, due credit should be given to the European Brothers for their accomplishment. One of the reasons for their success has been their ability to secure access to enormous funding. If in the first phase of its expansion in Europe, the Brotherhood received most of its funding from Saudi Arabia and other countries in the Arab Gulf, by the 1980s, it had created its own, extremely sophisticated financial network, which contributed significant funding for its activities.

Over the years, the Brothers established various financial institutions, mostly in London, Geneva, and Luxembourg, which were directed by Western-educated Ikhwan (Brothers) according to the principles of Islamic banking.[8] This financial viability allowed the European Brothers to intensify their activities in each European country and establish an array of transnational organizations, all of which worked together to create a global revivalist network and build ties with Western institutions. No competing movement or organization, including those sponsored by Muslim governments, has had the possibility or the ability to count on comparable resources.

Yet, funds are just one of the secrets to the European Brothers' success. The energy, commitment, and vision of its members are equally, if not more, important than material resources. Unlike most Muslim immigrants, the European Brothers were scions of well-educated families and graduates of some of Europe's most prestigious universities and professional community organizers with excellent communication and linguistic skills. Moreover, directly following the personal example of Banna and the writings of other Islamist thinkers such as Said Abu al-Ala al-Mawdudi, Said Ramadan, Said Hawwa, or Yusuf al-Qaradawi, the European Brothers perfectly understood the importance of building institutions.

Islamist scholars have often explained their emphasis on institution-building with their vision of Islam as a social religion. Al-Qaradawi has written influential treaties on "organized collective work," which he interprets as a duty "ordained by religion and necessitated by reality."[9] From the very beginning, the European Brothers adopted this view and established an impressive network of specialized organizations, each devoted to a well-defined goal and inserted in a corporation-like structure. Organizations devoted themselves to all the possible needs of the Muslim population, from the purely religious to the more mundane. Umbrella organizations at the national and international level were soon created to coordinate activities.

If ample funding and unrelenting activism are the cornerstones of the European Brothers' success, their extreme flexibility should also be considered an important aspect of their modus operandi. Basing their actions on the understanding that sacrifices and accommodations need to be made in order to achieve their goals, the Brothers have displayed a remarkable propensity to avoid dogmatisms and tailor their actions according to the circumstances. Cognizant of their position of relative powerlessness toward them, the European Brothers have decided to avoid unnecessary clashes with European establishments. Unlike Salafists and other radical trends, the Brothers take confrontational positions only when the benefits deriving from such stance are deemed to outweigh the negative consequences.

The European Brothers have displayed a remarkable ability to change positions with time, based on a very tactical calculation of what behavior could most benefit their agenda. In the first years of their existence, in fact, the Ikhwan organizations took very hard and confrontational positions on various issues that involved the Muslim community. These attitudes appear to have been dictated not only by the strong views of the leaders of these organizations but also by their desire to make themselves known and gain primacy within the Islamic community. Particularly telling in this regard is the approach of the UOIF over the veil issue.

Having witnessed how the confrontational stance used by various British Islamist organizations during the 1988 Rushdie affair had significantly improved their standing in the community, the following year the French

Ikhwan decided to imitate the tactics of their British Brothers when an opportunity presented itself in France. As the first nationwide controversy over the use of the *hijab* in public schools erupted in 1989, the UOIF, at the time a relatively young and powerless organization, became the most active defender of the right to wear the veil. Hoping to attract the sympathies of the Muslim community, while showing relative disinterest in pursuing a constructive dialogue with the French government, the UOIF organized several protests against the ban and declared that "the Muslims of France could not accept such attacks on their dignity."[10]

Fifteen years later, having reached a position of prominence within France's organized Islam, UOIF has completely changed tactics and strives to gain the trust of authorities. Realizing that it can obtain more by working within the system rather than against it, the UOIF has decided to avoid head-on confrontations with the government, which can only cause setbacks to its agenda. Therefore, in March 2004, when the French parliament passed a new controversial law banning all religious symbols and apparel in public schools, the UOIF kept remarkably quiet, abstaining from participating in the protests that were organized not only in France but throughout the world.

Azzam Tamimi, a leader of the British wing of the European Brotherhood who was harshly critical of this decision, explained that the UOIF opted for this more moderate position as it is "against any activity that could cause a confrontation with the public powers."[11] If in 1989 the issue of the *hijab* constituted a perfect opportunity to make the UOIF known to the French Muslim community as a strenuous defender of the honor of Muslims, fifteen years later, it constituted a dangerous trap to avoid. Since the law was passed with overwhelming and bilateral support, the UOIF saw no practical gain in challenging the establishment.

Another example of the European Brothers' flexibility is their ability to forge tactical alliances with the most disparate political forces. Since its early days, the European Brotherhood has established good relationships with other Islamist movements that operate in Europe, from the Pakistani Jama'at-e-Islami to the Turkish Milli Görüş. However, the European Brothers have gone well beyond these predictable alliances, often teaming up with all sorts of political forces that, according to the circumstances, best served their agenda.

Particularly noteworthy in that sense is, in recent years, the close cooperation between the European Brothers and some of the most extreme fringes of the left and the anti-Iraq War movement. Despite enormous ideological differences on social issues, the Brothers consider that the advantages they obtain by working with the extreme left far outweigh the risks involved with being accused of betraying their principles.

The success obtained by the European Brothers is particularly noteworthy considering the small numbers of members their organizations have attracted. While in each country they do control an ever-growing network of mosques and organizations, the membership numbers of all European

Brotherhood–linked organizations are limited to a few thousand members and represent a negligible fraction of the Muslim population. Yet, in the highly fragmented panorama of Muslim organizations operating in Europe, the Brothers far outpace competing trends and groupings, if not by membership by funding, organization, and activism.

Thanks to these characteristics the European Brothers perfectly fit the dynamics developed by what in social sciences is known as resource mobilization theory.[12] Formulated in the 1970s, the theory argues that a social movement's or an organization's likelihood to obtain its goals and overshadow competing forces depends largely on its ability to acquire resources to spread its message.[13] Whether an organization (and particularly its leadership) can establish a well-functioning structure, attract external financial support, capture the media's attention, and forge alliances with those in power determines its success no less than the validity of its ideas, goals, and grievances.

Applied to European Muslim communities, resource mobilization theory explains a fact on the ground: Organizations with historical and/or ideological links to the Muslim Brotherhood have often overshadowed other Muslim organizations in influencing the Muslim community and establishing relations with European governments. Most Muslim organizations operate only at the local level and can count on only limited means. Thanks to their politically motivated activism and ample funding, Brotherhood-linked organizations, on the other hand, have established an impressive network of mosques, think tanks, organizations, charities, and publications, which operate in each European country and transnationally. Even though they enjoy only limited direct support from the Muslim population, they constitute an extremely active and vocal presence and, as such, have managed to gain a position of prominence (in some cases, predominance) among Western Muslim organizations.

ASSESSING THE AIMS

Assessing the aims of the organizations created by members and sympathizers of the Brotherhood, particularly decades after their foundations, is challenging and controversial. An initial issue is constituted by the identification of such organizations with the Muslim Brotherhood. When speaking about Brotherhood networks in Europe, confusion often arises when analyses and speculations are met with an undeniable fact: there is no formal Muslim Brotherhood organization in Europe. There is no group with such name in any European country, nor is there any secret organization that identifies itself with it. Moreover, many of the individuals and organizations that are commonly identified by governments and commentators as "members of the Muslim Brotherhood" or "affiliated with the Muslim Brotherhood" often vigorously challenge such characterizations, in some cases, even by legal means.

Such behavior is easy to understand. In the West having an affiliation with the Brotherhood is not illegal, as it is in some Middle Eastern countries.

Yet, being linked to the Brotherhood, even on a purely ideological level, has consequences on how an organization is perceived and, consequently, on its access to European political establishments.

Before assessing the European Brothers' aims, it is therefore necessary to solve this terminological controversy. Today, the term Muslim Brotherhood can simultaneously encapsulate various realities. It is still an organization in Egypt, where it has a formal structure and even participates in the elections as a party. It is also an organization in various Middle Eastern scountries, where some outfits do consider themselves as the local branches of the Muslim Brotherhood. However, most notably, the Brotherhood is today also a global ideological movement in which like-minded individuals interact through an informal, yet very sophisticated, international network of contacts based on personal, financial, and, most importantly, ideological ties. Muhammad Akif, the current *murshid* (guide) of the Egyptian branch of the Muslim Brotherhood describes it as "a global movement whose members cooperate with each other throughout the world, based on the same religious worldview—the spread of Islam, until it rules the world." "We do not have an international organization," adds Akif, "we have an organization through our perception of things."[14]

In essence, the Western Brotherhood is composed of connections and collaborations established around a network of personal relationships.[15] It hardly corresponds to a well-defined master plan or a finely tuned conspiracy, but it originates from the interaction of a small group of smart, educated, and extremely motivated individuals united by a common ideology and driven by a deep belief in a religious/political worldview who slowly came together and found ways to cooperate. Rather than an organization of card-carrying members, it is a movement whose affiliation is determined by a series of personal contacts and, mostly importantly, a shared ideology or, in the words of a senior Brotherhood leader in Europe, a "common way of thinking."[16]

Even given, however, the fact that those operating in Europe are not subsidiary branches of any Middle East–based organization and that an affiliation to the movement is not based on any formal membership, it is fair to call them Muslim Brotherhood legacy groups or New European Brothers, since they trace their roots and ideology in the organization. Each organization belonging to the movement acts independently, adapting its actions to the environment in which it operates, but a lowest common denominator of commonly accepted principles and goals unites all of them.

Yet, even assuming that the identification of Brotherhood entities in European countries can be rendered a moot issue by referring to the Brotherhood as a movement rather than a structured organization, the most controversial source of debate surrounding the Brothers comes from the assessment of their aims. One factor that makes such assessment particularly challenging is the Brothers' continuous evolution. Initially, they perceived Europe simply as a convenient base of operation from which they could reorganize their struggle, whether through *da'wa* or violence, against secular regimes in the Middle East. As Europe's Muslim population surged, the movement focused on providing it with an environment that would help it retain its Islamic identity in non-Muslim societies. Naturally, the Islamic identity the Brothers wanted European Muslims to have is not just any Islamic identity, but rather one that conforms to their own view of what is appropriate, even divinely mandated.

Taking advantage of their superior organizational apparatus, the Brothers have tried to do what any competing organization finding itself with such edge would have done: exert strategic influence both internally and externally. Within the Muslim community the European Brothers have attempted, often with remarkable degrees of success, to exercise a sort of cultural hegemony, shaping and defining what Islam should be. Generally portraying themselves as defenders of the interests of Muslims in Europe, the Brothers have tried to occupy the entire Muslim space, putting their ideological stamp on any Islam-related issue, be it strictly religious or more properly political. This position of apparent predominance, derived by a phenomenal organizational apparatus rather than by genuine massive support of the Muslim community, has also allowed the European Brothers to be accepted, in many cases, as privileged interlocutors of European governments and elites.

It is nevertheless undeniable that Islamist thinking is in constant evolution. As the helm is being passed to a new generation of European-born and educated activists, the nature and aims of the organizations established forty years ago is changing. The unique status of Muslims as free minorities in non-Muslim countries has led Islamists in the West to confront issues and adopt positions that are very different to those of their counterparts in the Muslim world.[17] The New European Brothers seem no longer preoccupied with creating Islamic states in the Muslim world but rather focus on social and political issues concerning Muslims in the Europe. They now attempt, at least publicly, to portray themselves as facilitators of the integration of European Muslim communities, working to forge a sense of citizenship in which belonging to a European nation and Muslim faith can coexist; in which Muslims can be model citizens while being loyal to their faith.

Assessing the veracity of these claims is the challenge currently facing European policy-makers. Are the New European Brothers' pro-integration claims to be believed? Or are they just empty words for the consumption of Western ears? Can they be government interlocutors, reliable middlemen who can facilitate the integration process while still promoting their conservative interpretation of Islam? Is their purported moderate and prointegration position based on heartfelt convictions or on strategic calculations of the advantages such stance could bring to the movement? Is their ideology compatible with life in a secular Western democracy? Can they even be used as allies in contrasting the phenomenon of violent radicalization among Western Muslims?

The answers to these questions have crucial repercussions on the policies of European countries, determining how they interact with forces that have gained positions of significant influence within European Muslim communities. Whether the New European Brothers and, by extension, the global

Muslim Brotherhood movement, are considered potential friends, deceitful enemies, or anything in between is an extremely important assessment that would shape short- and long-term decisions in matters that span from foreign policy to domestic integration issues. Yet, the policymaking of virtually all European countries on the issue can be described only as schizophrenic, characterized by an apparent inability to reach a common assessment of non-violent Islamism, and constantly swinging between the "optimist" and the "pessimist" view of the movement.

Optimists argue that, over the last thirty years, the Muslim Brotherhood and affiliated Islamist movements have gone through a process of autoreform through which they have completely rejected the use of violence and embraced most democratic ideals.[18] This new generation of democratic-minded Islamists, argue the optimists, represents a powerful and genuinely moderate force that the West should embrace.[19] While some of their views might be different from ours, they argue, they do not pose a threat to the West, but, rather, they can be ideal partners in accomplishing the common goal of spreading democracy in the Muslim world. Moreover, they could even become allies in the fight against extremist groups such as al-Qa'ida, an objective that most optimists believe to be a mutual interest of the Brotherhood and the West.[20] The New European Brothers, representing offshoots of such reformed movement, are consequently seen by most optimists as bridgeheads between Western societies and religiously conservative Western Muslims—moderate forces that can foster integration and combat violent radicalization while preserving the Islamic identity of Western Muslim communities.

Pessimists, on the other hand, argue that the aims of the Brotherhood have changed little throughout the movement's history and that the Brothers are simply engaged in a cleverly architected public relations campaign to dissimulate their real aims. The Brothers, argue pessimists, make no qualms in publicly expressing their full support of democracy and human rights and rejecting violence in order to become part of the system, but, in reality, they are simply pursuing a "Trojan horse" tactic in order to destroy democratic systems from within. This deceitful approach is, according to pessimists, particularly sophisticated in the West. The pessimists argue that in the West, violence and confrontation have been replaced by a cleverly engineered mix of penetration of the system through a process of dissimulation and simultaneous radicalization of the Muslim population. Brotherhood leaders publicly proclaim the group's dedication to integration and democracy, represent themselves as mainstream, and portray themselves as the representatives of the various European Muslim communities in the media and in dialogues with European governments. Yet, when speaking Arabic, Urdu, or Turkish before their fellow Muslims, they often drop their "moderate" facade and embrace radicalism. While Brotherhood representatives speak about interfaith dialogue and integration on television, the group's mosques preach hate and warn worshippers about the evils of integration into Western society.

It is noteworthy that intelligence agencies and security officials from most European countries side firmly with the pessimists' view of the New European Brothers. Among the many negative assessments released by European agencies, particularly noteworthy for its completeness is that of the Algemene Inlichtingen-en Veiligheidsdienst, (AIVD), Holland's domestic intelligence agency:

> ...Not all Muslim Brothers or their sympathizers are recognizable as such. They do not always reveal their religious loyalties and ultra-orthodox agenda to outsiders. Apparently cooperative and moderate in their attitude to Western society, they certainly have no violent intent. But they are trying to pave the way for ultra-orthodox Islam to play a greater role in the Western world by exercising religious influence over Muslim immigrant communities and by forging good relations with relevant opinion leaders: politicians, civil servants, mainstream social organizations, non-Islamic clerics, academics, journalists and so on. This policy of engagement has been more noticeable in recent years, and might possibly herald a certain liberalization of the movement's ideas. It presents itself as a widely supported advocate and legitimate representative of the Islamic community. But the ultimate aim—although never stated openly—is to create, then implant and expand, an ultra-orthodox Muslim bloc inside Western Europe ....[21]

Despite such firm warnings from intelligence agencies, policy-makers in all European countries swing erratically from the pessimist to the optimist position. A telling example is represented by the internal debate within the British government over the relationship with the Muslim Brotherhood. In several public speeches during his time in office, former prime minister Tony Blair identified the Brothers as the ideological forefathers of modern Islamist terrorism, and various British top security officers have highlighted the impact of their philosophy on the radicalization of young British Muslims.[22]

Yet, other parts of the British government take a different stand, as perfectly exemplified by a 2005 internal memorandum from the Foreign Office on the visit to London of the above mentioned Yusuf al-Qaradawi, the undisputed spiritual leader of the global Muslim Brotherhood movement. While the Foreign Office admitted that al-Qaradawi's open support for suicide bombings in Iraq and against Israel was troubling, it also acknowledged that "they are not unusual or even exceptional amongst Muslims," both in the Middle East and the United Kingdom. Endorsing the cleric's visit to the United Kingdom, the Foreign Office praised al-Qaradawi's role in "promoting mainstream Islam" and suggested that "having individuals like Qaradawi on our side should be our aim."[23]

The British government's inability to formulate a cohesive position translates into seemingly incomprehensive policy discrepancies. In 2008, the Home Office decided to deny a visa to al-Qaradawi, stating that it would not "tolerate the presence of those who seek to justify any acts of terrorist violence or express views that could foster inter-community violence," and various ministries have recently cut the funding to organizations with ideological links to the Brotherhood and Jama'at-e-Islami, such as the Muslim Council of Britain.[24]

On the other hand, the Home and Foreign Office have been sponsoring programs such as *The Radical Middle Way*, a series of nationwide speaking engagements of several influential Muslim speakers, including former self-avowed Muslim Brotherhood representative to Europe Kamal Helbawy and several Brotherhood-leaning scholars and activists.[25] Like most European countries, the British government's attitude toward the Muslim Brotherhood seems almost schizophrenic. This inability to assess the European Brotherhood cohesively and, consequently, craft a consistent policy toward it, constitutes a serious failure of most European governments, which can severely hamper their efforts to combat radicalization and promote integration among their Muslim communities.

NOTES

1. While many books have been written on the Muslim Brotherhood and its early activities, the most comprehensive and widely read book remains Richard P. Mitchell, *The Society of the Muslim Brothers* (New York: Oxford University Press, 1969).

2. Jocelyne Cesari, *When Islam and Democracy Meet: Muslims in Europe and in the United States* (New York: Palgrave Macmillan, 2004), p. 143.

3. Arguably, the first Brotherhood leader to understand the new role of the Brothers in the West was Said Ramadan, founder of the Islamic Center of Geneva and a key figure in Brotherhood networks worldwide.

4. Gilles Kepel, *Muslim Extremism in Egypt* (Berkeley and Los Angeles, CA: University of California Press, 1986), pp. 62–63.

5. Jørgen Nielsen, *Muslims in Western Europe* (Edinburgh: Edinburgh University Press, 2004), pp. vii, 8–21, 24–27, 40–44.

6. Xavier Ternisien, *Les Frères Musulmans* (Paris: Fayard, 2005), pp. 190–192.

7. Joel S. Fetzer and J. Christopher Soper, *Muslims and the State in Britain, France and Germany* (New York: Cambridge University Press, 2005), pp. 6–10.

8. Sylvain Besson, *La Conquête de l'Occident* (Paris: Seuil, 2005).

9. Yusuf al Qaradawi, *Priorities of the Islamic Movement in the Coming Phase* (Swansea, UK: Awakening Publications, 2000).

10. Gilles Kepel, *Allah in the West: Islamic Movements in America and Europe* (Stanford: Stanford University Press, 1997), p. 187.

11. Ternisien, *Les Frères Musulmans*, p. 127.

12. See Anthony R. Oberschall, *Social Conflict and Social Movements* (Englewood Cliffs, NJ: Prentice Hall, 1973) and John D. McCarthy and Mayer N. Zald, "Resource Mobilization and Social Movements: A Partial Theory," *The American Journal of Sociology*, 82(6) (May 1977) 1212–1241.

13. Myra Mae Ferree, "The Political Context of Rationality: Rational Choice Theory and Resource Mobilization," in Aldon D. Morris and Carol McClung Mueller (eds.), *Frontiers in Social Movement Theory* (New Haven, CT: Yale University Press, 1992).

14. Ternisien, *Les Frères Musulmans* pp. 110–111.

15. Olivier Roy, *The Failure of Political Islam* (Cambridge, MA: Harvard University Press, 1996), pp. 110–113.

16. Author's interview with Yussuf Nada, Campione d'Italia, July 14, 2008.

17. Samir Amghar, "Europe Puts Islamists to the Test: The Muslim Brotherhood (France, Belgium and Switzerland)" *Mediterranean Politics*, 13(1) (March 2008) 63–77.

18. See, for example, Carry Wickham, "Democratization and Islamists—Auto-Reform," *Ikhwanweb (official English language website of the Muslim Brotherhood)*, June 15, 2006, http://www.ikhwanweb.com/Article.asp?ID=4112&SectionID=81 (accessed October 13, 2008).

19. See, for example, John L. Esposito, *The Islamic Threat: Myth or Reality* (New York and Oxford: Oxford University Press, 1999) and Raymond William Baker, *Islam without Fear: Egypt and the New Islamists* (Cambridge, MA: Harvard University Press, 2003).

20. Remarks of Prof. Marc Lynch, George Washington University, May 12, 2008; remarks reiterated on Prof. Lynch's blog: http://abuaardvark.typepad.com/abuaardvark/2008/05/assessing-the-m.html (accessed October 9, 2008).

21. AIVD, *The Radical Dawa in Transition: The Rise of Islamic Neoradicalism in the Netherlands*, https://www.aivd.nl/actueel-publicaties/aivd-publicaties/the-radical-dawa-in.(accessed December 5, 2009).

22. See, for example, Tony Blair, "A Battle for Global Values," *Foreign Affairs* (January/February 2007), p. 80.

23. British Foreign Office internal memo on Yusuf al-Qaradawi, July 14, 2005.

24. Vikram Dodd, "Controversial Muslim Cleric Banned from Britain," *Guardian*, February 7, 2008; interview with British official, London, January 2008.

25. For a list of speakers, see The Radical Middle Way's website: http://www.radicalmiddleway.co.uk/scholars.php (accessed October 23, 2008).

8

THE VERY MODEL OF A BRITISH MUSLIM BROTHERHOOD

David Rich

The British Muslim community has not always been fertile territory for the Muslim Brotherhood. British Muslims are mainly South Asian in origin, and consequently, the space for Islamist political activity is dominated by groups linked to Jama'at-e-Islami (JI). The gathering in Britain of Islamist exiles fleeing persecution and prosecution in their home countries during the 1990s brought a significant Muslim Brotherhood (MB) leadership cadre to the United Kingdom. However, with only a small Arab population making up a minority within the Muslim community—and with few mosques or other institutions under MB control—it has taken all of their tactical pragmatism, strategic flexibility, and political opportunism to establish some influence on Muslim politics in Britain.

NEW MUSLIM COMMUNITIES

Although Britain's first mosque was constructed in Woking in 1889, a Muslim community of significant size did not begin to emerge in Britain until mass immigration from the Commonwealth in the 1950s. This brought Pakistani—particularly Kashmiri—Muslims to Britain, followed by successive waves of Muslim immigration from South Asia, Turkey, northern Cyprus, East and sub-Saharan Africa, the Arab world, the Balkans, and elsewhere. As a result, Britain now has one of the most diverse Muslim communities in the world. More accurately, Britain has many different Muslim communities, defined, and often divided, by national origin, ethnicity, language, and sectarian differences. In total, some 2 million Muslims now worship in approximately 1,700 mosques.[1]

It did not take long for Islamist political organizations to try to establish a foothold in this new outpost of Muslim life. JI established several institutions in Britain in the 1960s and 1970s—of which the Islamic Foundation, UK Islamic Mission, and a collection of organizations based in the East London Mosque are now considered mainstream pillars of British Muslim life—while happily maintaining their JI connections and still promoting the works of JI founder Abu al-Ala al-Mawdudi, MB founder Hasan al-Banna, MB ideologue Sayyid Qutb, and other important JI and MB figures.

It would prove harder for the MB itself, however, to make an impression on this new community. While the JI groups had a natural UK constituency in the new South Asian communities whose members still felt the strong pull of their home countries, MB activists have always had to rely on the universal appeal of their Islamist ideology and "*umma*-centric" worldview, for which the younger generation of Muslim students was, from the start, an obvious target audience.

The Muslim Student Society, established in 1961, has been the closest group to the MB, regularly featuring leading Brotherhood speakers at its conferences. However, it has been a marginal group compared to the Federation of Student Islamic Societies (FOSIS), formed the following year. FOSIS has come to be seen as the representative body for Muslim students in the United Kingdom, and it has been courted constantly by the MB. One of its early activists, Ziauddin Sardar, recalls how "Two of the most influential organizations of the global Islamic movements vied with each other to capture our souls: the Muslim Brotherhood of Egypt and Jammat-e-Islami of Pakistan."[2]

Hasan al-Banna's son-in-law, Said Ramadan, the former secretary of the MB who in 1961 had established the Islamic Center of Geneva as a European focus for MB activity, was a regular visitor to FOSIS in the 1970s. This relationship has endured, but the MB still finds itself in competition with others. For the most part, and in a pattern replayed across the Muslim community, the MB has had more impact in providing ideological direction than organizational control. When FOSIS published Hasan al-Banna's "Letter to a Muslim Student" to give out to Muslim students across Britain, it was published not by an MB publishing house but by the JI-aligned Islamic Foundation.

In 1976, Said Ramadan joined the Executive Committee of the Islamic Council of Europe (ICE), a body set up three years earlier by Salem Azzam, a Saudi diplomat in London. Azzam was Egyptian by birth, the son of an Egyptian MP and the great-uncle of al-Qa'ida leader Ayman al-Zawahiri. Intended by the Saudis to be a vehicle for *da'wa* (proselytizing) in Europe, it had the grandiose aim of being the self-declared "supreme co-ordinating body of Muslim organizations in Europe, representing 25 million Muslims."[3]

Azzam used the ICE to bring together thinkers and activists from Islamist political movements to try to create a "theoretical basis for an Umma-wide Islamic political movement."[4] The ICE's work fit this global vision. It published, in 1981, a Universal Islamic Declaration of Human Rights, as well as an Islamic Constitution, both of which were intended to counter the secular basis of most Muslim-majority societies at that time.

Alongside Ramadan on the Executive Committee was Kurshid Ahmad, a former leader of the JI and its most senior figure in the United Kingdom, and other Muslim activists from across Europe and the United Kingdom. Ramadan had previously worked with Mawdudi in Pakistan, and Britain would prove, in later years, to be a place of fruitful collaboration between followers of the two major Islamist movements.

THE 1990S: THE CHALLENGE FOR ISLAMISTS

Even as late as the 1980s, however, all Islamist activity in the United Kingdom still reflected the attitude that Britain and the rest of Europe was part of *Dar al-Kufr* (land of unbelief), a hostile environment in which Muslims were only a temporary presence. This would change in the late 1980s, as a new generation of British-born Muslims reached maturity. At the same time, the defeat of the Soviet Union in Afghanistan, claimed by the Arab and Afghan *mujahidin* as a victory for Islam, and the collapse of Communism a year later led to a global surge in Islamist confidence. In the eyes of the MB, Europe now became *Dar al-Islam* (land of Islam), where Muslims were at home and should be able to live under Shari'a.[5]

The start of a new decade provoked a bout of this new thinking in the FOSIS magazine, *The Muslim*. Titled "Islamic Work 1990's: A Decade of Challenge," the opening article set the scene:

> While capitalism and communism are now setting suns, a historical turning point is about to knock on the door of the world. This ageing world is poised to embark upon a new era under the leadership of an entirely new civilization dawning on the horizon. Indeed for that matter, any ideological system which is able to offer hope and the required leadership will eventually lead mankind to the path. Could it be Islam? This is a challenge.[6]

The article went on to warn that the Muslim world was still beset by too many internal problems and divisions to achieve this goal. The plan for how to overcome these obstacles and meet the challenge, however, was set out by another article in that issue by the leading MB theologian Yusuf al-Qaradawi. Islamic work, he explained, means "the organized collective work which seeks to attain a certain status for Islam by virtue of which it becomes the director of life as a whole and as a leader of society in all aspects." For this, he clarified for his British Muslim audience

> Islamic workers [need] to understand that the future is theirs, that the future belongs to this religion, and that Islam will inherit all these civilizations. These civilizations may have reached the moon but they have certainly failed to provide humanity with happiness.

In a work plan that consciously echoed Communist strategy, al-Qaradawi identified "laborers" and women as key groups to target for "Islamic awakening," in addition to identifying and training an elite vanguard "culturally, spiritually, militarily, socially and politically .... Islamists must pay special attention to the preparation of competent cadres."[7]

The development of "competent cadres" was a problem for the MB in Britain that was beginning to be solved by this time. By the late 1980s, the phenomenon that later came to be known as "Londonistan," whereby Britain gave refuge to Islamists from across the Arab and Muslim world, was under way. Both violent jihadists and nonviolent Islamists settled in London and other British cities. There, they were able to continue their opposition to Arab regimes from under the shelter of British democracy. Many of these activists were senior MB figures from the Arab world, and their presence in the United Kingdom quickly led to the formation of Islamist political, propaganda, and fundraising activities in Britain.

The attitude of the British government was that so long as the focus of the Islamist exiles remained their home countries, and they did not plan to set off bombs in the United Kingdom, they were free to continue their activities unmolested by the British authorities. Many of the exiles had arrived via France, where the authorities were much less tolerant of Islamist political work, a difference between Britain and France that endures to this day.

British governmental neglect was compounded by a naive curiosity within civil society about Islamism. Many of the new arrivals sat alongside British policy-makers to hear Rashid Ghannouchi, the leader of the Tunisian al-Nahdhah party and one of the more important MB-aligned Islamist scholars in the United Kingdom, address the Royal Institute of International Affairs at Chatham House in 1995. Ghannouchi expressed his wonder at "The scene of a fundamentalist, who prefers to be described as an Islamist, addressing an audience of prominent political thinkers and policymakers in the United Kingdom."[8] Yet, few of those thinkers and policy-makers possessed, at that time, the critical tools to understand or challenge the global vision of Ghannouchi and his Islamist comrades, still less their local impact on the politics of the British Muslim community.

FROM GLOBAL TO LOCAL

The flaw in the Londonistan policy was in its assumption that British Muslims would not be influenced by the ideas of the MB and others, despite their emphasis on loyalty to the umma rather than to Britain, their need for Shari'a and the Caliphate, and the glorification of jihad and martyrdom. Many young British Muslims, victims of prejudice and discrimination by the majority population, were torn between the dual identities of their British nationality and the folk Islam of their parents' generation, neither of which answered their fundamental questions about themselves and their place in the world. For this generation, the new arrivals from the Arab world offered an alternative model of Islamic strength, honor and unity, fighting to establish an Islamic order in a godless world, a virtual community with which they were proud to identify.

The Islamic Society of Britain (ISB), established in 1990 to serve this new generation of British Muslims, was heavily influenced by Egyptian and Palestinian MB activists in Britain.[9] *Trends*, the magazine of their youth wing, Young Muslims UK, frequently published favorable articles about jihadist movements and ideologues. In 1994, one edition featured the MB on its cover; another focused on Hamas, and a third had an interview with the Sudanese MB leader Hasan al-Turabi. Warnings from those inside and outside Britain who foresaw the impact these exiles would have on Islamist politics in Britain fell on deaf ears throughout the 1990s.

Of all the MB leaders and other activists to arrive in Britain from the Arab world, Kamal Helbawy has done more than any other to push the MB into the public arena. An MB member since the age of twelve, he was part of the migration of Egyptian MB activists who fled to Saudi Arabia in the 1970s. After helping to found the World Assembly of Muslim Youth (WAMY), Helbawy moved in 1988 to Kurshid Ahmad's Institute of Policy Studies in Pakistan, where he was responsible for all MB activities in Afghanistan and Pakistan. Finally, in 1994, he moved to the United Kingdom, where he served as the MB's official spokesman in the West.[10]

Despite the fact that he is from the older generation of the Egyptian MB, Helbawy has always understood the opportunities available to Islamists in the open societies of the West and has lamented the caution and secrecy that many Arab Islamists have brought with them from their experiences in their home countries. "The International Organization," he told one interviewer,

> ... needs to work openly and meet with public figures; as it is, only the secret services know when its main figures come and go. There's no proper research center anywhere in the West, or a TV channel. We need to create a global forum for dialogue and to increase our activities.[11]

In pursuit of this open face, in September 1995 Helbawy announced the creation of a Muslim Brotherhood Information Center, based in London

> To store, classify and disseminate authentic information in different languages on Islam, Islamic issues, and movements, especially the Muslim Brotherhood .... To maintain an up-to-date file on the Muslim Brotherhood in particular and other contemporary Islamic movements in general, in order to provide authentic information and data to the press and others.[12]

The MB already had a publishing imprint, the International Islamic Forum, based in the United Kingdom, and produced its *Risalat al-Ikhwan* newsletter and *al-Da'awa* magazine in Britain.

This project, conducted in a combination of Arabic and English, had a focus mainly on Egypt and other Arab countries. It came to an abrupt end in 1997, when Helbawy found himself at odds with the MB leadership in Egypt and became estranged from the movement. In its place he and other MB exiles in the United Kingdom founded the Muslim Association of Britain (MAB), which emerged from internal divisions within the ISB over the extent of Arab influence in an organization intended to serve the needs of British Muslims. The MAB has retained a strong Arab influence and has come to be regarded as the British branch of the MB in all but name. Never a large organization—membership went from about 400 in September 2001 to around 800 to 1,000 by 2003—the MAB revolutionized political Islam's role in the United Kingdom by shifting it to a more anti-Western, anti-Israel, and anti-semitic outlook.[13]

It was able to exert this influence by exploiting the hesitancy of the dominant Muslim body in the United Kingdom, the Muslim Council of Britain (MCB), after the crisis of September 11, 2001 and the consequent invasions of Afghanistan and Iraq led by the United States. The MCB had been established in 1997, in response to a demand from the government to have a single point of contact for their dealings with the Muslim community, similar to that served by the Board of Deputies of British Jews. While claiming leadership of the British Muslim community, it was dominated by JI-linked groups, many of which had been in the forefront of Muslim political activism against the publication of Salman Rushdie's *Satanic Verses* in 1988.

The MCB's position as the government's main Muslim interlocutor left it caught between two conflicting demands after the September 11 crisis: the government wanted its backing for the invasion of Afghanistan, a proposition to which most of the politically active parts of the Muslim community were opposed. While the MCB faltered, the MAB seized the initiative, opposing the war in Afghanistan and taking the lead in organizing Muslim opposition to Israel.

In April 2002, with the second intifada at its height, the MAB organized a demonstration and rally against Israel in central London. This brought a level of public anti-Israel and even anti-semitic sentiment onto the streets of Britain that had rarely been seen before. Many demonstrators carried the flags of Hizballah, Hamas, and the MB itself; some even dressed as suicide bombers or carried placards equating the Star of David with the swastika. MB speakers including Azzam Tamimi—a former spokesman for the MB in Jordan and now the most vocal supporter of Hamas in Britain[14]—and Kamal Helbawy joined speakers from the Palestine Solidarity Campaign and other left-wing organizations.

The MB flavor of the event was summed up at the end, when Rashid Ghannouchi led prayers for the whole demonstration. The MAB's claim to have drawn 100,000 demonstrators[15] from around the country left an impression on many inside and outside the Muslim community, including the senior officers from the Stop the War Coalition (STWC), a new organization formed to oppose the war in Afghanistan and the impending war in Iraq, who spoke at the event.

THE MB AND THE LEFT

The main constituent part of the STWC was the Socialist Workers Party (SWP), a Trotskyite group that dominates most far-left activity in Britain. While the SWP normally manages to outmaneuver other far-left factions, they met their match in the MAB. After initially refusing an invitation to affiliate with the STWC, the MAB proposed instead an equal partnership, on the MAB's terms. According to one MAB leader, Anas al-Tikriti:

> MAB "spoke to Stop the War and we said to them, we will join you; however we will not become part of your coalition, we will be a separate and independent entity but we will work together with you on a national basis as part of the anti-war movement." This reassured MAB that it would not "melt into that big coalition" that was known to be "led by the Left." They would remain a distinct and autonomous bloc, able to shape the agenda.[16]

This equal partnership meant that MAB could ensure that the previously secular environment of a far-left political campaign now made faith-sensitive accommodations, such as gender-segregated meetings and *halal* food. They also stipulated their limits on who could join the STWC. Although they were now in partnership with far-left groups with whom they disagreed on most fundamental issues, and with some comrades they had at times been in violent conflict in their own countries, they made their limits clear: "While they could overcome misgivings about sharing platforms with some groups (such as socialists and atheists), they could never do so with others (Zionists and Israelis in particular)."[17]

For the anti-Zionist SWP this would not be a problem. One question over which the MAB differed with their new partners in the STWC was whether Iraq or Palestine should be the dominant issue of their campaigns. It is an indication of the importance that this issue played in the worldview of the MAB that for their demonstration in September 2002, they viewed the dual slogan of "no war in Iraq, justice for Palestine" as a compromise, distracting from the centrality of Palestine as "the cause of all problems in the Middle East." At the demonstration itself, the MAB leaflets placed "Freedom for Palestine" above "Stop the war in Iraq," while the STWC leaflets had the slogans in the opposite order.[18] Despite these differences of emphasis, anti-Zionism and opposition to Western foreign policy were the founding principles of the left-Islamist alliance and remains its energizing core.

Both sides of this alliance have been influenced by the analysis, prescriptions, and language of the other. This is not just another example of the political opportunism and adaptability common to both Islamists and the far left. Many Islamist participants in the antiwar movement were profoundly affected by their collaboration with non-Muslims from leftist, Christian, and other groups. Salma Yaqoob, a close political ally of MP George Galloway and Soumaya Ghannouchi, daughter of Rashid Ghannouchi, are two British-based Islamists who have merged the language of leftist anti-imperialism with their own Islamist outlook. Yaqoob speaks for many when she argues that this offers a new pathway for Muslim political engagement:

> The dominant character of Muslim radicalization in Britain today points not towards terrorism or religious extremism, but in the opposite direction: towards political engagement in new, radical and progressive coalitions that

seek to unite Muslim with non-Muslim in parliamentary and extra-parliamentary strategies to effect change. What is unique about British Muslim radicalism in the European context is the degree to which it has overlapped, intertwined and engaged with indigenous non-Muslim radicalism post-9/11 ... [a] sea [of] change ... has taken place in the transformation of Muslim ideas of citizenship through participation in the anti-war movement.[19]

Despite their common ground, the relationship between Islamists and the left has not always been an easy one. Tariq Ramadan—Said Ramadan's son and Hasan al-Banna's grandson—is perhaps the most prominent Islamist in the European anti-globalist movement. He has been, at times, wary of the way the old left has approached this relationship:

Convinced that they are progressive, they give themselves the arbitrary right to proclaim the definitively reactionary nature of religions, and if liberation theology has contradicted this conclusion, the possibility that Islam could engender resistance is not even imagined ... unless it's to modernity. In the end, only a handful of "Muslims-who-think-like-us" are accepted, while the others are denied the possibility of being genuinely progressive fighters armed with their own set of values.[20]

The radicalizing impact of the MB on anti-Israel campaigning in Britain has come not just by its framing of Israel/Palestine as the central problem through which all other foreign policy issues should be understood but also via the uncompromising nature of the MAB line which comes straight from its Hamas roots. The MAB slogan "Palestine must be free, from the river to the sea" is now ubiquitous in anti-Israel demonstrations in the United Kingdom. The MAB has also promoted support for Palestinian suicide bombing. One leading MAB activist, Muhammad Sawalha, was a Hamas activist before and after moving to Britain in 1990.[21] Another, Azzam Tamimi, publicly expressed his wish to carry out a suicide bombing in Israel, saying: "If I can go to Palestine and sacrifice myself I would do it ... it is the straight way to pleasing my God and I would do it if I had the opportunity."[22]

Kamal Helbawy has repeatedly echoed the views of al-Qaradawi and the late Shaykh Yasin of Hamas that Israeli civilians are different from the civilians of other countries because all Israelis are past, current, or future soldiers and that suicide bombings in Israel should therefore not be thought of as terrorism.[23] At times, too, a level of anti-semitism slips into the MAB's discourse that is rarely seen in public anti-Israel campaigning. The MAB newsletter *New Dawn* greeted the outbreak of the second intifada in October 2000 by reproducing the notorious anti-semitic hoax "The Jewish Threat on the American Society," supposedly a report of a speech by Benjamin Franklin but in fact written by the American Nazi William Dudley Pelley in the 1930s.[24]

None of this could distract the leaders of the STWC from the political potential of the huge numbers of people who marched against the war in Iraq. As war became imminent and public opposition to the government's policy swelled, veteran far-left activists, who had spent their political careers leading small numbers of people in campaigns that had little or no impact, found themselves at the head of a national campaign that had tapped into previously untouched constituencies, both Muslim and non-Muslim. The MAB's role as the leading Muslim organizer of this campaign pushed what was previously a marginal Islamist group into a position of political leadership in the Muslim community. They still controlled few mosques and had only a narrow grass-roots structure, but their influence at the top of the community, both within and as an alternative to the MCB, had grown immeasurably.

The question of how to tap into this new political constituency led naturally to involvement, direct and indirect, in election campaigning. The MAB had already identified the need "to prove to political circles that Muslims can be mobilized into becoming an influential block in any future elections."[25] The most obvious electoral expression of this new left-Islamist movement was the formation of Respect–The Unity Coalition, an electoral alliance between the SWP, the MAB, and other far-left, Islamist and Muslim community groups. Best known for the 2005 election of George Galloway in Bethnal Green and Bow, Respect was in the end a short-lived experiment that held only a brief attraction for the MAB. [26]

Engagement with the kind of radical leftist movements advocated by Salma Yaqoob was no substitute for the patronage and influence available through involvement in mainstream politics. By 2004, the MAB was already moving away from Respect and into the orbit of a far more powerful figure of the British left: the mayor of London, Ken Livingstone. A relationship that would eventually do a great deal of damage to both parties first came to public attention in July 2004, when the City Hall hosted the MAB-arranged visit to London of Yusuf al-Qaradawi. When Livingstone came under attack for this, his stubborn defense of al-Qaradawi as a moderate—despite the latter's homophobia, anti-semitism, theological justification for suicide bombings, support for female genital mutilation, and other views—appalled not just many of Livingstone's political allies on the left, particularly gay rights' groups, but also much of the London electorate in general.

Livingstone, though, was, in the words of a London magazine, "more interested in the Muslim vote and thought that by pandering to al-Qaradawi he could get it."[27] This fit a wider pattern of Livingstone's mayoralty, by which he extended his patronage to many different community groups across London in return for their support. The MAB's communalist attitude to elections was clear from its first electoral intervention in 2004, which took the form of a fatwa issued in their support by Shaykh Haitham al-Haddad, a Wahhabi shaykh in London. Haddad ruled that voting was halal but that choosing who to vote for

requires [such] a deep and meticulous understanding of the political arena ... that individuals should avoid involving themselves in this process and rather should entrust this responsibility to the prominent Muslim organizations that have sufficient experience and the ability to determine the issue according to the interests of the Muslims.

The "prominent Muslim organization" that al-Haddad recommended to Muslim voters was the MAB, which had "done a great service by preparing a list of candidates whom they believe will best represent the interests of Muslims in the event they are elected."[28]

Unfortunately for Livingstone, the MAB, lacking a large grassroots base, was incapable of delivering significant numbers of votes. This should have been apparent to the mayor's office by the time of the 2005 general election, when the MAB did little actual campaigning, simply preferring to issue another list of candidates around the country for Muslims to support. In neither the year 2004 nor the year 2005 did the MAB's public support have any noticeable impact on the voting patterns for their chosen candidates.

In 2008, when Livingstone was next up for reelection, his MB allies put together a more sophisticated campaign, but this public support was exploited by Livingstone's opponents to remind the wider electorate of his unpopular embrace of al-Qaradawi. What Livingstone had lost in the support of many on the left his new Islamist allies were incapable of replacing. Mobilizing Muslims to demonstrate about Iraq or Palestine proved easier for the MB than delivering enough votes in London to keep its patron in office. When Livingstone lost the election to his Conservative challenger, Boris Johnson, one senior Conservative MP declared it to be the death of communalist vote-harvesting: "There's no such thing as the Muslim block vote, to be delivered up to suitably grateful candidates by key special interest groups."[29]

THE PIOUS AND THE POLITICAL

Al-Qaradawi's 2004 visit to London was not just a chance for him to meet the mayor. His visit was primarily for a gathering of the European Council for Fatwa and Research (ECFR), a body formed in 1997 to provide religious rulings that would be relevant for Muslims living in Europe. Run by al-Qaradawi and Faysal Mawlawi, the leader of the MB in Lebanon, the ECFR was created by the Federation of Islamic Organizations in Europe (FIOE),[30] a Europe-wide network of MB-linked groups, based until 2008 at the headquarters of the Islamic Foundation, one of the main JI-aligned bodies in Britain. Although conceptually similar to the Islamic Council of Europe, the FIOE, chaired by an Iraqi exile in Britain, Ahmad al-Rawi, has proved to be much bigger and more effective.

The FIOE website lists twenty-eight member organizations, many of which are both well-known in their own right and known to have links to the international MB.[31] In addition to the ECFR, which provides religious rulings, the FIOE has the following member organizations: an associated financial base, the European Trust; an academic arm, the European Institute for Human Sciences, with campuses in Wales and France; a youth wing, the Federation of Muslim Youth and Student Organizations, which claims thirty-seven member organizations across Europe; and other divisions for women, media professionals, and imams. Al-Qaradawi's 2004 visit to London included a trip to Ireland, where he established the International Association of Muslim Scholars.

This growing MB network reflects the feeling of many in the MB—including al-Qaradawi, Mawlawi, and Helbawy—that providing a new, relevant framework for European Muslim life will give new energy and meaning to the movement. Al-Qaradawi's international popularity via satellite TV, his history of innovative rulings on a wide range of questions about life for Muslims in the West and his prominent role in the Islamic finance sector make him ideally placed to lay the foundation for a kind of non-territorial Islamic state and direct Muslim life in the West.[32]

However, this occasional clash in values between Muslim minority and non-Muslim majority can pose a serious obstacle to al-Qaradawi's European ambitions. He retains his important role as a religious authority for Hamas and frequently expresses his support for jihad against British and other Western forces in Iraq and Afghanistan. His views on homosexuality, aspects of gender relations, and other social issues, although considered progressive compared to the rulings of some *ulama*, still diverge widely from the social norms of wider British society.

This long-term work is in some ways the more important part of the MB's activities in Britain. While the FIOE's work rarely drew public scrutiny, the MAB's political activities brought increasing attention onto the presence of the movement in Britain. As a small political clique projecting disproportionate influence, the MB had begun to resemble, in its political methods, the kind of Trotskyite fraction that would have been familiar to Ken Livingstone's advisers at City Hall. Some of the older MB leaders in Britain had become increasingly nervous at the MAB's public opposition to the government, which they felt would jeopardize their educational and spiritual work.

There were examples of cooperation with government. In December 2005, the MAB was drawn into efforts to secure the release of Norman Kember, a British hostage in Iraq. Anas al-Tikriti, a MAB leader, was dispatched to Iraq, and the MAB managed to persuade al-Qaradawi and other MB leaders to call for Kember's release. (He was later freed by British troops.) Despite this, the generational divide within the MAB led, in December 2005, to the election of a new president and executive, effectively removing the younger political activists such as Anas al-Tikriti and Azzam Tamimi from positions of power. This internal split, "pitting the pious against the political firebrands," as the *Economist* put it,[33] led directly to the formation of the British Muslim Initiative (BMI), by Muhammad Sawalha, Tamimi, al-Tikriti, and a handful of others who wanted to ensure that their political activism, particularly in the antiwar movement, did not die away. There is some disagreement about how amiable the split was at the time,[34] but there is no doubt that it has created a convenient division of labor, which allows the work of the ECFR to continue out of the public and media eye, while the BMI ensures that the MB still has influence in the Muslim community's overt political campaigning.

Although the MB has failed to exert political influence in terms of votes, it has been much more successful in influencing opinion, both inside and outside the Muslim community. In October 2004, Muhammad Sawalha, then a director of the MAB, established Islam Expo, a project to create a combined political conference and Islamic cultural festival on a massive scale. The first Islam Expo event took place in summer 2006, by which time Sawalha and the other organizers had left the MAB to form the BMI. A second Islam Expo was held in summer 2008. Both drew tens of thousands of Muslims, attracted as much by the cultural attractions as the religious and political speeches. While the Islam Expo website for 2008 concentrated on the cultural and educational purpose of the event,[35] the goals of those behind Islam Expo, listed in Companies House documents, include the overtly political purpose: "To change the perception of key decisionmakers from the world of politics, media and commerce about Islam."[36]

At the 2008 event, this took the form of a seminar on "Understanding Political Islam," which featured a host of MB and other Islamist speakers. The seminar was co-organized by several groups, including BMI and the left-leaning think tank Demos and was a clear expression of the MB's new political position: after the London subway bombing, and with a growing terrorist threat from home-grown Salafist-jihadist networks, the MB are the Islamists with whom you can do business. The seminar included non-Muslim advocates of cooperation with the MB: Robert Leiken[37] was one speaker, while the seminar was co-organized by Alistair Crooke's Conflicts Forum.

Crooke is a former MI6 officer who created Conflicts Forum in 2004 to "engage and listen to Islamists, while challenging Western misconceptions and misrepresentations of the region's leading agents of change."[38] In practice, Conflicts Forum is much more an advocate of Islamism than a neutral space for dialogue. One Conflicts Forum document identifies the need "to shift the debate on Islamism from a predominantly defensive posture to a positive assertion of Islamist values and thinking."[39] Another document sets out how this will be done:

> We aim to find the visual imagery, and the metaphors appropriate in a secular society to generate the "oh, I get it now!" moment for Western viewers in terms of the Islamist critique of Western modernity, and their alternative vision. This will require investing Islamist concepts with a new significance and meaning that provokes recognition and a positive response from Western audiences.[40]

Crooke himself, in a lecture in Beirut in 2008, expanded on the Islamist critique of Western individualism as "diminishing man himself" before calling for

> a resistance in the West; a resistance from within ... to think afresh, to go back to some of the foundations of Western culture not simply to diminish or criticize them, but this is the means by which we can step beyond our present impasse.[41]

Crooke's acceptance of MB and wider Islamist thinking is plain; just as Islamism is a political ideology, distinct from the religion of Islam, so he is perhaps the clearest example of somebody who is politically an Islamist without being a Muslim.

The scale of Islam Expo certainly impressed many. Tens of thousands of people, mostly but not exclusively Muslims, passed through the doors of the event in both 2006 and 2008. The 2008 event was even promoted via advertisements on the sides of London buses. However, this was not a reflection of any increased grassroots capacity of the MB in Britain; rather, it was a consequence of their political organization and their ability to access funding that is rarely available to moderate, non-Islamist groups.

The 2006 Islam Expo cost over £1.1 million to produce, which was paid for entirely by grants from the following: the Qatari National Council for Culture, Arts and Heritage (£967,442), in reality, an arm of the government of Qatar; and the Greater London Authority (£200,000), then under the control of Ken Livingstone. The 2008 event was paid for by a second Qatari grant of £2 million.[42] Similar grants have been given by the Scottish government to the BMI's equivalent in Scotland, the Scottish Islamic Foundation,[43] to hold similar events in Scotland. This external funding is the reason why the BMI, a political clique with no membership beyond its core activist group,[44] can organize an event in London that attracts tens of thousands of British Muslims. Similarly, the activities of the FIOE and ECFR are funded by Middle Eastern money, mainly from Dubai and Kuwait.[45] There is much resistance in the British Muslim community to the idea that the British government should use its patronage to try to shape the future of British Islam; meanwhile, there are foreign governments pouring huge amounts of money into doing just that.

SET A THIEF TO CATCH A THIEF

MB figures in Britain have tried hard to present themselves as potential allies in counterterrorist work, an idea that was taken up most notably by the Muslim Contact Unit (MCU) of the Metropolitan Police, under the leadership of Detective Inspector Robert Lambert (now retired). In particular, the police used the MB in its efforts to take control of the North London Central Mosque, better known as Finsbury Park Mosque, which had become notorious under the leadership of the hook-handed Abu Hamza al-Masri for its connections to several convicted and suspected terrorists. After expelling Abu Hamza and his supporters from the mosque, the police handed it over to Sawalha and his MB colleagues, on the understanding that they had the physical strength and credibility with local Muslim youth to prevent the mosque from falling back into Salafist-jihadist hands.

MB activists had not always seen themselves as allies of the British state against the likes of Abu Hamza. In 1999, when a group of Abu Hamza's followers (including his son and stepson) were arrested in Yemen for plotting terrorist attacks against Western targets in the country, Azzam Tamimi had speculated in a Muslim student magazine whether this was in fact part of a more sinister British government plot against British Muslims:

> Could it be that the harm caused to Islam and the Muslims by Abu Hamza and his likes is something which certain circles within the British official establishment would welcome? This is not a naïve question. Islam is now the fastest growing religion in the country and it gains more converts every day .... Is it not likely that by tolerating—in the name of democracy and freedom of expression—extreme wings of the Muslim community the government may be preparing the ground for denying democratic rights to the community as a whole? Is it not possible that the long-term objective might be to curb the spread of Islam and the growth of Islamic influence in British public life?[46]

Still, Tamimi and other MB activists overcame their mistrust to form a partnership of sorts with the police in London, which the MCU claims "empowered and facilitated direct and successful intervention by hard-line Salafi and various Islamist groups to reduce the threat of terrorist recruitment."[47] In return, a level of respectability, validation, and other political benefits could be derived from working as police advisers on counterterrorism. The MAB is also part of a government-backed project, the Mosques and Imams National Advisory Body (MINAB), to improve mosque governance, develop the skills of imams, and encourage mosques to become hubs of community cohesion. However, the limited potential of such partnerships ought to be recognized. They are only relevant for the immediate needs of a counterterrorism strategy that looks no further than preventing the next bomb on British soil. There is no doubt that the MB, in Britain, is wholly opposed to the idea of terrorist attacks in Britain. This is partly for pragmatic reasons, as it jeopardizes their nonviolent Islamist work[48] but also because they genuinely believe that violence cannot be justified in Britain, today.

British forces in Iraq or Afghanistan, though, are another matter; Ahmad al-Rawi, Rashid Ghannouchi, and Ali Sadr al-Din al-Bayanuni, the London-based head of the Syrian MB, all signed a public statement in August 2004 supporting attacks against coalition forces in Iraq.[49] Suicide bombings in Israel, too, will not be condemned by UK-based Brotherhood leaders, despite the fact that two years prior to the London subway bombs, two British Muslims with connections to that network carried out a suicide bombing in Tel Aviv. Of course, justifying suicide bombings by Palestinians in Israel is subtly different from encouraging British Muslims to travel to Israel to carry out terrorist attacks themselves, but this sort of distinction is indicative of the MB's conditional support for counterterrorism, which could never extend to a theological or ideological refutation of martyrdom via suicide bombings *per se*.

Other parts of MB ideology directly undermine the long-term needs of social cohesion in Britain. The idea that the MB can be a useful—even an indispensable—partner against jihadist terrorism in Britain is partly related to their strength in some Arab countries and the lazy assumption that this strength and influence automatically transfers to the British Muslim community. A series of leaked internal government documents[50] revealed the extent to which discussions within the Foreign & Commonwealth Office over whether to escalate their contacts with the MB in Egypt ran in parallel with discussions about whether the MB could be a partner for moderation in the United Kingdom. However, it is a failure of leadership to assume that the sole alternatives for young British Muslims are either the Salafist, jihadist, or MB frameworks, as opposed to any of the other Muslim or secular choices available to them in Britain.

A Very British Brotherhood

Britain is still the location of Arab-facing MB activity. The Syrian MB leadership opened a formal office in London in 2007. Egyptian MB activists in Britain joined other exiled Islamists in 2005 to form the Save Egypt Front, which has held protests in London against the Egyptian government. Azzam Tamimi and Anas al-Tikriti are involved with a London-based Arabic TV station, Al-Hiwar, which promotes the MB perspective on Arab affairs. However, it is their work within the British arena, such as Islam Expo or the MCU, which represents a maturing of MB political activity in Britain and a growing self-confidence. They are not yet at the stage advocated by Kamal Helbawy of operating as an open organization under the MB name, but there is little attempt to disguise the fact that the MAB, BMI, and other similar groupings are aligned with the MB school of thought, although not, it is often stressed, under its organizational direction.

What is striking are the many different areas of British public life relating to the Muslim community—political, educational, policing, cultural, and others—in which MB ideas and activists exert some influence. The MB's willingness and ability to work with a wide range of partners, Islamist and non-Islamist, Muslim and non-Muslim, compounds their strength, generating influence beyond their numbers, but is also a sign that the MB in Britain is far from a single, homogeneous movement. It also provides evidence, like the work of the ECFR, that the MB increasingly derives its energy and dynamism from its work in the open societies of Europe, away from the stagnant leadership in Egypt. The MB has always been open to Western influences and has always been prepared to work with other political forces, but the MB experience in Britain has been particularly marked by the osmosis of political ideas and language between previously separate, even opposed, political extremes.

Whereas the alliance with the far left surprised many, collaboration with JI-linked organizations such as the Islamic Foundation or East London Mosque that dominate Islamist activity in Britain is both natural and unavoidable and has been of great benefit to the MB. Anas al-Tikriti now runs a body called the Cordoba Foundation, in which Abdallah Faliq, who has a background in the British JI-linked organizations, holds a senior position. Faliq is also a trustee of the JI-linked East London Mosque and director of training at Kamal Helbawy's Center for the Study of Terrorism (CFSOT), a think tank established by Helbawy as "an independent research, training and consultancy organization, dedicated to the in-depth study of Islamic resurgence, democratisation and extremism in the Muslim world."[51]

With positions in the JI-linked Islamic Forum of Europe and Tariq Ramadan's European Forum, Faliq's portfolio is a good example of how MB and JI activities often complement each other or even merge into one in Britain. Helbawy has also explored alliances with Iranian and other Shi'a groupings and in November 2008 visited Lebanon to discuss his ideas for Muslim unity with Shaykh Na'im Qasim, deputy secretary general of Hizballah.[52]

Tariq Ramadan is one of the more influential Islamist voices in Britain in the debate over the future of Muslims in Europe. Ramadan manages to play the roles of academic, political activist, evangelist preacher, and government advisor all at once. He speaks eloquently about the right of, and need for, Muslims to integrate into European society, but typically, it should be on their terms only. He cites approvingly Faysal Mawlawi's classification of the whole world as *Dar al-Da'wa* (land of proselytizing),[53] but adds his own nuance by labeling the whole world, and particularly the West, as *Dar al-Shahada* (land of testimony).[54]

Bassam Tibi has called this "cover language" for the idea that Europe is an Islamic space rather than a civilization of its own.[55] Ramadan insists that, for Muslims, "loyalty to one's faith and conscience requires firm and honest loyalty to one's country"[56] but warns that this cannot possibly be because the latter is the equal of the former:

> Philosophically speaking, the "Muslim identity" answers the question of being and as such it is basic and fundamental, since it justifies life itself. The concept of nationality, as understood in industrialised countries, is of a completely different nature …. Muslim identity is an answer to the question "Why?" while national identity answers the question "How?" and it would be senseless and foolish to expect geographical attachment to come first or to solve the question of being.[57]

Muslims, Ramadan explains, who think that "to be part of today's world is to adapt oneself to the Western way of life" are "Muslims without Islam."[58] This insistence on loyalty to the umma over and above nationality is common to MB thinking. Azzam Tamimi told a Muslim conference in Manchester that "I don't ever believe that there is something called European Muslims. We are Muslims in Europe not European Muslims. We have an identity, we have our *aqidah* [belief] we have a *shariah* and we have an Ummah that we are part of."[59] Ismail Patel of the BMI explained Islamophobia in British society as fear of this transnational identity:

> The concept of the umma … is what society fears. The umma transcends national borders. That is the fact. Muslims have a value system that we transcend towards. Muslims, wherever they are, they subscribe to these values, and when the values are threatened the fight back …. People fear Islam, and that is why they attack it.[60]

This hints at the true challenge of the MB in Britain and wider European society. The MB plays a role in spreading the ideology of martyrdom and religious violence, but it is a nonviolent movement in Britain; its activities in the United Kingdom would not justify legal proscription. Rather, it poses a political challenge and should be treated as such: "Islamism," writes Tibi, "has found a safe haven in the European democracies, contesting their values while simultaneously making full use of civil rights that the Islamist model of 'God's rule' clearly despises."[61]

Efforts to co-opt the MB as a partner in democratic processes are likely only to strengthen it, both by validating its politics and giving it de facto recognition as the representative voice of British Muslims without inducing any serious ideological change. Instead, the ideas of the MB ought to be challenged and political alternatives offered. This is unlikely to be success-ful as long as the small number of MB activists (and, for that matter, the larger number of JI activists) in Britain can call upon millions of pounds of funding from overseas, while non-Islamist Muslims lack similar resources or organizational capability.

Sidney Hook wrote, in a different time and context, of the difference between heresy—"A set of unpopular ideas or opinions .... The right to profess and advocate heresy of any character ... is an essential element of a liberal society"—and conspiracy—"which seeks to attain its ends not by normal political or educational process but by playing outside the rules of the game ... conspiracies cannot be tolerated without self-stultification in a liberal society."[62]

The MB certainly propagates heresies against liberal democracy; its entire ideology is a rejection of fundamental liberal democratic values. The MB has also acted conspiratorially in Arab countries but currently lacks the organi-zational cohesion to be considered a conspiracy in Britain. It should not be assumed that this will always be the case or that government and civil society will avoid making the mistakes that could help it become one.

NOTES

1. Paul Jump, "Charity Commission Struggles to Register Mosques," *Third Sector,* December 3, 2008. There are several demographic and sociological surveys of Muslims in Britain. A useful sample can be found on the website of the Muslim Council of Britain at http://www.mcb.org.uk/library/statistics.php (accessed December 4, 2008).
2. Ziauddin Sardar, *Desperately Seeking Paradise: Journeys of a Sceptical Muslim* (London: Granta, 2004), p. 29.
3. "Islamic Council of Europe: Progress and Plans," *Impact International,* September 10–23, 1976, p. 14
4. "Salem Azzam (1924–2008)," *The Muslim Weekly,* February 22, 2008, p.15.
5. Gilles Kepel, The War for Muslim Minds (Cambridge, MA: Harvard University Press, 2004), p. 254.
6. "Islamic Work 1990's: A Decade of Challenge," *The Muslim,* 25(1) (January 1990–March 1990), p. 6.

7. Yusuf Qardhawi, "The Future Horizon," *The Muslim*, 25(1) (January 1990–March 1990), pp. 13–15.

8. Rached Ghannoushi, "The Conflict Between the West and Islam: The Tunisian Case: Reality and Prospects," May 9, 1995.

9. Ed Husain, *The Islamist* (London: Penguin, 2007), pp. 166–167,

10. All biographical information from "Profile: Dr. Kamal Helbawy," Islamism Digest, 2(10) (October 2007) 7. Islamism Digest is the journal of the Center for the Study for Terrorism (CFSOT), of which Helbawy is chairman.

11. Wendy Kristianasen, "A Row in the Family," *Le Monde diplomatique*, April 2000.

12. Muslim Brotherhood website, http://Muslim-Brotherhood.com/mbicobj.html (accessed April 19, 1997).

13. Richard Phillips, "Standing Together: The Muslim Association of Britain and the Anti-War Movement," *Race & Class*, 50(2) (October 2008); Michael Whine, "The Advance of the Muslim Brotherhood in the UK," *Current Trends in Islamist Ideology* (Washington, DC: Hudson Institute, 2005), p. 35.

14. "Tamimi, 51, said he is a supporter but not a member of Hamas and is close to leaders such as Mashaal ... Tamimi said: 'I am someone who is closely associated with the movement. I don't have an official capacity, but I help as much as I can within the limits of the law.'" Orly Halpern, "Exclusive: Hamas Working on 'New Charter,'" *Jerusalem Post*, February 16, 2006.

15. MAB Press Release, April 13, 2002. Police estimated that between 10,000 and 15,000 people attended the demonstration. See "Angry Scenes at Anti-Israel Demo," http://news.bbc.co.uk/1/hi/uk_politics/1928071.stm (accessed December 8, 2008).

16. Phillips, "Standing Together," p. 104.

17. MAB officials have shared platforms with anti-Zionist Israeli and Jewish speakers.

18. Phillips, "Standing Together," p. 104.

19. Salma Yaqoob, "British Islamic Political Radicalism," in Tahir Abbas (ed.), *Islamic Political Radicalism: a European Perspective* (Edinburgh: Edinburgh University Press, 2007), pp. 279–280.

20. Tariq Ramadan, "'Alter'-Globalisers Challenge of Diversity," *Insight*, 2(4) (September/October 2003).

21. "Faith, Hate and Charity," *Panorama*, BBC One, July 30, 2006, transcript available at http://news.bbc.co.uk/1/hi/programmes/panorama/5234586.stm (accessed December 8, 2008).

22. *Hardtalk*, BBC One, November 2, 2004, transcript available at http://www.geocities.com/martinkramerorg/Documents/TamimiHardtalk.htm (accessed December 8, 2008).

23. For example, "How to Deal with Britain's Muslim Extremists? An interview with Kamal Helbawy," *Spotlight on Terror*, vol. 3, no. 7 (August 5, 2005). More recently, "British Islamist Kamal Al-Hilbawi and Liberal Nabil Yasin Debate Whether Israeli Children Constitute Legitimate Military Targets," BBC Arabic TV, October 17, 2008, transcribed and translated by MEMRI TV, clip no. 1922.

24. *The New Dawn*, no. 2 (October/November 2000); for the history of the Franklin hoax, see "The Franklin Prophecy," http://www.america.gov/st/pubs-english/2007/November/20071116144849atlahtnevel0.359524.html (accessed December 8, 2008).

25. "The Campaign So Far," *Inspire* special edition, September 28, 2002, p. 17.
26. Respect split into two competing parties in late 2007: Left Alternative, dominated by the SWP, and Respect Renewal, led by Salma Yaqoob and George Galloway.
27. "Mayor Culpa," *Private Eye*, March 21, 2008.
28. Haitham al-Haddad, "Why Vote, and Who To Vote For?" http://www.sunna-honline.com/library/contemporary/0037.htm (accessed November 19, 2008).
29. Paul Goodman, "Boris Johnson Defeated Islamic Extremists as well as Ken Livingstone," http://conservativehome.blogs.com/platform/2008/05/paul-goodman-mp.html (accessed May 3, 2008).
30. For a detailed investigation of FIOE, see Steve Merley, "The Federation of Islamic Organizations in Europe," NEFA Foundation, October 1, 2008.
31. Ibid., p. 4.
32. Reuven Paz, "The Coronation of the King of the Golden Path: Sheikh Qaradawi Becomes Imam *Al-Wasatiyyah* and a School and Movement by Itself," *PRISM Occasional Papers*, 5(3) August 2007.
33. "Who Speaks for British Muslims?" *The Economist*, June 17, 2006.
34. Phillips, "Standing together," p. 109.
35. About IslamExpo, http://www.islamexpo.com/aboutus.php? id=&art=1 (accessed November 21, 2008).
36. Memorandum of Association of Islam Expo Ltd., Companies House, October 7, 2004.
37. "Cooperation (with the Muslim Brotherhood) in specific areas of mutual interest—such as opposition to al Qaeda, the encouragement of democracy, and resistance to expanding Iranian influence—could well be feasible." Robert S. Leiken and Steven Brooke, "The Moderate Muslim Brotherhood," Foreign *Affairs* (March/April 2007), p. 120.
38. "What is Conflicts Forum?"http://conflictsforum.org/what-is-conflicts-forum/ (accessed December 10, 2008).
39. "Report from Conflicts Forum Mobilisation Workshop, London: 18-21st October 2007," http://thekeynetwork.org/reports/Conflicts-Forum-Workshop-Report-Nov-07.pdf (accessed December 10, 2008).
40. *Cultures of Resistance*, vol. 1, no. 1 (July 2008), p. 6.
41. Alistair Crooke, "The Paradox of Islamist Dialogue," *Cultures of Resistance*, 1(1), pp. 21–22.
42. All financial data from Companies House records for Islam Expo Ltd.
43. For example, Eddie Barnes, "SNP Gives More Funding to Ally's Islamic Group," *The Scotsman*, August 10, 2008; Iain Harrison, "Row over £215k 'Terror Link' Festival," *Scottish Sunday Times*, October 12, 2008.
44. "BMI is a political organization founded by a group of activists in 2006. It does not have a membership, nor does it cover aspects of a British Muslim's life beyond politics (such as MAB does)." Anas al-Tikriti, "A New Conservative London: What's Next?" IslamOnline Live Dialogue, May 5, 2008, http://www.islamonline.net/livedialogue/english/Browse.asp?hGuestID=vZ6iIh (accessed December 10, 2008).
45. Merley, "The Federation of Islamic Organization in Europe," p. 10.
46. Azzam Tamimi, "The Yemeni Hostage Drama: Embroiling Islam and British Muslims," *The Reality Magazine*, Spring Term 1999.
47. Salwa El-Awa, Robert Lambert, et al, "Police Partnership with Muslim Communities: Key in Countering Terrorism," *Arches Quarterly*, 2(1) (Summer 2008), p. 32.

48. Kepel, *The War for Muslim Minds*, p. 254–255.

49. "Muslim and national scholars and personalities denounce the American and Israeli crimes in Iraq and Palestine," *al-Quds al-Arabi*, August 23, 2004, p. 4 (trans. Muslim World News). The statement had ninety-three signatories, including MB General Guide Muhammad Mahdi Akif, Yusuf al-Qaradawi, Faysal Mawlawi, and other leading MB figures from several countries; leaders of Hamas, Hizballah, and Palestinian Islamic Jihad; Kurshid Ahmad and other JI leaders.

50. Martin Bright, *When Progressives Treat with Reactionaries* (London: Policy Exchange, 2006).

51. "CFSOT: About Us," http://www.cfsot.com/index.php?thm=about (accessed December 10, 2008).

52. "Lebanese Hezbollah Deputy Chief Meets Islamic Unity Forum Team," BBC Monitoring November 13, 2008.

53. According to Ramadan: "The notion of *da'wa* is often understood as the expression of the inherent Islamic tendency towards proselytism and the will to convert. This notion conveys the idea of presenting and explaining the Message of Islam for purposes of conversion, but this has to be a free act, one which is between God and the person's own heart." Tariq Ramadan, *To Be a European Muslim* (Leicester: Islamic Foundation, 1999), p. 152.

54. Ibid., pp. 142–150.

55. Bassam Tibi, *Political Islam*, World Politics and Europe (Oxford: Routledge, 2008), p. 159.

56. Ramadan, *To Be a European Muslim*, p. 172.

57. Ibid., p. 163.

58. Ibid., pp. 185–186.

59. "Justice a Call to Humanity—Dr. Azzam Tamimi," http://www.islamicforumeurope.com/live/ife.php?doc=articleitem&itemId=327 (accessed November 29, 2006).

60. "Coalition Launched to Defend Religious Freedom," *The Muslim Weekly*, June 8, 2007, p. 3.

61. Tibi, Political Islam, p. 154

62. Sidney Hook, "Heresy, Yes—But Conspiracy, No," *Democratiya*, No.15 (Winter 2008); originally published in *New York Times Magazine*, July 9, 1950.

9

THE MUSLIM BROTHERHOOD IN FRANCE

Farhad Khosrokhavar

The French branch of the Muslim Brotherhood, like the branches in other European countries, aims to establish an Islamic government and substitute the prevailing secular laws. In Europe, including France, the Muslim Brotherhood has used peaceful methods and even denied that it is seeking such an outcome. The organization's declared aim instead is to "re-Islamize" Muslims and direct them as to how to behave religiously in countries where they are in minority and seek ways to preserve and abide by Islamic faith. The group also mobilizes Muslims on political issues elsewhere, in particular, over the Palestinian, Iraqi, Bosnian, and Afghan questions.

In France, the Muslim Brotherhood branch encounters specific problems, given the political system, which is based on the secularism of state and society. Referred to as *laïcité*, this system implies strict separation of church and state with religion limited to the private sphere. Thus, ideally, no religious symbol should be displayed in the public sphere or embodied in government institutions, especially those at the heart of citizen-building, such as government schools.[1] Muslim Brotherhood organizations must manage this issue in order to gain public recognition. Their official aim is not so much to put the official secularism into question as to propose a more religious-friendly definition of it.

The Brotherhood's influence in France has been manifold and deep among many Muslims. Two types of influences can be distinguished—at the individual level and at the institutional level. On the institutional level, two organizations deeply influenced by the Egyptian Muslim Brotherhood are the Union of Islamic Organizations in France (UOIF) and the Muslim World League. The UOIF is the main representative of the Muslim Brotherhood in France and one of the most potent Islamic organizations in the country. It is the French branch of the Federation of Islamic Organizations in Europe (FIOE), which is partly funded by Saudi Arabia and the United Arab Emirates, and whose aim is to promote an Islam adapted to the European context. The UOIF is assisted by the European Council for Fatwa and Research, which studies and edicts "collective *fatwas* to answer questions for

Muslims of Europe and solve their problems, in accordance to the rules and aims of the *sharia*."[2]

UOIF AND OTHER ORGANIZATIONS

The UOIF was formally founded in 1983 by two students, Tunisian Adallah Ben Mansour and Iraqi Mahmoud Zouheir. The UOIF has a strong base among Muslim youth—particularly students—and the middle classes. It encompasses more than 100 local associations and owns around thirty mosques in cities all over France. UOIF has divided France into twelve regions by the, and each region has its own representative. The UOIF is directly connected to the other European organizations attached to or inspired by the Muslim Brotherhood ideology and structure.

The umbrella group includes many organizations, the most important among them being the Young Muslims of France (Jeunes Musulmans de France, JMF), Muslim Students of France (Etudiants Musulmans de France, EMF), the French League of Muslim Women (Ligue Française de la Femme Musulmane, LFFM), Imams of France (Imams de France), the European Institute of Human Sciences (Institut Européen des Sciences Humaines, IESH), and the Welfare and Charity and Rescue Committee for the Palestinians (Comité de Bienfaisance et de Secours aux Palestiniens, GBSP).

One of the UOIF's important subsidiaries is the IESH, located at Château-Chinon, which opened its doors in 1990. In IESH, future UOIF imams are educated, which includes training in the Arabic language. This institute trained more than 300 imams between 1990 and 2004. Every year, the UOIF gathers its members and sympathizers at the Bourget locality near Paris, where thousands of people meet and listen to religious personalities and political figures. In 2003, then Interior Minister Nicolas Sarkozy spoke about Islam in France and the necessity for women to take off the veil in their official identity card photos.

The UOIF is one of the most significant representatives within the French Council of Muslims (Conseil Français du Culte Musulman, CFCM), an organization set up in 2003 to represent Muslims and serve as the direct contact with the French government on questions concerning the problems of Muslims in France (halal meat, the education and training of imams, cemeteries, construction of new mosques, and the like). In 2005, elections results for the CFCM gave ten out of forty-three seats to the UOIF, a decrease of three seats from the first elections in 2003. The National Federation of French Muslims (Fédération Nationale des Musulmans de France, FNMF) won nineteen seats (three more than in 2003). The Great Mosque of Paris won ten seats (three fewer than in 2003).

In terms of its priorities, the UOIF singles out a number of themes, some related to the situation of Muslims worldwide and others related to the daily life of French Muslims. The first category mostly concerns Muslims' fate in the Middle East, for example the wars in Iraq and Afghanistan as well as the Palestinian question. During the war in the Gaza Strip, in December 2008, the

UOIF issued a public statement asking to "stop the massacre of the Palestinian people" and "to stop the genocide against the population of Gaza."

Thami Breze, president of the UOIF, went to Rafah on the Gaza–Egypt border with representatives of the Federation of Islamic Organizations in Europe to show support for its population there. It called the Gaza bombings "a crime against humanity."[3] At the same time though, the group was careful not to say anything that would inspire a direct conflict with French Jews who supported Israel. The group denounced Islamophobia, anti-semitism, and racism. The UOIF's intent was thus to mobilize French Muslims against the Israeli attacks on Palestinians without bringing the conflict onto the streets of France, since many young Muslims in poor suburbs of French cities might be inclined to accept broader anti-semitic ideas.[4] This stance contributed to limiting violence within France itself.[5]

Rather than incite conflict in France, it can be argued that the UOIF tried to engage in nonviolent demonstrations. Similarly, the UOIF tries to cope with drug-dealing, theft, and other criminal offenses in poor districts by trying to impose a religiously based discipline on those who dwell there by integrating them into a more pious lifestyle. Of course, this is only effective among those who are willing to accept religious views or participate in organizational activities. Other disaffected young Muslim males may express their rage in confrontational terms toward people and institutions (the police, bus drivers, firemen, and more generally, all government officials, employees, and minorities such as Jews).

Attempts to show responsibility and even French patriotism are important themes in the UOIF's activities. For example, on November 7, 2005, the UOIF issued a *fatwa* condemning the civil unrest going on then, saying that "it is strictly forbidden for any Muslim...to take part in any action that strikes blindly at private or public property or that could threaten the lives of others." Thousands of cars were burned during that period by young people, Muslims or otherwise, in protest against alleged police violence, social segregation, racism, for financial gain or simply in order to create a festival atmosphere.

Another subject where UOIF is particularly active is giving religious advice on Muslim daily life in a non-Muslim country. A key issue here is the mobilization of UOIF followers on the headscarf matter.

In 2003, a French law banned "ostentatious religious signs" in government-sponsored schools. This law translates into a ban on the scarf at every public meeting sponsored by the state or at any official gathering. Through legal counsel, the UOIF helped Muslim girls who did not want to comply with the ban at school. In January 2009, it issued a *fatwa* decrying as discriminatory the treatment of Muslim women who had been barred from wearing the headscarf while being employed as childcare workers at places housed in school buildings. The UOIF also encouraged and helped them to take legal action.[6] This has become an important symbolic issue in France, with public opinion viewing Muslims who take off or do not wear the scarf as "moderates" and those who insist on its necessity as "fundamentalists." The UOIF has also explored to change the law.

An example of combining legal rulings and politics can be seen in the demonstration organized against Israel during the Gaza war in December 2008. For those Muslims who took part in the demonstration, there was a conflict between participating fully and performing all the daily prayers at the prescribed times. There was thus a necessity to perform the noon and the afternoon prayers at noon rather than separately or to put together the evening and night prayers at night in order to take part fully in the demonstration. The UOIF provided and justified a dispensation in reference to two rules. First, taking part in the demonstrations was "fighting against the evil" and could be vindicated under the Islamic saying of "Commending the Good and Forbidding the Evil" (*amr bi ma'ruf and nahy an al munkar*). As for the simultaneous performance of the two daily prayers, be it those of noon and afternoon or those of evening and night, it could be justified under another Islamic saying, namely that passersby in the street would be inconvenienced if the Muslims prayed in the street at noon or in the evening.[7] According to the *hadith* (sayings of Muhammad), Muhammad did not intend to disturb the pedestrians of his time. The UOIF ruled that so too Muslims today should not disturb French non-Muslims by praying in the street and thus giving them a derogatory picture of Allah's religion.

In this respect, the UOIF combines social mobilization and religious devotion in a single act by providing religious justification for both in reference to Islamic tradition as well as a concern for the image of Islam in a non-Islamic land.

Other topics are less political or social and strictly pertain to finding a compromise between Islamic religious prescriptions and the secular laws of France. The third National Conference of Imams promoted by the UOIF and held on March 15 and 16, 2008, under the title, "Marriage between the Traditional (Islamic) Procedures and the French Law" sought to give Islamic legitimacy to secular marriage procedures in the French municipalities.

The Internet has been utilized to provide a "simplified *fiqh*" (Islamic jurisprudence) for devout Muslims. The UOIF closely cooperates with the European Council for Fatwa and Research in Dublin, whose prominent members, such as Yusuf al-Qaradawi, are among the best-known Brotherhood spiritual advisors on the daily problems of Muslims in secular European environments.

Among the topics addressed in these discussions are the following: the substitution of Islamic lending to the usual banking practices that are considered "usury" (*riba*); intermarriage between Muslims and non-Muslims; the daily prayers and their timing; and Islamic rituals that are difficult to implement in a French environment (including ablutions before prayers and the performance of the daily prayers themselves).

Another subject that mobilizes the UOIF as well as other Muslim organizations is the promotion of Islamic schools. Catholic, Protestant, and Jewish private schools in France abide by the rules set by the Ministry of National Education but have a degree of freedom toward religious observance far higher than in the government-sponsored schools. The French public's suspicion toward these Muslim associations makes the generalized acceptance of the Islamic schools a matter of debate in the country. There are only a few of them authorized within France itself.

While itself not a Muslim Brotherhood organization directly, the Muslim World League (MWL) is a conduit for Brotherhood influences. It is one of the largest Islamic nongovernmental organizations in the world, founded in 1962 in Mecca by Prince Faysal with the support of twenty-two countries. Its French branch is La Ligue Islamique Mondiale (LIM).

The LIM contributes to the construction of mosques and Islamic centers and other cultural activities. In the suburbs of Paris, the Evry mosque, for example, was built with the cooperation of the LIM and the Hassan II Foundation. In the same fashion, the grand mosque in the city of Lyon that opened in 1994 was financed by the LIM as a personal gift of Saudi Arabia's King Fahd. In the West, MWL often cooperated with Muslim Brotherhood-type organizations since the latter have more influence on European Muslims than the Salafi-Wahhabi message from Saudi Arabia itself.[8]

The LIM, which is close to the UOIF as well as to the FNMF, was founded in 1985. It is currently the most important member of the CFCM in terms of the number of people elected to its governing board.[9] It joins forces with other Islamic associations to press charges against people or organizations that allegedly slur Islam, as in the lawsuit against the French writer Michel Houellebecq, who, in an interview in 2002, called Islam the coarsest religion on earth, or against the magazine *Charlie Hebdo* that published the caricatures of the Muhammad in 2007 to support the Danish journal that initiated the controversy.

The LIM's influence is largely institutional and economic, and it does not directly have any influence in France comparable to that of the UOIF. The competition between the two institutions, however, does not prevent their close cooperation.

LEADERSHIP

Many prominent Islamic individuals have been directly influenced by Muslim Brotherhood ideology even if are not members of that group. Tariq Ramadan is one of them. He denies any formal link to the Muslim Brotherhood, but his modern approach to Islam and his attempt at "updating" it without renouncing its core message is inspired by the Muslim Brotherhood in many respects.

Both Ramadan[10] and the UOIF have been accused of using a "double language": a supposedly "democratic" mind-set toward French non-Muslims and a fundamentalist, anti-*laïcité* attitude with regard to French Muslims.[11] The main objection, in France, is that the UOIF and those intellectuals who sustain it put into question—without expressing it explicitly—the secular state and its laws, in particular regarding the public sphere that should be free from religious symbols.

The "hypocrisy" lies in the fact that not only what they say is different according to the audience to whom they are saying it, but also in their aim at promoting Islam as a public norm—that is, against the secular state and its citizenship rules and, even more so, against democracy and its equality and freedom. In part, many Muslim Brotherhood offshoots in the West do promulgate their aim to impel the Islamization of the West. However, the picture regarding the group in France is more complex.

The first and major point, according to which the UOIF has a double nature,[12] is in part true. Yet, it is also accurate to say that the organization has taken a democracy-friendly attitude toward major issues such as anti-semitism, gender, the problem of believers versus nonbelievers, the allegiance to human-made law that is, by definition, different from the law of God, or other topics where the traditional Islamic tenets contradict rules of democracy.

The attitude of the UOIF has been to support new ideas that might soften the traditional orthodox stance without denouncing it directly or rejecting it. If it were to choose the second attitude, many of its sympathizers might be tempted to opt out in favor of other Islamic organizations (Tabligh, neo-Salafist groups, or others). As for their end goal and the establishment of an Islamic state, one might surmise that a long involvement in European politics might change it de facto, without any explicit change on their part.

This, in turn, is in direct relation to the situation of Muslims caught between the highly secular Europe where they live and their places and families of origin. External society pushes Muslims either toward total secularization or the espousal of Islamic attitudes that mark a sharp break with those of their parents, who were often functionally illiterate and more likely than not highly traditional.

In this context, young people of Muslim origin have in most cases no religious culture or any ability to be informed through family channels on Islamic matters. A de facto secularization coupled with a sense of guilt and self-disrespect characterizes many young Muslims in France. They seek a renewed sense of religion as a means of self-respect. This cannot be achieved other than through self-imposed restrictions and the rejection (moderate or violent) of the secular norms that have led to their alienation from their roots and sense of honor and dignity.

Fundamentalism becomes attractive in this sense: in contrast to the denial of real citizenship and a sense of uprootedness, it opposes a universal construction of Islam, independent of specific cultures (they do not master the language and the culture of their own parents or grandparents) and ambivalently at odds with the secular societies in which they do not feel at home. Islamic rigorism becomes a substitute to a second-rate citizenship in a highly secular environment.

The UOIF, the FNMF, Tabligh, and the neo-Salafist movements in France offer a new sense of dignity through allegiance to an "intransigent" religious feeling. Most of the Muslims in France are of working-class background and deeply resent the denial of citizenship to them—despite their having a French passport—as a sign of deep disrespect toward them. Their cultural uprootedness—they know very little about Islam or the countries of their parents or grandparents—and their immersion into a permissive, largely secular world has entailed estrangement of their own parents and French society.

The UOIF insists on Muslims learning Arabic and becoming immersed in the religious ambience of Islam. Teaching Arabic and reading the Koran become part of the education and acculturation for the young culturally uprooted second- or third-generation Muslims who discover a new identity through this learning, different both from the surrounding French milieu and the culture of parents who spoke at best an Arab dialect and had only a sketchy knowledge of the Koran. Fundamentalism becomes a prodding toward self-discipline in religion—daily prayers, learning Arabic, reading the Koran, performing pious acts—that distinguishes the new self from the lax one in a permissive society where nonreligious attitudes are positively reinforced.

Given the need for roots and the failure of mainstream society to provide them, the appeal of fundamentalism through associations like the UOIF (for the lower-middle classes) or Tabligh and neo-Salafist organizations (for the lower classes, the so-called excluded jobless youth) is therefore potent. These organizations cannot be attractive unless they hold to a rigorous religious framework to stand in contrast to the permissive secular European environment. In France, the attraction is heightened by the tangible target of *laïcité*.

The UOIF finds itself in a double-bind: to win legitimacy in a nonreligious society, it has to be "open-minded"; to captivate the Islamic youth, it has to be counter-laïque. The "double discourse," be it from the UOIF or from the Muslim intellectuals who appeal to a wider audience, arises from the need to close in an imaginary way this unbridgeable gap between the two mind-sets. The optimistic view emerging is that this ambivalent attitude will ease the future understanding between the two worlds. The pessimistic attitude would stress the double standard and the hypocrisy of this type of attitude that forestalls the "reality shock" for Muslims and perpetuates the dogmatic attitudes of the past, staving off the adjustment in the mind-set of the Muslims to the European setting.

For a long time, this ambivalence will be part of the coexistence between the non-Muslim French and France's Muslim minorities. This ambivalence is rooted in the social status of Muslims. Unlike their American counterparts, who are middle or upper-middle class, Muslims in France are of the lower or lower-middle classes in an overwhelming majority. They do not share, in their core, the "American dream" of their counterparts in the United States. Fundamentalism is for them a way of escaping dissolution in the ultrasecular France, on the one hand, and the building up of an identity in a situation of economic uncertainty or precariousness, on the other hand.

Their ambivalence toward French society is based on a malaise that has no foreseeable end to it. The fascination for a tiny minority of them to jump completely from a fundamentalist attitude toward Islamic radicalism is real.[13]

Tareq Oubrou is a Muslim scholar, president of the mosques within the regional Association des Musulmans de Gironde (AMG) who also belongs to the UOIF. He is active in deterring young Muslims from adhering to the extremist brands of Islam and legitimizing the submission of Muslims to the people's law (instead of God's law) by referring to the "fiqh of the minority."

In non-Muslim societies, according to the *hadith*, he argues, one has to submit to the prevailing laws and adapt Islamic prescriptions to it. That is why he proposes performing the prayers all at once if for any reason a Muslim cannot do them separately during the different times of day and night. In the same vein, he looks for solutions to gender issues in Islam. He has propounded new ways of reading the Islamic duties in light of modern life and has brought the individual's decisions and adaptations as a major yardstick, in conjunction with the *umma* (Islamic community).[14]

His "fiqh of the minority" is in opposition to the *"fiqh al-aqalliya,"* whose proponents imply that the West must recognize Islamic laws governing the relations between Muslims, who must be treated as a legally separate group. For Oubrou, obedience to the rules of the society, even though they are not Islamic by nature, is part of the moral pact between Muslims and others in non-Muslim societies. *Fiqh* is subordinated, in his perspective, to ethics, and the latter is the ground upon which Muslims and non-Muslims can find common denominators independently of religion. Metaphysics and ethics, from this standpoint, are over jurisprudence, and *fiqh* can adapt to them without putting the Islamic creed into question.

In spite of his open stance toward to the secular world, Oubrou's views are subject to much ambivalence. His relation to gender and his view of Islam cannot entirely submit to the secular standpoint without seeing Allah's religion lose its specificity. Other intellectuals, such as Hassan Iquioussen or Tariq Ramadan, assert their views in a more explicit way and are exposed to criticism and suspicion by secular people.

The malaise of a "mutually distrustful coexistence" can best describe the situation of the Muslim Brotherhood organizations and intellectuals in France. On the one hand, in civil society they are the targets of acerbic critics regarding their attitude toward religion and its scope, democracy and its legitimacy, and personal freedom and its limits, as well as the degree to which Islamic norms and prescriptions should be followed or tolerated within civil society and government institutions.

Unlike Great Britain and Holland, where multiculturalism grants Muslims many rights, France denies such things as their recognition as a religious community, tolerance toward their holidays, the wearing of a headscarf by civil servants (in Britain), or of religious insignia (the beard) by male policemen. In France, the main bone of contention is the *laïcité* and the way these Muslim associations have to cope with it.

CONCLUSION

Although the UOIF or personalities like Tariq Ramadan or Tareq Oubrou deny any direct link to the Egyptian Muslim Brotherhood, they are deeply influenced by the Brotherhood in terms of ideology, thought, and political views. As in the Egyptian case, they believe that democracy (and more generally, parliamentary political systems) are not antithetical to Islam. They also believe that the Islamization of society can be achieved through peaceful means from action at the grassroots' level. In both cases, they can be accused of insincerity by the opponents.

Their role is ambivalent at best. On the one hand, they prevent the passage to Islamist extremism by Muslims. On the other, they propose an "Islamic alternative" to the secular democratic political system. This alternative oscillates between creeping Islamization that instrumentalizes democracy for other ends and a "democratic compromise" that reconciles Allah's religion with the pluralist political system.

In the West, where Islamization cannot reasonably go beyond certain levels, organizations like the UOIF challenge the secularization of young Muslims, push them toward becoming "born-again Muslims," combine Islamic identity and fundamentalism in order to save Allah's religion from dissolution into secular European societies, and harness youth identity into a framework that can control and mobilize them on specific social, political, and cultural topics.

In France, the role of the UOIF and like-minded Islamic organizations is to create a distinct identity that will push toward the preservation of Allah's religion in an ultrasecular environment and create solidarity with other Muslims around the world without bringing the conflicts that split the Muslim world back to France in a violent manner.

Muslim Brotherhood associations play yet another role: they contribute to creating an imaginary *umma* that extends from Europe's shores to the limits of the Muslim world with new ties and a homogeneous religious view, independent of the specific cultures of the countries where they are established. Unlike the Wahhabi type of transnational organizations marginal in Europe, the only two types of transnational "fundamentalist" Muslim associations that have taken root in Europe are the loosely connected Muslim Brotherhood associations and the Tabligh, which is highly centralized and has a strong pyramidal organization, with its head at Duisebury, England.

These two types of transnational associations in part compete with each other and in part have different audiences: UOIF-like associations, inspired by the Muslim Brotherhood in Egypt and loosely in touch with it, aim at the new lower-middle and middle-class Muslims, whereas Tabligh mainly entices lower-class Muslims who mostly have lost the hope for economic and social integration into European societies.

Wahhabi-type associations prosper in the Sunni Muslim world where they can attract many sympathizers who accept strict Islamic orthodoxy. In Europe, their local versions seduce only a marginal part of the Muslim community due to its stringent rules and its way of life that is too alien to European Muslims.

The UOIF and similar organizations propose an ambivalent compromise between orthodox Islam, on the one hand, and the secular and pluralist

French society, on the other. Their aim is to gain recognition, in the long run, in the French public sphere as a major representative of French Muslims. Even if some of their leaders harbor pan-Islamic ideas, the "ordeal of reality" pushes them toward the recognition of the French brand of secularism (*laïcité*) and a compromise with it. This prevents them from officially espousing radical stances toward major social, cultural, or political events in society. Ambivalence is part of the institutional interplay with society, which is multifaceted by necessity.

NOTES

1. John R. Bowen, *Why the French Don't Like Headscarves* (Princeton and Oxford: Princeton University Press, 2007).
2. See www.nationmaster.com/encyclopedia/UOIF.
3. See www.uoif-online.com/webspip/spip.php?
4. Some Jewish organizations in France characterize the UOIF as being anti-semitic and pro-*jihad* in reference to its relations to Yusuf al-Qaradawi and the Egyptian Muslim Brotherhood. See Simon Wiesenthal Center, "The True Face of the UOIF: Antisemitism, Advocacy and Financing of Terrorism, and the Call to *Jihad*," www.wiesenthal.com/atf/cf/{DFD2AAC1-2ADE-428A-9263-35234229D8D8}/trueUOIF.pdf.
5. According to *Haaretz*, "The incidents included a stabbing of a young Jewish man by two masked car thieves outside Paris, and two firebombing attacks against synagogues in Saint Denis, a northern suburb of Paris, and in Strasburg." See "Jewish Agency: Anti-Semitic Acts in Jan. 2009 Triple Last Year's Records," *Haaretz*, January 25, 2009, www.haaretz.com/hasen/spages/1058555.html. According to another account "A total of 55 anti-semitic incidents occurred in France since the start of Israel's Operation Cast Lead in the Gaza Strip, said President of the French Jewish Students' Union Raphael Haddad on Monday." See "France: 55 Anti-Semitic Acts Since the Start of Cast Lead," *Yediot Aharonot*, January 14, 2009, www.ynet.co.il/english/articles/0,7340,L-3655372,00.html.
6. See *"Le Comité 15 mars et les libertés*," February 3, 2009, www.uoif-online.com.
7. According to Ibn Abbas quoted in the reliable *(sahih)* Saying of the Prophet as reported by the compiler Muslim. See comite15mars.net.
8. See Johannes Grundmann, *Islamische Internationalisten–Strukturen und Aktivitäten der Muslimbruderschaft und der Islamischen Weltliga* (Wiesbaden: Reichert Verlag, 2005).
9. See earlier text about the number of the members of each Muslim organization within the CFCM.
10. For Caroline Fourest, Ramadan is a war leader and the political heir of his grandfather Hasan al-Banna, his discourse being often just a repetition of the discourse that al-Banna had at the beginning of the twentieth century in Egypt. According to her, Ramadan presents al-Banna as a model to be followed. From her perspective, "Tariq Ramadan is slippery. He says one thing to his faithful Muslim followers and something else entirely to his Western audience. His choice of words, the formulations he uses—even his tone of voice—vary, chameleon-like, according to his audience." See Caroline Fourest, *Brother Tariq:*

The Doublespeak of Tariq Ramadan (New York: Encounter Books, 2008). This picture is too Machiavellian to be entirely true.

11. "Qu'est-ce que l'UOIF?" éditions de l'Archipel, Collection l'information citoyenne dirigée par Claude Perrotin, Paris, 2006. Riposte Laïque, *Face à une charte islamique européenne, il faut une résistance laïque et féministe européenne,* January 16, 2008, www.ripostelaique.com/Face-a-une-charte-islamique.html.

12. See Fiammetta Venner, *OPA sur l'Islam de France : Les ambitions de l'UOIF,* Calmann-Lévy, May 2005.

13. See for this complex web of ambivalence and the appeal to jihadism Farhad Khosrokhavar, *Inside Jihadism, Understanding Jihadi Movements Worldwide* (New Haven, CT: Yale Cultural Sociology Series, Paradigm Publishers, 2009).

14. Tariq Oubrou, "La Shari'a de minorité : réflexions pour une intégration légale de l'islam," in F. Frégosi (ed.), *Lectures contemporaines du droit islamique- Europe et monde arabe*(Strasbourg: PUS, 2004); Leila Babès et Tariq Oubrou, *Loi d'Allah, loi des hommes–liberté, égalité et femmes en Islam* (Paris, Albin Michel, 2002). See, for a summary, Alexandre Caeiro, "An Imam in France Tareq Oubrou," *ISIM Review,* vol. 15 (Spring 2005).

10

THE MUSLIM BROTHERHOOD IN GERMANY

Guido Steinberg

The Muslim Brotherhood gained its first foothold in Germany when the Geneva-based Egyptian Said Ramadan (1926–1995), a close confidant and son-in-law of Muslim Brotherhood founder Hasan al-Banna, took over the Islamic Center in Munich (Islamisches Zentrum München) in 1960.

Arab students in Munich who wanted to build a new mosque had contacted him in 1958.[1] Ramadan had to leave Egypt after the Free Officers' government crackdown on the Muslim Brotherhood in 1954. From exile in Geneva, he laid the foundations for the emergence of the Brotherhood network in Europe. Munich became an early center of these efforts. In the 1950s and 1960s, West Germany became an increasingly popular destination for Arab students who studied engineering, medicine, and sciences at its universities. Ramadan himself studied law at Cologne University and earned his PhD in 1959 with a thesis on Islamic law.[2]

A trusted aide of Ramadan, the Syrian-Italian Ghalib Himmat, who had arrived in the 1950s to study in Munich, and who later became a wealthy businessman, took over the Islamic Center. Under his leadership, it became the Brotherhood's early headquarters in Europe. Ever since, Germany has remained a focal point of the Brotherhood's activities in Europe.

From the Islamic Center in Munich grew the Islamic Community in Germany (Islamische Gemeinschaft in Deutschland [IGD]), the main representative of the Brotherhood, headed by Himmat until 2001. The IGD has remained the German branch of the Muslim Brotherhood and the most important organization of Arab Islamism in Germany.

The Muslim Brotherhood in Germany has from its inception in the 1960s been divided between the Egyptian Brotherhood, with its headquarters in Munich, and the Syrian Brotherhood, with its headquarters in Aachen. Both have at times cooperated intensively but still have remained as separate entities. While the Egyptian Muslim Brotherhood has gained in importance, the Syrian branch has reduced its public visibility in recent years.

THE EGYPTIAN MUSLIM BROTHERHOOD AND THE ISLAMIC COMMUNITY IN GERMANY

Since the end of the 1990s, the Islamic Community in Germany (IGD) has gained influence among the German Muslims. The organization became especially important after Ghalib Himmat resigned in late 2001. He stepped down because of his close connection to the Switzerland-based Al Taqwa bank, which had come under intense scrutiny after the September 11 attacks because of its alleged financing of terrorist organizations, most notably Palestinian Hamas, Algerian Islamic Salvation Front (Front Islamique du Salut, FIS), and Usama bin Ladin's al-Qa'ida. In November 2001, the U.S. treasury and UN Security Council listed Himmat as a terrorism financer.[3]

The Al Taqwa bank has been correctly labeled "the Bank of the Muslim Brotherhood," and it is therefore very likely that it had financial dealings with Brotherhood offspring like Hamas and the FIS. Concrete evidence was scarce, however, and proof for its financing of al-Qa'ida is highly dubious. As a consequence, investigations into Himmat's business dealings in Switzerland and Italy were dropped in 2005 and 2007, respectively. However, as a result of his designation, Himmat became undesirable as the IGD's chairman.

His successor was the German-Egyptian Ibrahim Faruk al-Zayat, born in 1968, who has since led the organization. Although unknown to the wider public, Zayat is the gray eminence of German Islamism. German security services have frequently named him as head of the Muslim Brotherhood in Germany—a claim Zayat himself frequently denied. In fact, he also denies being a member of the Brotherhood and has sued authors and journalists for claiming that he is.[4]

The IGD is structured as an umbrella organization of Arab mosque associations in Germany. Its headquarters remains in the Islamic Center in Munich, but it controls other Islamic centers in Frankfurt (Main), Marburg, Nuremberg, Stuttgart, Cologne, Münster, and Braunschweig, and possibly other cities. Although German security sources speak of only 1,300 members of the organization, it is more influential among German Muslims than this number might suggest. One indicator is the IGD's yearly meetings, where up to several thousand predominantly young Muslims participate.[5]

The IGD controls a number of affiliated associations, the most influential of which seems to be the Islamic Center Cologne (Islamisches Zentrum Köln) and the German Muslim Students Association (Muslim Studenten Vereinigung in Deutschland). The Islamic Center in Cologne was founded in 1978 and has been closely connected to the Turkish Islamic Community Milli Görüş, which has its headquarters in Cologne as well. The embodiment of these connections is Ibrahim al-Zayat, the head of the center since 1997, who has established close ties with the Milli Görüş leadership in Germany, especially Mehmet Sabri Erbakan, born in 1967, the former Turkish prime minister Necmettin Erbakan's nephew and head of Milli Görüş from April 2001 until October 2002.[6]

Zayat rose to prominence as a leading member in several Islamist youth groups, most notably the German Muslim Students Association, which includes several Muslim student associations at German universities. It was founded in 1964 in Munich and was then closely connected to the Islamic Center situated in Munich. Today, it is located in Cologne. In 1997, Zayat became its head and Mehmet Erbakan his deputy. Since the 1990s, Zayat has become the symbol of the IGD's enhanced cooperation with Turkish circles.

THE SYRIAN MUSLIM BROTHERHOOD AND THE ISLAMIC CENTER AACHEN

The Islamic Center Aachen, a town close to the Belgian and Dutch borders in the country's far west, serves as the headquarters of the Syrian Muslim Brotherhood in Germany. In the 1960s, Arab students studying at the Technical University in Aachen started constructing the Bilal mosque. In 1978, the Islamic Center Aachen was founded as the body responsible for the mosque association.

Its head was Isam al-Attar, born in 1927, the former head of the Syrian Muslim Brotherhood who left his native country in the 1950s. The Islamic Center Aachen became the headquarters of the Syrian Muslim Brotherhood in Europe in the 1970s and 1980s. From the 1970s, the Brotherhood spearheaded an insurgency against the regime of Syrian president Hafiz al-Asad, which culminated in a civil war from 1979 to 1982. Several writers have accused the center of having become the headquarters for the Syrian Islamists' insurgency against the Asad regime.[7]

The Damascus government shared that interpretation and sent secret agents who targeted the Syrian Muslim Brothers in Germany. In their most publicized attack, they killed Attar's wife in his Aachen home in March 1981.[8] After the Syrian troops subdued an uprising in the city of Hama in the spring of 1982, however, the insurgency quickly lost momentum and the Brotherhood's center in Aachen some of its former importance. Attar continued activities in Belgium and France and remained a highly respected personality in Islamist circles in Western Europe.[9] Nevertheless, he seems to have lost his political importance in the early 1980s.

The Islamic Center in Aachen maintained close relations with the Munich center just as the Syrian Muslim Brothers were closely connected to their Egyptian colleagues in Switzerland. Both Egyptians and Syrians cooperate in the Central Council of Muslims in Germany.[10] Some critics consider its general secretary, the German-Syrian Aiman Mazyek, born 1969, as the Syrian branch's most important representative on the Central Council. Nevertheless, the Syrians and the Islamic Center Aachen insist on their independence from the more powerful Egyptian branch. Just like the IGD, they hold an annual conference. However, while the IGD conference takes place in different cities every year, the Islamic Center Aachen organizes its conferences in Aachen only—showing the limited appeal of the Syrian branch of the Brotherhood. The yearly meetings regularly attract around 500 participants.[11] The Center publishes a print and online journal in Arabic, *al-Ra'id* (*The Pioneer*), founded by Isam al-Attar in the 1970s.[12]

THE CENTRAL COUNCIL OF MUSLIMS IN GERMANY

Close relations between the Egyptian and Syrian Muslim Brotherhood were formalized in 1994, when their supporters jointly founded the Central Council of Muslims in Germany (Zentralrat der Muslime in Deutschland, ZMD), the umbrella organization of the Muslim Brotherhood in Germany. The IGD is its most influential member group.

The Central Council has between 15,000 and 20,000 members but claims to represent all Muslims in Germany. Its head until February 2006 was the Saudi-born Nadeem Elias, born 1945, a prominent member of the Islamic Center Aachen (Islamisches Zentrum Aachen) and a former member of the IGD.[13] Nadeem Elias embodies the Syrian Brotherhood's Saudi connection, most notably to the Muslim World League in Mecca, to which the Islamic Center Aachen and the Central Council are closely related, although relations seem to have weakened in recent years. While the Central Council is smaller than its Turkish equivalent, the Islamic Council for the Federal Republic of Germany, Elias succeeded in becoming the most prominent Muslim representative in Germany from the late 1990s.

After his resignation, however, a convert, Axel Köhler, born 1938, took over the presidency of the Central Council, narrowly defeating Ibrahim al-Zayat in the vote. Köhler seems to have been a compromise candidate in order to prevent Zayat's election. That choice was logical insofar as Köhler has a reputation of being relatively moderate, while the German media frequently criticizes Zayat because of his connections to the Brotherhood.

Among the German public, the Muslim Brotherhood is often alleged to be a key factor of modern jihadism and criticized because of its antisemitism. Therefore, Zayat's election could have threatened the Central Council's public standing. It is unclear whether the choice of Köhler indicates any major rupture within the Central Council. For the time being, it rather seems as if Zayat preserved his old position of gray eminence to the organization. Köhler is much less visible than his predecessor Elias, and its general secretary, Aiman Mazyek, has become an important public face of the organization.

GOALS, STRATEGIES, AND ACTIVITIES OF THE MUSLIM BROTHERHOOD IN GERMANY

Just as in other European countries, the German Muslim Brotherhood tries to establish itself as representative of all Muslims, mainly through the Central Council. It is very likely no coincidence that they named the organization based on the model of the Central Council of Jews in Germany (Zentralrat der Juden in Deutschland), which, since its inception in 1950, has successfully claimed to represent all Jews in the country and functions as a highly visible and powerful actor in German politics.[14]

Today, the relations between the German Muslim Brothers and Brotherhood organizations abroad have weakened. The first generation of Muslim Brothers in exile still had strong connections to their home countries—with personalities like Isam al-Attar playing a leading role in movements opposing the governments of their home countries. The new generation of leaders has mostly been born in Germany. In fact, some leading members of the Central Council and IGD like Zayat and Mazyck have German mothers—quite unlike their counterparts in the Turkish Islamist organizations—and are therefore more strongly oriented toward Germany than the older generation.

The IGD and the Central Council aim at establishing an autonomous space in German society where Muslims can live their lives according to the tenets of Islamic law (*Shari'a*) as interpreted by the Brotherhood and its representatives in Europe. Implicitly, as these organizations claim to represent all Muslims in Germany, they aim at controlling these spheres of Muslim life. In the German public, this vision is often depicted as one of a Muslim "parallel society" and rejected by large parts of the political spectrum, especially on its conservative side.

In order to reach this goal, the IGD and the Central Council follow a two-pronged strategy. First, they build the necessary infrastructure to promote their vision of Muslim faith and culture in Germany. In a country where mosques are often situated in poor backyards, they promote the construction of modern mosques and cultural centers for their constituencies. These projects often meet with problems, as large parts of the German public reject the building of big mosques, especially when the builder-owners are suspected of entertaining strong ties with the Muslim Brotherhood.

For instance, in 2006, Inssan, a small Muslim association in Berlin, was denied a construction permit for a cultural center with a mosque because it was (correctly) suspected of acting as a front for the IGD.[15] When Inssan then tried to get a construction permit in another district of the German capital, a citizens' action committee protested and tried to thwart the project.[16] Partly as a consequence of these suspicions, leading functionaries deny being members in or entertaining close relationships with the Muslim Brotherhood.

Second, the Central Council and IGD frequently demand to be recognized by the federal and the state governments as the main representatives of Muslims in Germany and as privileged partners in all matters pertaining to them. Until 2006, Nadeem Elias had been successful in positioning himself as a moderate Muslim leader and a partner in religious dialogue. Although suspicions concerning his person and the Central Council remained, he was accepted by large parts of the public as the representative of Muslims in Germany. And although the federal and state governments are aware of the strong Muslim Brotherhood influence on the Central Council, some have nevertheless opted to enter into a dialogue with it.

When the Interior Ministry convened the German Islam Conference (Deutsche Islamkonferenz) in September 2006, the Central Council was one among five Muslim umbrella organizations represented. The conference was planned to work out a binding agreement on guidelines for the interaction between Muslims and non-Muslims in Germany. Quite ironically, when Ibrahim al-Zayat appeared at the conference in May 2007, politicians protested his presence, but not the representation of the Central Council.[17]

THE ARAB MUSLIM BROTHERHOOD AND TURKISH MILLI GÖRÜŞ

The organizations of the Muslim Brotherhood in Germany closely cooperate with some of their Turkish counterparts, most notably the Milli Görüş (National Vision/Perspective) movement. In fact, this movement might be considered a Turkish branch of the Muslim Brotherhood. Its founder, former Turkish prime minister Necmettin Erbakan, born in 1926, was heavily influenced by the Muslim Brotherhood's ideology. Just as Erbakan and his movement stood in close contact with Muslim Brotherhood officials in the Arab world, the organizations affiliated with the Milli Görüş movement in Germany have followed suit. Representatives of both the Muslim Brotherhood and Milli Görüş have cooperated in different organizations in Germany and abroad. Furthermore, there are indications that this cooperation has been intensifying at an European level in recent years.

Since the 1970s, Milli Görüş has been the most influential and biggest Islamist movement among German Muslims of Turkish origin. Since 1995, it has been called Islamic Community Milli Görüş (Islamische Gemeinschaft Milli Görüş [IGMG]). The Federal Office for the Protection of the Constitution (Bundesverfassungsschutz), the German domestic intelligence service, counts about 27,000 members of this organization, although the actual numbers might be higher.[18]

Since its foundation in 1976, the organization, originally called Turkish Union Europe (Türkische Union Europa/Avrupa Türk Birliği), repeatedly changed its name. In 1985, the Milli Görüş Association in Europe (Vereinigung der neuen Weltsicht in Europa/Avrupa Milli Görüş Teşkilatları, AMGT) was founded, and in 1995 parts of this organization were named Islamic Community Milli Görüş. It is commonly known as either Milli Görüş or IGMG and has its headquarters in Kerpen, a small city close to Cologne. It is an umbrella organization for a wide variety of associations all over Germany, which are connected to it in different ways. About 300 mosque associations are affiliated with the IGMG in Germany.

Although Necmettin Erbakan's Felicity Party (Saadet Partisi)[19] has lost most of its influence in Turkey to Prime Minister Recep Tayyip Erdoğan's Justice and Development Party (Adalet ve Kalkınma or AK Party), it has retained its influence on the German IGMG. However, younger members who grew up in Germany gained importance and challenged the dominance of the "older guard" of Turkey-oriented functionaries in the 1990s.

However, while people like the general secretary of IGMG since 2002, Oğuz Uçüncü, born in 1969, try to present themselves as willing to integrate into German society, the traditional Islamist leadership with stronger connections to Turkey is still influential. The current president of Milli Görüş, Osman Döring (or Yavuz Karahan) is unknown to the German public but remains influential within the organization.

Relations between the IGMG and the IGD are strong. Their embodiment is Ibrahim al-Zayat, who is married to Sabiha Erbakan, sister of Mehmet Sabri Erbakan, Necmettin Erbakan's nephew.[20] Mehmet Erbakan has been a leading functionary in the IGMG in the 1990s and, from April 2001 until October 2002, headed the organization. All three have been active in the German Muslim Students Association. When Zayat became its head in 1992, Mehmet Erbakan became his deputy. It is highly doubtful whether Zayat would have been able to build his position without these family connections.

Zayat has established himself as the central figure in the Islamist real estate business. He is the chief representative of the European Mosque Construction and Support Company, which administrates about 300 IGMG mosques in Germany.[21] Besides, he is the director of a private company called "Spezial-Liegenschafts-Management" based in Cologne, and which buys real estate for mosque constructions and advises mosque associations in legal and financial matters.[22]

THE ISLAMIC COUNCIL AND THE COORDINATION COUNCIL FOR MUSLIMS IN GERMANY

In 1986, the IGMG founded the Islamic Council for the Federal Republic of Germany (Islamrat für die Bundesrepublik Deutschland), with its headquarters in Cologne, as a larger umbrella organization.[23] Milli Görüş is by far the biggest member group and the president of the Islamic Council has always been one of its members. Most observers regard it as being an IGMG's front organization.

Just like the Central Council, the Islamic Council aims at gaining official recognition as a major representative of Muslims in Germany. However, due to its lack of success, it often cooperates with the Central Council in order to push through common aims. It came closer to gaining official recognition when it was invited to the German Islam Conference in September 2006. However, both the Islamic and the Central Council criticized the predominance of individual Muslim thinkers—some of them avowed secularists—and the relatively weak roles of the Muslim umbrella organizations, which held only five out of fifteen seats.[24]

In order to assert themselves in this environment, in April 2007 four of the five organizations founded the Coordination Council of Muslims in Germany (Koordinierungsrat der Muslime in Deutschland). It claims to represent the Muslims in Germany and has been quite successful in establishing itself as the main contact for German institutions in all matters pertaining to Muslim life in the country. The Turkish DITIB (Religious Affairs

Turkish-Islamic Union), the German branch of the Presidency of Religious Affairs (Diyanet İşleri Başkanlığı) in Ankara, is the strongest member of the council.[25] The Central and the Islamic Council have thereby compromised their goal of being accepted as the sole representatives of Muslims in Germany but have gained a privileged position in German religious politics.

THE GERMAN MUSLIM BROTHERHOOD AND ITS INTERNATIONAL CONTACTS

The German organizations affiliated with the Muslim Brotherhood have long-established contacts with other Muslim Brothers and like-minded groups in the Middle East and—in recent years—increasingly with European organizations close to the Muslim Brotherhood.

One of the most controversial questions regarding the Muslim Brotherhood in Germany is the nature of relations to the Muslim World League (Rabitat al-Alam al-Islami). The Muslim World League was founded in Mecca in 1962 as an organization of Muslim scholars and intellectuals. Although it is often described as a "Wahhabi" institution, it is rather the institutional embodiment of a rapprochement of the Saudi Arabian religious establishment and the Islamist Muslim Brotherhood.[26]

The Muslim World League is officially labeled a nongovernmental organization, but the influence of the Saudi state is such that it should rather be considered a governmentally operated NGO (GONGO) or para-state organization. It draws most of its finances from the Saudi government, and—even more importantly—reflects Saudi Arabian government interests. In fact, the most important functionaries of the organization are Saudi citizens and its acting head, the general secretary, has always been a Saudi national.[27]

The League and its affiliated organizations are instruments of Saudi religious foreign policy insofar as Riyadh tried to build international and transnational religious ties in order to promote the official Saudi Arabian interpretation of Islam in order to counter attacks on the legitimacy of Saudi rule—first by Nasserist Egypt and later by revolutionary Iran. Even before the foundation of the Muslim World League, the Islamic University of Medina was established in 1961. It was designed as the educational center of Saudi religious foreign policy. Students from the peripheries of the Muslim World—South and Southeast Asia, Africa, and increasingly Europe—study here and then carry Wahhabi teachings to their home countries.

The World League's influence became an issue of contention in Germany, when in 2003, it was reported that Christian Ganczarski, a German convert and later al-Qa'ida member, was given a scholarship to study at the Islamic University in Medina in 1991. Allegedly, Nadeem Elias was present when a delegation of the World League screened young applicants in the Islamic Center in Aachen. The case highlighted the strong connections between the World League and Muslim Brotherhood institutions in Germany. Since then at least a dozen Germans have enrolled in the Islamic University of Medina.

A second organization close to the World League is the World Assembly of Muslim Youth (WAMY). Although it is not organizationally affiliated with the World League, it maintains extensive contacts with the organization and shares its religious-political goals. WAMY's staff is largely drawn from the Muslim Brotherhood, while it is financed by Saudi Arabian sources. Established by the World League in Riyadh in 1972, where it still has its headquarters, its general secretary is a Saudi national too. WAMY's declared aim is to "preserve the identity of young Muslims" and build the necessary infrastructure to promote Muslim culture. In practice, WAMY coordinates the activities of a multitude of Muslim student and youth organizations around the world; it runs schools, orphanages, hospitals, and educational centers; and it tries to form future Muslim elite by granting scholarships for Saudi universities.[28] The head of the IGD and the Islamic Center Cologne, Ibrahim al-Zayat, has served as the European and Germany representative of WAMY since the 1990s.[29]

The German organizations affiliated with the Muslim Brotherhood are part of a wide and constantly growing network of European institutions. The IGD is an important member of the Federation of Islamic Organizations in Europe (FIOE), an umbrella for all major national associations affiliated with or sympathetic to the Muslim Brotherhood. It was founded in 1989 and has been based in Brussels since 2007, after having moved its headquarters from Britain. Its importance grew with the increasing "Europeanization" of its member organizations. Just like its member organizations in their respective national societies, it aims at representing all Muslims in Europe.[30]

However, while institutions like the Central Council and the IGD had some success in lobbying the German government, the FIOE has not established itself as an important factor on the European level. Again, Ibrahim al-Zayat is an important functionary in this organization. He represents the German Brotherhood as a member of its board of directors, responsible for public relations.[31] Zayat was also the co-founder of the Forum of European Muslim Youth and Student Organizations (FEMYSO) in 1996 and served as its president until 2002. Other Germans held and continue to hold important positions. FEMYSO is an organization closely connected to the FIOE and seems to have extensive links to WAMY as well. It has its headquarters in Brussels and represents organizations from some two dozen European countries. It claims to represent the Muslim youth in Europe and lobbies the European Union on youth issues.[32] Its establishment is a logical result of the Brotherhood's focus on the recruitment and education of the Muslim youth in Europe.

CONCLUSION

The Muslim Brotherhood in Germany has strengthened its position in Germany since the end of the 1990s. Its organizational efficiency has placed it at the center of German religious policy. Through the Central Council of Muslims in Germany, it is represented as one of the four major players in the

German Islam Conference and will most likely remain one of the main actors among Muslims in Germany for the foreseeable future. The founding of the Coordination Council for Muslims in Germany in 2007 proved that the IGD and the Central Council were ready to compromise in order to expand their influence in German politics. As only one among four strong umbrella organizations, the Central Council will be able to influence German religious policy toward Muslims, but it will have to compromise with its three Turkish counterparts.

Perhaps this move indicates that the IGD and the Central Council have realized that the role of any Arab organization will remain limited in a country where the overwhelming majority of Muslims is of Turkish descent (about 2.5 million out of 3.5 million). The dominance of the Turkish organizations is made acceptable, however, by the fact that the Arab Muslim Brotherhood entered a close alliance with the Turkish Islamists of Milli Görüş some years ago. It remains to be seen whether this alliance will persist, especially because the Islamist scene in Turkey itself has been in upheaval since the founding of Prime Minister Erdoğan's Justice and Development Party in 2001. The long-term repercussions of this move on the Islamist scene in Germany have not become clear yet.

However, even in cooperation with the Turkish Islamists, the German Muslim Brotherhood has not generated any mass following, although its ideas are popular among a wider spectrum of German Muslims. With a membership of not more than 20,000, the Central Council and the IGD will only play a major role in German religious policy if they succeed in enhancing their public standing through cooperation with the German federal or sixteen state governments. As it seems from the history of the German Islam Conference, the federal government is—for the time being—willing to grant them a limited role.

Ibrahim al-Zayat has established himself as both the gray eminence of German Islamism—among Arabs and Turks as well—and the leading German voice in the European Muslim Brotherhood movement. He has not yet, however, managed to establish himself as a leading Muslim representative vis-à-vis the German government and the general public. His strong affiliation with the Muslim Brotherhood has proved to be a serious public relations disadvantage and might keep him from reaping the fruits of the work he has done behind-the-scenes since the early 1990s. In order to reduce this weak spot, Zayat—like other important Muslim protagonists—has steadfastly denied any affiliation with the Muslim Brotherhood. It is exactly this lack of transparency that has raised doubts about the motives and aims of the Muslim Brothers in Germany.

NOTES

1. On the early history of the center, see Ian Johnson, "The Beachhead: How a Mosque for Ex-Nazis Became Center of Radical Islam," *Wall Street Journal*, July 12, 2005.

2. The first English edition of the text was published in 1961. Said Ramadan, *Islamic Law: Its Scope and Equity* (London: Macmillan, 1961). The thesis has been published in numerous German and English editions.
3. Lorenzo Vidino, "The Muslim Brotherhood's Conquest of Europe," *Middle East Quarterly*, 12(1) (Winter 2005), http://www.meforum.org/article/687.
4. In 2007, German newspapers reported that the head of the Egyptian Muslim Brotherhood, Mahdi Akif (who had served as head of the Islamic Center in Munich from 1984 to 1987), had called Zayat "the head (*ra'is*) of the Muslim Brethren in Germany." *Die Welt* (Hamburg), February 26, 2007. Zayat published a counterstatement in *Die Welt* (Hamburg), April 10, 2007.
5. On the conference in 2007, see Bundesministerium des Innern, *Verfassungsschutzbericht 2007*, Berlin 2008, p. 214. The reports of the German domestic intelligence agency (Office for the Protection of the Constitution) can be downloaded from http://www.verfassungsschutz.de/de/publikationen/verfassungsschutzbericht/. The states (*Länder*) publish their reports as well.
6. On the Turkish Islamists in detail, see Guido Steinberg, "Germany," in Barry Rubin (ed.), *Global Survey of Islamism* (in print).
7. Karl Binswanger, "Fundamentalisten-Filz—Getrennt marschieren, vereint schlagen? "in Bahman Nirumand (ed.), *Im Namen Allahs: Islamische Gruppen und der Fundamentalismus in der Bundesrepublik Deutschland* (Köln: Dreisam 1990), pp. 129–148 (143).
8. Ibid., pp. 129–132.
9. According to Brigitte Maréchal, the Da'wa mosque in Paris and the Al-Khalil mosque in Brussels were affiliated with Attar and the Syrian Brotherhood. Brigitte Maréchal, *The Muslim Brothers in Europe* (Leiden: Brill, 2008), p. 62.
10. Until 1981, the Islamic Center Aachen had been a member of the IGD. Johannes Grundmann, *Islamische Internationalisten* (Wiesbaden: Reichert Verlag, 2005), p. 59.
11. On the congresses, see the yearly reports of the Office for the Protection of the Constitution in North Rhine-Westphalia, http://www.im.nrw.de/sch/41.htm#. On the conference in Aachen 2007, see Innenministerium des Landes Nordrhein-Westfalen, *Verfassungsschutzbericht des Landes Nordrhein-Westfalen über das Jahr 2007*, Düsseldorf 2008, p. 185.
12. www.alraid.de.
13. A short biography in Arabic can be found on the website of al-Ra'id, http://www.iid-alraid.de/Alraid/aboutauthor/Nadeem.pdf.
14. See the website of the organization, www.zentralratdjuden.de.
15. *Frankfurter Allgemeine Zeitung*, August 4, 2006. ("Wir müssen die gemäßigten Muslime schützen.") The association's website is: www.inssan-ev.de.
16. *Tagesspiegel* (Berlin), April 16, 2008. The project was later thwarted but for reasons not related to the Islamism debate.
17. See for example the interview with the conservative parliamentarian Kristina Köhler (CDU) in *Frankfurter Allgemeine Zeitung*, May 11, 2007 ("Sie täuschen uns in der Maske der Medienprofis").
18. Bundesministerium des Innern, *Verfassungsschutzbericht 2007*, Berlin 2008, p. 217.
19. After Erbakan was forced to resign as prime minister in June 1997, his Welfare Party was prohibited. In 2001, he founded the Felicity Party.
20. Sabiha al-Zayat (b. 1970) herself is a leading Islamist functionary and mainly covers women's issues. Officially, she heads the "Center for Islamic Women's

Research and Women's Advancement" in Cologne, teaches Islamic hermeneutics and didactics there.

21. Europäische Moscheebau und Unterstützungsgemeinschaft e.V. (EMUG).
22. *Frankfurter Allgemeine Zeitung*, May 11, 2007. Oğuz Uçüncü has a leading position at "Spezial-Liegenschafts-Management."
23. The headquarters was moved from Bonn to Cologne in 2005.
24. The other organizations were the non-Islamist Religious Affairs Turkish-Islamic Union (Türkisch Islamische Union der Anstalt für Religion/Diyanet Işleri Türk Islam Birliği, DITIB), the Federation of Alevi Communities in Germany (Almanya Alevi Birlikleri Federasyonu), and the Federation of Islamic Cultural Centers (Verband der Islamischen Kulturzentren, VIKZ).
25. See the internal rules of procedure as published on the website of the Central Council, http://islam.de/files/misc/krm_go.pdf.
26. Reinhard Schulze, *Islamischer Internationalismus im 20: Jahrhundert: Untersuchungen zur Geschichte der Islamischen Weltliga* (Leiden: Brill, 1990).
27. The current general secretary is Abdallah ibn Abd al-Muhsin al-Turki, a Wahhabi scholar.
28. Grundmann, *Internationalisten*, pp. 93–95.
29. Steve Merley, *The Federation of Islamic Organizations in Europe*, NEFA Foundation October 1, 2008, p. 25, http://www.nefafoundation.org/miscellaneous/FeaturedDocs/nefafioereport1008.pdf. In a 2005 interview with the *Wall Street Journal*, Zayat stated that he was a members of WAMY's board of trustees and its representative in Germany. *Wall Street Journal*, December 29, 2005.
30. Maréchal, *Muslim Brothers*, p. 63f.
31. Merley, *Federation of Islamic Organizations in Europe*, p. 25.
32. Lorenzo Vidino, "The Muslim Brotherhood's Conquest of Europe," in *Middle East Quarterly* ,12(1) (Winter 2005), http://www.meforum.org/article/687. Steve Merley, *The Federation of Islamic Organizations in Europe*, NEFA Foundation October 1, 2008, pp. 14–17, http://www.nefafoundation.org/miscellaneous/FeaturedDocs/nefafioereport1008.pdf.

11

THE MUSLIM BROTHERHOOD IN NORTH AMERICA

Alyssa A. Lappen

Although the name Muslim Brotherhood is never used explicitly in North America by its adherents, and connections to the organization are denied publicly, the Brotherhood has a large number of institutions and supporters in the United States and Canada. Their objectives and ideologies are similar to that of the Brotherhood elsewhere in the world. In 2005, the Egyptian Brotherhood's leader Muhammad Mahdi Akif referred to his group as "the largest organization in the world," whose members cooperated globally "based on the same religious worldview—the spread of Islam, until it rules the world." He added, "Jihad is the only way to achieve these goals."[1] According to Akif, Western democracies are corrupt, "false," and determined "to destroy the [Islamic] nation, its faith and tradition."[2] Akif also called the United States "a Satan that abuses the religion" and predicted that it would "collapse soon." He also stated he had "complete faith that Islam will invade Europe and America."[3]

The Brotherhood first reached North America in an organized way in 1963 through the founding of the Muslim Students Association (MSA) at the University of Illinois at Champaign-Urbana.[4] The MSA created a host of front groups, such as the following: the Islamic Medical Association (IMA) in 1967; North American Islamic Trust (NAIT) in 1971; the Herndon, Virginia-based International Islamic Institute of Thought (IIIT) in 1981; the Islamic Society of North America (ISNA) in 1982; and the Committee on American-Islamic Relations (CAIR) in 1994, among others.[5]

In August 2008, despite many such connections, ISNA claimed always to have disavowed Brotherhood associations.[6] For example, Sayyid Syeed, ISNA Secretary General from 1994 to November 2006,[7] had made donations to the Holy Land Foundation (HLF) and had defended designated terrorist and Hamas Chief Musa Marzuk, who was deported to Jordan in 1997.[8]

The powerful Brotherhood theoretician Yusuf al-Qaradawi, along with Brotherhood Finance Chief Yusuf Nada, has reportedly funded MSA and other groups.[9] Al-Qaradawi, a major stockholder in the Al Taqwa bank (which Nada heads) is also a foreign terrorist and was barred from entering the country in 1999. He has also chaired the terrorist-funding Union of Good "charity," Qatar National Bank, its al-Islami subsidiary, Qatar Islamic Bank, and Qatar International Islamic Bank.[10] MSA leaders included the Iraqi Kurdish-born, engineers Ahmad Totonji, Jamal Barzinji, and Jamal Badawi[11] educated in the United Kingdom. By 1983, a $21 million headquarters was built for the group on a former farm near Indianapolis, Indiana.[12]

In November 1977, the MSA convened the First International Conference on Islamization of Knowledge in Lugano, Switzerland. Its second conference was held in Islamabad, Pakistan in 1983; its third conference in 1984 in Kuala Lampur, Malaysia; and its fourth in 1987 in Khartoum, Sudan. The meetings concluded, "Islamization of knowledge" was an "epistemological and civilizational necessity" for Muslims and for "mankind at large."[13]

Throughout the 1980s, the Brotherhood's North American supporters published a number of books promising, for example, to Islamize Western thinking.[14] Hundreds of other books and articles outlined the group's plans, including 24 IIIT "Islamization of Knowledge" books.[15] The California-based Institute of Islamic Sciences, Technology, and Development (IISTD) published twelve titles, including *Islamization of Knowledge and Higher Education*.[16]

The Brotherhood's basic plan for North America can be traced back to a program first drafted at the MSA's Lugano meeting in 1977. *Towards a Worldwide Strategy for Islamic Policy* instructed Brothers to think, educate, and act to establish "an Islamic power [government] on the earth."[17] They should engage internationally "with flexibility at a local level," temporarily accommodating non-Muslim values but never violating "basic [Islamic] principles...." Further, they should avoid disproportionate "confrontation" with potentially harmful adversaries until the time was ripe.[18]

A further refinement was introduced in 1987 by Egyptian Brotherhood General Guide Muhammad Hamid Abu al-Nasr and reiterated by his successor Muhammad Akram in 1991. "On the General Strategic Goal for the Group in North America" ordered North American Brothers to seek the economic, cultural, and political overthrow of the United States and the West through the "establishment of the global Islamic State." After "settling" Islam "and its Movement [as] a part of the homeland it lives in," the group would make Islam "stable in the land," enabled "within the souls, minds and the lives of the people," and " 'entrenched' in the soil ...." This grand mission was "a grand *Jihad* in eliminating and destroying Western civilization from within and 'sabotaging' its miserable house by their hands and the hands of the believers ...."[19]

The method was to employ flexibility (*muruna*)[20] and concealment (*taqiyya* or *kitman*)[21] in order to spread Islam. Thus, the North American Brotherhood branch maintained at least twenty-nine groups would provide fronts for its efforts. They included the MSA, Muslim Youth of North America (MYNA), the Muslim Arab Youth Association (MAYA), the ISNA Fiqh Committee (now, FCNA), the Islamic Education Department (IED), the Islamic Book Service (IBS), the Muslim Businessmen Association (MBA), and the now defunct HLF (originally the Occupied Land Fund). The MB created the Islamic Circle of North America (ICNA), IIIT, IMA, the ISNA, the Muslim American Society (MAS), the NAIT,[22] and the Muslim Public Affairs Council (MPAC).[23] The MAS runs the Qaradawi-chaired Islamic American University (IAU), a teacher and imam correspondence school[24] in the Detroit area. The Brothers' supporters also control large numbers of North American mosques and Islamic centers, which serve as a means to spread its doctrine and gain recruits.[25]

While the Brotherhood's fronts often seek to portray themselves as moderate, the background of activists and the ideology offered often betrays its actual vision. For example, in 2008, for the seventh anniversary of the September 11 attacks, the ICNA chose New York-based Imam Siraj Wahhaj to market "Subway Project" on the popular YouTube video-sharing website and proposed a $48,000 ad campaign to promote Islam to millions of daily on the New York City system. Elected officials protested. Wahhaj was an unindicted coconspirator in the 1993 bombing of World Trade Center and had defended the operation's imprisoned mastermind, Shaykh Umar Abd al-Rahman.[26] In 1991, Wahhaj condemned the U.S. liberation of Kuwait from Iraqi control as one of the "most diabolical plots" in history.[27]

ICNA's own website shows its support for the Muslim Brotherhood and radical Islamist thinking.[28] In this context, ICNA reveres the teachings of Muslim Brotherhood founder Hasan al-Banna, as well as parallel thinkers and groups, including Pakistan's Jama'at-e-Islami (JI) founder Said Abu al-Ala al-Mawdudi (1903–1979), Iranian revolutionary Ayatollah Ruhollah Musavi Khomeini, and the harshly anti-American Egyptian Brotherhood ideologue Sayyid Qutb. From April 1999 through 2007, ICNA's website honored them and dozens more on a list of "Great Leaders."[29] ICNA's Young Muslims group also runs jihad camps and conferences.[30]

INVOLVEMENT IN TERRORISM

The incitement to hatred or violence in the texts of Brotherhood front groups has also led to actions by some of their members. In May 2007, London authorities extradited Fahad Hashmi—a Queens, New York–raised Pakistani, Brooklyn College graduate, and ICNA activist—to New York, eleven months after he attacked Heathrow Airport officers while attempting to flee to Pakistan. Hashmi had allegedly assisted al-Qa'ida in Afghanistan by transporting military gear,[31] recruiting terrorists, and conducting such operations himself.[32] Connected to a London bomb plot,[33] Hashmi was awaiting trial in late 2008.[34] He was allegedly aided by Pakistani former Brooklyn College student Muhammad Junaid Babar, a confessed al-Qa'ida agent, who helped plan a 2003 assassination plot against the then Pakistan president Pervez Musharraf.[35]

In May 2007, the U.S. Department of Justice identified ISNA and its Brotherhood parent organization as unindicted coconspirators for allegedly funding terrorism through Hamas and the HLF.[36] The HLF case was declared a mistrial when jurors could not reach a verdict,[37] but the case has since been retried, and in November 2008, all its defendants were found guilty.[38]

One of the most explicitly radical Brotherhood front groups has been the Islamic Association for Palestine (IAP), created to give direct support to the Palestinian Islamist group Hamas and its terrorist operations. In 1994, former IAP Public Relations Director Nihad Awad and Omar Ahmad cofounded CAIR.[39] In 2004, a federal court ordered IAP (with Hamas and HLF) to pay $156 million in damages for the 1996 Jerusalem murder of David Boim, a seventeen-year-old U.S. citizen.[40]

While CAIR was enormously successful in gaining favorable media coverage, it had numerous links to Brotherhood network members and groups, along with supporters of Hamas and Islamic Jihad, and even some who backed al-Qa'ida. A number of CAIR activists and even officials have been indicted and convicted of involvement with terrorist groups. CAIR also raised funds for the Hamas-linked HLH and Global Relief Foundation "charities" and, in 2003, was allegedly funded by the Brotherhood's IIIT.[41]

POLITICAL AND GOVERNMENTAL CONNECTIONS

From 1990, the Brotherhood's influence grew dramatically. Despite its radical ideology, international connections with radical Islamist groups, involvements in fund-raising for terrorists, direct involvement of some activists or officials in terrorism, and virulent denunciations of U.S. policies, Brotherhood network members achieved remarkable success in terms of mainstream political connections. For example, despite being an unindicted coconspirator in the 1993 bombing of World Trade Center and having made statements in favor of terrorist groups and operations, Wahhaj was invited to deliver Islamic invocations at both the U.S. House of Representatives and Senate.[42]

For over a decade, the U.S. government employed only Brotherhood programs to certify Islamic clergymen for U.S. military or prison chaplaincies.[43] Ironically, in doing so, it approved the curricula of an international organization outlawed by several U.S. allies, including Egypt and many other Muslim countries.[44] Moreover, U.S. government let the Brotherhood's Hartford Seminary Duncan Black Macdonald Center for the Study of Islamic Studies and Christian–Muslim Relations program use U.S. prisons as a place for radical recruitment. Through 2003, the Brotherhood's American Muslim Foundation (AMF), American Muslim Armed Forces and Veterans Affairs Council (AMAFVAC), and Graduate School of Islamic and Social Sciences (GSISS) controlled Hartford's institute, which is now headed by ISNA's Dr. Ingrid Mattson.[45]

All this occurred despite President Clinton's order 12947 of January 24, 1995, naming Hamas a foreign terrorist organization and his prohibition on all subsequent "transactions with terrorists ...."[46]

Before his twenty-three-year prison sentence for terror-funding, al-Qa'ida agent, former AMF chief, Fiqh Council of North America (FCNA) trustee, and American Muslim Council (AMC) founder Abdurahman Alamoudi[47] regularly visited the White House while Clinton and George W. Bush were in office.[48] In addition, Alamoudi donated $1,000 and the AMC $50,000 to Hillary Clinton's New York senatorial campaign (funds she subsequently returned).[49] Former MAS communications director and AMC and CAIR employee Ismail (Randall) Royer pleaded guilty to sending recruits to Pakistani terror-training camps managed by Lashkai-e-Taiba, a Brotherhood outgrowth and designated foreign terrorist group.[50] Further, in 2000, Alamoudi supported Hamas and Hizballah at a rally opposite the White House.[51]

Nevertheless, Alamoudi, naturalized in 1996, maintained political connections, as did CAIR director Awad.[52] In 1997—two years after Clinton's executive order—a White House civil rights advisory board appointed Awad to the President's Commission on Aviation Safety and Security. After September 11, Awad visited President Bush,[53] while Orange County Islamic Society Imam Muzammil Siddiqui—an associate of convicted terrorist Abdel Rahman, supporter of Hizballah, and a proponent of turning America into an Islamist state—led prayers at the Washington National Cathedral.[54]

Even convictions of CAIR officials failed to deter U.S. officials.[55] In January 2006, the U.S. State Department requested policy proposals from Awad and other CAIR executives, including a "World Report on Islamophobia."[56] In June 2006, CAIR challenged U.S. immigration policies. The Department of Homeland Security (DHS) then hosted individuals with radical Islamist connections on an inside tour of sensitive U.S. customs areas at Chicago's O'Hare International Airport.[57]

In June 2007, one month after designating CAIR a Brotherhood arm and unindicted terror-funding coconspirator,[58] the Department of Justice canceled an event on law enforcement partnerships with Muslim minorities.[59] Yet, in August 2007, following objections from two U.S. congressmen and several U.S. attorneys, the department cosponsored an Islamic convention with ISNA.[60]

In March 2008, the Iraqi-born Michigan CAIR chief Muthanna al-Hanooti was charged with conspiracy as an unregistered agent of Saddam Hussein's Iraqi regime. Hanooti allegedly arranged for three U.S. congressmen to visit Iraq before the March 2003 invasion and receive financing from Iraq's intelligence agency under the cover of receiving two million barrels of Iraqi oil to sell internationally.[61]

In September 2008, former Secretary of State Madeleine Albright and former Special Middle East Envoy Dennis Ross were among the participants in a report advocating official U.S. contacts with Muslim Brotherhood groups in the Middle East.[62] Also participating in this United States–Muslim Engagement Project was ISNA's Mattson.[63]

In June 2008, the Brotherhood's network achieved its greatest single success in national politics when Senator Barack Obama appointed Chicago corporate lawyer Mazen Asbahi as his Muslim outreach advisor. Asbahi quickly resigned, however, after reports of his eight-year-long connection with Illinois Imam Jamal Said and the Saudi-funded NAIT Bridgeview Mosque Foundation, both Brotherhood affiliates and unindicted terrorist funding coconspirators.[64] In 2000, Said raised funds to memorialize a suicide bomber.[65] Asbahi also briefly served on the "Shari'a-compliant" board of the NAIT's Allied Asset Advisors money management firm, where Said was a trustee in 2005.[66] Asbahi denied having Brotherhood links. Yet the Egyptian Brotherhood's website (http://www.ikhwanweb.com) defended Asbahi[67] and, while denying any formal connection, admitted to holding similar ideological positions.[68]

In August 2008, the Democratic National Convention welcomed participation by ISNA. The presidential nominee Obama invited Muslim convert and ISNA President Mattson to speak at an interfaith prayer service at the convention.[69] Critics noted her radical ideas and denial of a terrorist threat within the United States from foreign-directed domestic Islamists.[70] In January 2009, she delivered the Muslim invocation at the Obama inaugural.[71]

THE BROTHERS IN NORTH AMERICAN UNIVERSITIES AND CULTURE

The MSA national website includes a Muslim Code of Honor prohibiting "branding others as nonbelievers (*takfir*)"—thus rejecting a frequent radical Islamist concept—while defining proper Islam along normative lines including professing the "Supremacy of God, the prophethood of Muhammad ibn 'Abd Allah," the reality of a day of judgment, "the authenticity of the Holy Qur'an and facing Makkah (*qibla*) in daily prayers." A "Mutual Respect and Cooperation" pledge also vowed to "protect" U.S. Muslims from divisive and "inflammatory" literature and "misleading propaganda."[72]

MSA's Canadian Young Muslims of North America website also advocated "spreading the message of Islam (Da'wa)" and defined jihad as the "defense of Muslim lands." Yet, an additional basic goal mentioned was the "establishment of the Islamic State (*khilafah*)."[73] It recommended for study the radical writings of such Brotherhood luminaries as Hasan al-Banna, Abu al-Ala al-Mawdudi, Ahmad al-Rashid, Assam al-Bashir, and even Abdallah Azzam, who was the personal inspiration for Usama bin Ladin's jihad activities.[74]

In August 2007, MSA had 600 North American college chapters in five regions.[75] In 2008, it claimed to have 100,000 members. It recruited and promoted its brand of politically Islamist religion while pressuring universities to create footbaths for Muslim prayer preparation, special prayer rooms, and to provide halal food.[76] It also participated in monthly North American "Zonal Conference Calls"[77] and annual conferences. The August 2008 MSA gathering coincided with ISNA's Columbus, Ohio convention,[78] which was attended by thousands of people.[79]Among the ISNA speakers were former secretary general Syeed, ISNA trustee and MSA cofounder Badawi, Orange County Imam Siddiqui, and lecturer at University of California at Berkeley Hatam Bazian.[80] In 1999, in Santa Clara, Bazian had cited an Islamic hadith (tradition of Muhammad), linking Judgment Day to the extermination of all Jews.[81]

Brotherhood-associated individuals and groups such as the Council on Islamic Education (CIE) have since 1995 written chapters and curricula reaching U.S. schools in most states. In 2003, for example, the CIE published "A Teacher's Guide to Religion in the Public Schools" that encouraged public schools to neither "inculcate *nor inhibit* religion." The CIE also drafted numerous Jewish and Christian organizations as cosponsors.[82]

Dozens of U.S. textbooks and curricula were revised as a result, claimed *Textbook League* director William J. Benetta. One taught that Allah was the same "God of other monotheistic religions, Judaism and Christianity."[83] While some changes were aimed at equal treatment of Islam, others, concluded a 2008 study of textbooks, allowed apologist and misleading information that accorded with the Brotherhood's goals of presenting Islam as superior or above the kind of critical inquiry applied to other religions.[84]

In June, the Brotherhood received a major cultural introduction when New York University's Center for Dialogues, Brooklyn Academy of Music and Asia Society cosponsored a nine-day "arts" festival entitled *Muslim Voices: Arts & Ideas*. The event was hailed as "New York city's first Muslim arts festival."[85] The advisors included such Brotherhood supporters as Imam Feisel Abdul Rauf, NYU's Khalid Latif, ICNA affiliate and Muslim Consultative Network Chief Adem Carroll, and Saudi Princess Lubna Zaki Thunayan al-Saud.[86] Many of the 300 events at numerous New York cultural institutions—and on national television—were merely apologias and Islamic indoctrination. These included the following: a romanticized film on fourteenth-century Muslim historian Ibn Batutta; a Kuwaiti production of Shakespeare's *Richard III* as an "Arab Tragedy"; various exhibits and talks on mosques; several Koranic lectures, exhibits, and recitations; and a speech on the beauty of the Muslim veil (advanced most feverishly by extremists).[87]

ECONOMIC ACTIVITIES

The Muslim Brotherhood's most influential advisor, Yusuf al-Qaradawi, has stated: "Holy war...is an Islamic duty," and the charitable contributions Muslims are religiously commanded to give are best spent "fighting in the Way of Allah." Islamic charity is "*jihad* with money." God has ordered Muslims "to fight enemies with our lives and with our money."[88]

As remarked by the well-known Arab journalist and former *al-Sharq al-Awsat* editor Abd al-Rahman al-Rashid in 2004, such funding has fueled a vast "army of ... friends and associates, ideologists, organizers, supervisors, perpetrators, preachers, camps, positions, arms, print shops, hideouts, broadcasting stations and programs."[89]

Creating "an Islamic Economic system [is] a priority," instructed the 1982 plan for Brotherhood strategy. Brothers were to spend "sufficient effort," time, and "money" to further Islamic globalization; connect "with economic institutions adequate to support the cause" and "construct social, economic, scientific and health institutions [to] penetrate" services and control "local power centers." The development of "economic, social, and other specialized Islamic institutions" was designed to establish an eventual Brotherhood political rule.[90] Al-Qaradawi heralded Islamic finance, urging Muslims to spread *Shari'a*-based economics to promote victory.[91]

In 1987, the Pasadena, California–based LARIBA Finance House became the first U.S. Islamic bank. By 2005, it was operating in twenty-eight states. The United States hosted at least eight more stand-alone *Shari'a* (Islamic law) compliant financial institutions in 2007—Chicago's Devon Bank; Reston, Virginia's Guidance Financial Group; Houston's MSI Financial Services Corporation; Minneapolis's Neighborhood Development Center and Reba Free; West Falls Church, Virginia's SHAPE Financial Group; Ann Arbor's University Bank; and Nashville's World Relief. Bank of America, BNP Paribas, Citibank, Credit Suisse, HSBC, J.P. Morgan Chase, Lloyds TSB, Merrill Lynch, Standard Chartered, and UBS also offered Islamic banking. *Shari'a banks* sold Islamic mortgages to the later bankrupted Fannie Mae.[92]

Regulators were "open to Islamic financial products," New York Federal Reserve Board executive vice president William L. Rutledge said in April 2005. He promised to "hold Islamic financial institutions to the same high licensing and supervision standards" as conventional banks. Yet, the Federal Reserve lacked understanding of the religious laws it approved to regulate some banks and could not "take a stance on issues of *Shari'a* interpretation."[93]

The question, however, was to what extent the Brotherhood promoted *Shari'a* finance to meet religious requirements compared to its use for concealing money transfers and increasing the political leverage of the organization to promote its longer-term agenda. University of Southern California King Faisal Professor of Islamic Thought Timur Kuran wrote that "neither classical nor medieval Islamic civilization featured banks in the modern sense, let alone 'Islamic banks.'" *Shari'a* actually retarded economic development in many nations, he concluded, and strengthened radical Islamist political forces there.[94] In January 2008, Muslim Canadian Congress president Farzana Hassan complained to authorities that *Shari'a* finance was "nothing more than an attempt by Islamists, with backing from Middle Eastern Financial Institutions and their Western partners, to scare Muslim Canadians into believing that they should pay more to the banks and demand less in return as an act of religiosity."[95]

Saudi scholar Muhammad Najatallah Siddiqi acknowledged that *Shari'a* finance was part of a revolutionary program to replace the "excesses of capitalism"[96] by bringing in Islamic law, which would "create a safer, saner financial world," and "morally inspired" behavior.[97] Nevertheless, the Brotherhood's efforts involved serious financial risks[98] since *Shari'a* banking had far fewer regulatory and accounting protections than subprime mortgages. Moreover, Islamic banking purveyors admitted that *Shari'a* regulations could "override commercial decisions"; did not "standardize" documentation; and used complex "inter-creditor agreements" and "off-balance sheet financing."[99]

Another problem was the ability to conceal information about where money went, on what basis decisions were made, and whether moderate Muslims or radical Islamists were in control. One of the top advisors being used was a twenty-year veteran of Pakistan's *Shari'a* Supreme Court, former Judge Taqi Usmani.[100] He had connections with Taliban-related groups,[101] had endorsed suicide bombing, and, in 2007, advised U.K. Muslims to impose *Shari'a* law on that country when their numbers sufficed.[102] Usmani chaired the Dow Jones Islamic Index Shari'a board until July 2008[103] and served the Sharia Supervisory Board (SSB) of an NAIT Islamic fund.

Another such person was Yusuf Talal DeLorenzo, religious advisor to Pakistan's dictator Zia ul-Haq from 1981 to 1984, when he purported to establish an Islamist-based regime.[104] DeLorenzo directed education for the Virginia Islamic Saudi Academy, cited in 2008 by the U.S. Commission on International Religious Freedom for using textbooks inciting against non-Muslims.[105] He served the IIIT[106] and from 1989 was Fiqh Council of North America secretary.[107]

Other Islamic Shari'a authorities for U.S. banks who worked with Brotherhood groups included:

- Muhammad Kaiseruddin, tied to suburban Chicago's NAIT-controlled Bridgeview Mosque, where preachers condemned Western culture, praised suicide bombers, and incited members to be "Muslims against the world."[108] Kaiseruddin advised the Dow Jones Islamic Market Index.[109]
- NAIT trustee Abdallah Idris Ali,[110] ISNA president from 1992 to 1997,[111] affiliated with Saudi Arabia's MWL and WAMY, and Al-Haramain, a charity group which the U.S. Treasury designated in June 2008 as terrorist-funding.[112] Ali's Islamicity website denounced Christians and Jews and incited jihad to defeat the West.
- Bassam Osman, an NAIT trustee and reputed former chairman,[113] controlled the Islamic Academy of Florida terror-cell base.[114] Osman directed Oak Lawn, Illinois's Quranic Literary Institute, whose assets DOJ froze in 1988[115] and was chairman and president of Allied Asset Advisors (AAA), the Dow Jones Islamic Index Fund manager.[116]

The Muslim Brotherhood wants Islam to triumph over all other religions in North America, the heart of the Western world.[117] Despite being active in North America since 1963, until recently the group's influence and activities are still not well understood. Since it is so deliberately camouflaged in many ways, even asserting the Brotherhood's existence can be a controversial endeavor and much remains to be known.

NOTES

1. *Al-Sharq al-Awsat* (London), December 11, 2005, http://www.aawsat. com/english/ (subsequently removed), cited by Rachel Ehrenfeld and Alyssa A. Lappen, "The Truth about the Muslim Brotherhood," June 16, 2006, *FrontPage Magazine*, http://www.frontpagemag.com/Articles/Printable. aspx?GUID=55B2AEBA-09BD-44C5-8827-66B50ABA2693.
2. http://arabi.ahram.org.eg/arabi/ahram/2005/4/30/WRLD9.HTM and http://news.bbc.co.uk/hi/arabic/news/newsid_4554000/4554324.stm.
3. "New Muslim Brotherhood Leaders: Resistance in Iraq and Palestine is Legitimate; America is Satan; Islam Will Invade America and Europe," *MEMRI Special Dispatch*, No. 655, February 4, 2004.
4. "History of IIFSA," International Islamic Federation of Student Organizations (IIFSO), http://web.archive.org/web/19990202092801/www.iifso.org/hist. htm (accessed August 19, 2008); "Adopting IISTD Action Plan for (a) Muslim-Majority and (b) Muslim-Minority Countries Besides USA: Islamizing Higher Secular and Pseudo-Islamic Education Systems," *IISTD Newsletter*, vol. 1, no. 3 (Shaban 1419/December 1998), http://www.islamicscience.org/pages/english/A4.htm.
5. "Emerging Islamic Infrastructure," undated, The Pluralism Project at Harvard University http://www.pluralism.org/ocg/CDROM_files/islam/emerging_infrastructure.php (accessed August 22, 2008); Ehrenfeld and Lappen, "The Truth about the Muslim Brotherhood, Part II."; Joe Kaufman, "MSA, the Missing Co-conspirator," July 11, 2007, http://www.frontpagemag.com/articles/Read.aspx?GUID=482B28BF-86D4-440C-ADD7-49B07331DA2A; (accessed August 22, 2008).
6. "Setting the Record Straight," ISNA statement, August 9, 2008, http://www.isna.net/articles/News/SETTING-THE-RECORD-STRAIGHT.aspx (accessed August 22, 2008).
7. NCC Interfaith Relations, November 2006, http://nccinterfaith.blogspot. com/2006_11_01_archive.html (accessed September 15, 2008).
8. Stephen C. Coughlin, "Extremism and the Islamic Society of North America," International Assessment and Strategy Center, February 2007, http://www. strategycenter.net/docLib/20080127_Extremism_and_ISNA.pdf (accessed July 1, 2008); *U.S. v. Mousa Mohammed Abu Marzook*, http://www.usdoj.gov/usao/iln/indict/2004/marzook_et_al.pdf (accessed September 15, 2008).
9. John Mintz and Douglas Farah, "In Search of Friends among the Foes," *Washington Post*, September 11, 2004, http://www.washingtonpost.com/ac2/wp-dyn/A12823-2004Sep10?language=printer; http://www.masnet.org/aboutmas.asp (accessed August 21, 2008); Jonathan D. Halevi, "The Muslim Brotherhood: A Moderate Islamic Alternative to al-Qaeda or a Partner in Global *Jihad*," *Jerusalem Viewpoints*, November 2007, http://www.jcpa.org/JCPA/Templates/ShowPage.asp?DRIT=2&DBID=1&LNGID=1&TMID=111&FID=379&PID=0&IID=1920&TTL=The_Muslim_Brotherhood:_A_Moderate_Islamic_Alternative_to_al-Qaeda_or_a_Partner_in_Global_Jihad.
10. Jenny Booth, "Muslim Outrage As Yusuf al-Qaradawi Refused U.K. Visa," *Times Online*, February 7, 2008, http://www.timesonline.co.uk/tol/news/uk/article3325439.ece; "Sheik Yusuf al-Qaradawi: Theologian of Terror," Anti-Defamation League, November 9, 2007, http://www.adl.org/main_Arab_World/al_Qaradawi_report_20041110.htm?Multi_page_sections=sHeading_4;

http://www.aaoifi.com/forms/Conference2-%202007%20Brochure.pdf;
Qatar National Bank, *Annual Report 2005*, http://www.qnb.com.qa/cspor-
tal/BlobServer?blobcol=urlenglishdoc&blobtable=QNBNewDocs&blobkey=i
d&blobwhere=1193211043176&blobheader=application%2Fpdf (accessed July
15, 2005); *Qatar: An Investor's Guide 2003*, http://qnb.com.qa/csportal/Bl
obServer?blobcol=urlenglishdoc&blobtable=QNBNewDocs&blobkey=id&blo
bwhere=1196665802626&blobheader=application%2Fpdf (accessed July 15,
2008).

11. Coughlin, "Extremism and the Islamic Society of North America"; Joe
Kaufman, "Islamist in the Hall," *FrontPage Magazine*, April 16, 2008, http://
www.frontpagemag.com/Articles/Read.aspx?GUID=A7EABB5C-E929-40-
C1-92DB-925C630C7076; Zenyo Baran, "The Muslim Brotherhood's U.S.
Network," in Hillel Fradkin, Husain Haqqani, and Eric Brown (eds.), *Current
Trends in Islamist Ideology*, vol. 6, Hudson Institute, http://www.hudson.org/
files/documents/CT6%2520zeyno.pdf, p. 101.

12. Mintz and Farah, "In Search of friends among the Foes."

13. Amber Haque (ed.), *Muslims and Islamization in North America: Problems and
Prospects* (Beltsville, MD: Amana, 1999), pp. 18–23.

14. Leif Stenberg, "The Islamization of Science: Four Muslim Positions Developing
an Islamic Modernity," *Lund Studies on History of Religions, No. 6*, (New York:
Coronet Books, 1996), p. 364, from Center for Islam and Science, http://www.
cis-ca.org/reviews/4-pos.htm (accessed October 16, 2008).

15. "Islamization of Knowledge," http://iiit.org/Publications/Books/
EnglishPublications/tabid/181/Default.aspx.

16. IISTD website, http://www.islamicscience.org/pages/engMain.htm
(accessed October 15, 2008). See for example S. Waqar Ahmed Husaini,
"Towards Islamization of Studies and Research in North American
Universities: Challenges and Opportunities for Students and Scholars,"
February 2003, http://www.islamicscience.org/pages/english/bro-
ch1of%203.htm; Ahmad Husaini, "Towards Development of Islamic Medical
and Health Science through North American Secular Universities," February
2003, http://www.islamicscience.org/pages/english/broch3of%203.
htm; Ahmad Husaini, "Islamization of Social and Humanistic Sciences:
An Action Plan," http://www.islamicscience.org/pages/english/AcPL%20
1of%204.htm; S. Michael Craven, "The Muslim Rebuttal and Islamization of
Knowledge," *Christian Post*, February 6, 2008, http://www.christianpost.
com/article/print/20080206/the-muslim-rebuttal-and-the-islamization-of-
knowledge.htm.

17. Patrick Poole, "The Muslim Brotherhood 'Project,'" May 11, 2006, http://
www.frontpagemag.com/articles/readarticle.asp?ID=22416&p=1;   Rachel
Ehrenfeld and Alyssa A. Lappen, "Shari'a Finance and the Coming of the
Ummah," in Jeffrey Norwitz (ed.), *Armed Groups: Studies in National Security,
Counterterrorism, and Counterinsurgency* (Newport, RI: U.S. Naval War
College, June 2008), pp. 390–404, notes 9 and 27.

18. "The Project," cited by Ehrenfeld and Lappen, "The Truth About the Muslim
Brotherhood."

19. Mohamed Akram, "An Explanatory Memorandum on the General Strategic
Goal for the Group in North America, 5/22/1991," www.nefafoundation.org/
miscellaneous/HLF/Akram_GeneralStrategicGoal.pdf (accessed September 18,
2007).

20. Ikhwan website, http://www.ummah.net/ikhwan/; American Arab Encounters syllabus, Carnegie Mellon Department of History, Qatar, Fall 2005, http://www.qatar.cmu.edu/~breilly2/US-Arab/.

21. Amad Saad, "The Islamic Perspective of Concealment," Islamonline.net, undated, http://www.islamonline.net/servlet/Satellite?cid=1123996016 204&pagename=IslamOnline-English-AAbout_Islam/AskAboutIslamE/ AskAboutIslamE; Abdul H. Siddiqui, "Al-Taqiyya/ Dissimulation, Part I," undated, http://www.al-islam.org/ENCYCLOPEDIA/chapter6b/1.html.

22. Akram, "An Explanatory Memorandum on the General Strategic Goal for the Group in North America, 5/22/1991"; Steven C. Coughlin, "Analysis of Muslim Brotherhood's General Strategic Goals for North America Memorandum," September 7, 2007, http://www.investigativeproject.org/documents/misc/20. pdf (accessed May 8, 2008).

23. "Muslim Public Affairs Council Tries to Halt Congressman Sherman's Hearings," July 30, 2008, http://www.house.gov/list/press/ca27_sherman/ morenews/MPAC.html.

24. Muslim American Society website, http://www.masnet.org/..

25. Akram, "An Explanatory Memorandum on the General Strategic Goal for the Group in North America, 5/22/1991"; Coughlin, "Analysis of Muslim Brotherhood's General Strategic Goals"; Noreen S. Ahmed-Ullah, Kim Barker, Laurie Cohen, Stephen Franklin and Sam Roe, "Hardliners Won Battle for Bridgeview Mosque," *Chicago Tribune*, February 8, 2004 http://www. chicagotribune.com/news/local/chi-0402080265feb08,0,2047644,print. story (accessed August 21, 2008); Muhammad Hisham Kabbani, "Islamic Extremism: A Viable Threat to U.S. National Security, An Open Forum at the U.S. Department of State" January 7, 1999, http://www.islamicsupremecoun-cil.org/bin/site/wrappers/extremism_inamerica_unveiling010799.html.

26. Jeremy Olson, "MTA's Islam Ad Furor," *New York Post*, July 22, 2008, http:// www.nypost.com/seven/07222008/news/regionalnews/winner_takes_ allah_120938.htm (accessed August 4, 2008).

27. Mohamed Nimer, *North American Muslim Resource Guide: Muslim Community Life in the United States and Canada* (London: Francis & Taylor: 2002), p. 130; Patricia Sullivan, "W.D. Mohammed; Changed Muslim movement in U.S.," *Washington Post*, September 10, 2008, http://www.washingtonpost.com/wp-dyn/content/article/2008/09/09/AR2008090903408.html.

28. About ICNA, Islamic Circle of North America website, http://www.icna.org/ icna/about-icna/4.html (accessed September 4, 2008].

29. Joe Kaufman, "The Mullahs and the Islamic Circle of North America," *FrontPage Magazine*, November 15, 2007, http://www.frontpagemag.com/Articles/Read. aspx? GUID=1f61e755–9b4c-4057–91c7–3c612cad5ead; ICNA Khomeini bio, http://www.americansagainsthate.org/IranSupportedByICNA.htm.

30. Ibid.

31. Anemona Hartocollis and Al Baker, "U.S. Citizen Is Accused of Helping al-Qaeda," *New York Times*, June 6, 2006, http://www.nytimes.com/2006/06/08/ nyregion/08terror.html? _r=1&oref=slogin; "U.S. Announces First Extradition from U.K. on Terrorism Charges," May 26, 2007, U.S. Attorney, Southern District of N.Y., http://www.usdoj.gov/usao/nys/pressreleases/May07/ hashmiextraditionpr.pdf; Kati Cornell, "Jihadi's Airport Tantrum," *New York Post*, June 2, 2007, http://www.nypost.com/seven/06022007/news/ worldnews/jihadis_airport_tantrum_worldnews_kati_cornell.htm.

32. "Radicalization in the West: The Homegrown Threat," New York City Police Department, ibid.
33. Pete Williams, "U.S. Citizen Held in London as Terror Suspect," *NBC News*, June 8, 2006, http://www.msnbc.msn.com/id/13190589/.
34. Hartocollis and Baker, "U.S. Citizen Is Accused of Helping al-Qaeda"; "U.S. Announces First Extradition from U.K. on Terrorism Charges"; Cornell, "Jihadi's Airport Tantrum."
35. "Radicalization in the West: The Homegrown Threat," New York City Police Department.
36. "List of Unindicted Co-conspirators and/or Joint Venturers," United States of America vs. Holy Land Foundation for Relief and Development, also known as "HLF," Shukri Abu Baker, Mohammed el-Mezain, Ghassan Elashi, Haitham Maghawri, Akram Mishal, Mufid Abdulqader, and Abdulrahaman Odeh, CR NO. 3:04-CR-240-G, ECF, Attachment A in the U.S. District Court for the Northern District of Texas, Dallas Division, downloaded June 8, 2007 from Pipelinenews.com, http://www.pipelinenews.org/images/2007–05–29-US%20v%20HLF-ListCoConspirators.pdf.
37. William Mayer and Beila Rabinowitz, "Holy Land Foundation Prosecutors Move to Streamline Hamas Funding Terror Case," *PipelineNews.org*, September 3, 2008, http://www.pipelinenews.org/index.cfm?page=hlfid=9.3.08.htm; Daniel Pipes and Sharon Chadha, "CAIR: Islamists Fooling the Establishment," *Middle East Quarterly* (Spring 2006), http://www.danielpipes.org/article/3437; Paul Sperry, "CAIR's Dubai Sugar Daddy," FrontPageMagazine.com, March 1, 2006, http://www.frontpagemag.com/Articles/Read.aspx?GUID=B4CB72DB-F13C-4E06–9029-AC5E595FEC24; Paul Sperry, "The Terrorist Next Door," FrontPageMagazine.com, August 31, 2006, http://www.frontpagemag.com/Articles/Read.aspx?GUID=0DFC5616-C9DC-4108–8B79-E6452E975392; "Selected Government Exhibits & Documents from U.S. v. Holy Land Foundation," NEAF Foundation, undated, http://www.nefafoundation.org/hlfdocs.html.
38. Jason Trahan and Tanya Eiserer, "Holy Land Foundation Defendants Guilty on all Counts," *Dallas Morning News*, November 25, 2008, http://www.dallasnews.com/sharedcontent/dws/dn/latestnews/stories/112508dnmetholylandverdicts.1e5022504.html.
39. "CAIR National Board and Staff," http://www.cair.com/AboutUs/CAIRNationalBoardandStaff.aspx; "Nihad Awad, CAIR Executive Director," Pluralism Project at Harvard University, http://www.pluralism.org/events/interfaculty2003/guest_bios/awad.php. .
40. Art Moore, "CAIR Leader Convicted on Terror Charges," *WorldNetDaily*, April 14, 2005, http://worldnetdaily.com/news/article.asp?ARTICLE_ID=43805; "Jury Awards $156M to Family of Teen in Slain in West Bank," *USA Today*, December 9, 2004, http://www.usatoday.com/news/nation/2004–12-09-slaying-suit_x.htm.
41. Pipes and Chadha, "CAIR Founded by 'Islamic Terrorists'?"Joseph Goldstein, "Court Sheds Light on Terror Probe," *New York Sun*, March 24, 2008, http://www.nysun.com/national/court-sheds-new-light-on-terror-probe/73461/; http://www.pa-aware.org/resources/pdfs/Green_Quest_Brochure.pdf.
42. Mohamed Nimer, *North American Muslim Resource Guide: Muslim Community Life in the United States and Canada* (London: Francis & Taylor: 2002), p. 130; Patricia Sullivan, "W.D. Mohammed; Changed Muslim movement in U.S.,"

Washington Post, September 10, 2008, http://www.washingtonpost.com/wp-dyn/content/article/2008/09/09/AR2008090903408.html.

43. Vanessa E. Jones, "A Study in Comfort," *Boston Globe*, March 7, 2007, http://www.boston.com/news/globe/living/articles/2007/03/07/a_study_in_comfort/?page=full (accessed September 8, 2008); Tim Townsend, "At Hartford Seminary, a Military Matter," *New York Times*, October 12, 2003, http://query.nytimes.com/gst/fullpage.html?res=9F07EEDE133FF931A25753C1A9659C8B63&sec=&spon=&pagewanted=print (accessed September 8, 2008); Faculty Profile, Ingrid Mattson, http://macdonald.hartsem.edu/mattson.htm; Islamic Chaplaincy Program, http://macdonald.hartsem.edu/chaplaincy/program.html.

44. Lorenzo Vidino, "The Muslim Brotherhood in Holland," *Counterterrorismblog.org*, April 6, 2007, http://counterterrorismblog.org/2007/04/the_muslim_brotherhood_in_holl.php; Atef Dalgamouni, "Rise of the Muslim Brotherhood," *Al Jazeera*, February 14, 2008, http://english.aljazeera.net/focus/arabunity/2008/02/2008525185757654836.html.

45. J. Michael Waller, "Terrorist Recruitment and Infiltration in the U.S.: Prisons and Military as an Operational Base," U.S. Senate Committee on the Judiciary testimony, October 14, 2003, http://judiciary.senate.gov/testimony.cfm?id=960&wit_id=2719 (accessed September 4, 2008).

46. "Foreign Terrorists Designations Table," U.S. Department of State, December 30, 2004, http://www.state.gov/s/ct/rls/fs/2004/40945.htm; "Executive Order 12947," Jan. 24, 2995, http://www.historycommons.org/context.jsp?item=a012495executiveorder&scale=0#a012495executiveorder (accessed September 8, 2008).

47. "Abdurahaman Alamoudi Sentenced to Jail in Terrorism Financing Case," U.S. Department of Justice, October 15, 2004, http://www.usdoj.gov/opa/pr/2004/October/04_crm_698.htm (accessed September 4, 2008); "Treasury Designates MIRA for Support to al-Qa'ida," July 14, 2005, Department of Treasury, http://www.treas.gov/press/releases/js2632.htm (accessed September 8, 2008).

48. J. Michael Waller, "D.C. Islamist Agent Carried Libyan Cash," *Insight on the News*, October 27, 2003, http://findarticles.com/p/articles/mi_m1571/is_2003_Oct_27/ai_109128674/print (accessed September 8, 2008); "U.S.A. vs. Abdurahman Alamoudi a/k/a Abdulrahman Alamoudi, Abdul Rahman Al-Amoudi, Abdulrahman Mohamed Omar Alamoudi," U.S. District Court, Eastern District of Virginia, AO 91 (Rev. 5/85) Criminal Complaint, http://news.findlaw.com/hdocs/docs/terrorism/usalamoudi93003cmp.pdf (accessed September 8, 2008).

49. Dean E. Murphy, "Mrs. Clinton Says She Will Return Money Raised by a Muslim Group," *New York Times*, October 26, 2000, http://query.nytimes.com/gst/fullpage.html?res=9400E3D91031F935A15753C1A9669C8B63&sec=&spon=&pagewanted=all (September 8, 2008).

50. Ehrenfeld and Lappen, "The Truth about the Muslim Brotherhood."

51. "What Are the Lessons of the Abdurahman Alamoudi Case?" *National Review*, August 23, 2004, http://findarticles.com/p/articles/mi_m1282/is_16_56/ai_n13803161 (accessed September 4, 2008); Waller, "D.C. Islamist Agent Carried Libyan Cash."

52. "Nihad Awad: Apologists or Extremists," *Investigative Project*, undated, http://www.investigativeproject.org/profile/113.

53. "CAIR National Board and Staff."
54. John-Thor Dahlburg, "Religious Heads Question Interfaith Group's Intentions," *Los Angeles Times*, December 19, 2003, http://articles.latimes.com/2003/dec/19/nation/na-muslim19; Raffi Khatchadourian, "Azzaz the American," *New Yorker*, January 22, 2007, http://www.newyorker.com/reporting/2007/01/22/070122fa_fact_khatchadourian?currentPage=all.
55. Emerson, "The White House, CAIR and the OIC," July 5, 2007, *Counterterrorismblog.org*, http://counterterrorismblog.org/2007/07/the_white_house_cair_and_the_o.php (accessed September 8, 2008); Pipes and Chadha, "CAIR: Islamists Fooling the Establishment"; Sperry, "CAIR's Dubai Sugar Daddy"; Sperry, "The Terrorist Next Door"; "Selected Government Exhibits & Documents from U.S. v. Holy Land Foundation."
56. "CAIR Proposes World Islamophobia Report," *Islamonline.com*, January 14, 2006, http://www.islamonline.net/English/News/2005–01/14/article05.shtml (accessed September 8, 2008).
57. "Controversial Muslim Group Gets VIP Airport Security Tour," *World Net Daily*, August 18, 2006, http://www.wnd.com/news/article.asp?ARTICLE_ID=51573 (September 8, 2008).
58. "List of Unindicted Co-conspirators."
59. "Justice Department Cancels 'Muslim Outreach' Event with ISNA Imam," JihadWatch, August 9, 2007, http://jihadwatch.org/archives/017708.php.
60. "U.S. Sponsors Islamic Convention," *Washington Times*, August 21, 2007, http://www.washingtontimes.com/news/2007/aug/27/us-sponsors-islamic-convention/ (accessed August 1, 2008).
61. Art Moore, "Ex-CAIR Chief Indicted for 'Baghdad Jim' Junket," *World Net Daily*, March 27, 2008, http://www.wnd.com/index.php/index.php?pageId=60041 (accessed September 8, 2008); "Another Ex-CAIR Official in Legal Trouble," Investigative Project on Terrorism, March 26, 2008, http://www.investigativeproject.org/article/626.
62. Jeffrey Imm, "U.S.-Muslim Engagement Project Calls for Engagement with Muslim Brotherhood," Anti-Jihad Network, September 24, 2008, http://anti-jihad.org/blog/2008/09/engagement-with-mb/; "Changing Course: A New Direction for U.S. Relations with the Muslim World," *Report of the Leadership Group on U.S.-Muslim Engagement*, U.S.-Muslim Engagement Project, September 2008, http://www.usmuslimengagement.org/storage/usme/documents/Changing_Course_-_A_New_Direction_for_US_Relations_with_the_Muslim_World.pdf; "CAIR Welcomes Announcement of U.S. Envoy to Islamic Conference," CAIR Press Release, June 27, 2007, http://islamic-conference-news.newslib.com/story/1413–3215568/ and http://ccun.org/News/2007/June/28%20n/Muslim%20American%20News%20Briefs,%20June%2028,%202007.htm; "Bush to Speak at Islamic Center of Washington, D.C.," Little Green Footballs, June 26, 2007, http://littlegreenfootballs.com/article/26018_Bush_to_Speak_at_Islamic_Center_of_Washington_DC.
63. Frank Walker, "West Must Act to End Jihad: Imam," *Sydney Morning Herald*, March 21, 2004, http://www.smh.com.au/articles/2004/03/21/1079789939987.html.
64. "List of Unindicted Co-conspirators."
65. "Spinning the Asbahi Resignation," *IPT News*, The Investigative Project on Terrorism, August 7, 2008, http://www.investigativeproject.org/article/744 (accessed August 12, 2008).

66. Glenn R. Simpson and Amy Chozick, "Obama's Muslim-Outreach Adviser Resigns," *Wall Street Journal*, August 6, 2008.
67. Khaled Salam, IkhwanWeb, August 11, 2008, http://www.ikhwanweb.com/Article.asp?ID=17570&LevelID=1&SectionID=121.
68. "Egyptian Muslim Brotherhood Responds to GMBDR," *Global Muslim Brotherhood Daily Report*, August 14, 2008, http://globalmbreport.com/?p=1040 (reprinted August 18, 2008, http://www.familysecuritymatters.org/publications/id.904/pub_detail.asp).
69. Pat Ferrier, "Interfaith Service Kicks Off Convention," DNCC Blog, August 10, 2008, http://www.coloradoan.com/apps/pbcs.dll/article?AID=/20080810/UPDATES01/80810008/1002/NEWS01 (accessed August 22, 2008).
70. Frank Gaffney, "The Democrats' 'Soft' Jihadist," August 23, 2008, http://www.centerforsecuritypolicy.org/home.aspx?sid=140&categoryid=140&subcategoryid=141.
71. Josh Gerstein, "Obama Speaker Has Hamas Tie," Politico, January 17, 2009, http://www.politico.com/news/stories/0109/17562.html.
72. "The Muslim Code of Honor Pledge," http://www.msanational.org/codeofhonor/; "The Pledge of Mutual Respect and Cooperation," http://www.msa-national.org/pledge/.
73. Young Muslims UK, "The Importance of Collective Work: Jama'ah," Young Muslims of Canada, http://www.youngmuslims.ca/articles/display.asp?ID=11.
74. Ehrenfeld and Lappen, "The Truth about the Muslim Brotherhood."
75. "Muslim Students Association," *Investigative Project on Terrorism*, http://www.investigativeproject.org/documents/misc/31.pdf.
76. MSA National website, http://www.msanational.org/.
77. "Zonal Conference Calls on Topics Specific to Muslim Students," http://www.msanational.org/events/conferencecalls/.
78. "MSA National Conferences," http://www.msanational.org/events/conferences/; MSA National Continental Conference, 2008, "Celebrating the MSA Legacy: Moving Forward Together," August 2008, http://www.msanational.org/files/pdf/MSA_Program_08_26_08.pdf.
79. "A Time for Change: 45th Annual ISNA Convention," http://www.isna.net/articles/Press-Releases/RAMADAN-A-TIME-FOR-CHANGE-45TH-ANNUAL-ISNA-CONVENTION.aspx; 45th ISNA Annual Convention Program, http://www.isna.net/assets/conventions/programs/convention08programv3.0.pdf.
80. 45th Annual ISNA Convention Program; "Action Alert: Defend Free Speech Stop the Attacks on Dr. Hatem Bazian!" *A.N.S.W.E.R*, April 15, 2004, http://bellaciao.org/en/article.php3?id_article=720 and http://www.campus-watch.org/article/id/1126.
81. Coughlin, "Extremism and the Council of American-Islamic Relations (CAIR)," International Assessment and Strategic Center, January 2007, http://www.strategycenter.net/docLib/20080127_Extremism_and_CAIR.pdf.
82. Alyssa A. Lappen, "The Dawning of Dawa," *FrontPage Magazine*, July 15, 2003, http://www.frontpagemag.com/Articles/Read.aspx?GUID=5BC2FD27-3EF2-475D-9B49-575BAC744003; see revised "Teacher's Guide to Religion in the Public Schools," at http://www.alyssaalappen.org/wp-content/uploads/teachersguide.pdf.
83. Lee Kaplan, "Textbooks for Jihad," *FrontPage Magazine*, March 19, 2004, http://frontpagemag.com/Articles/ReadArticle.asp?ID=12645; "Islam and

the Textbooks: A Report of the American Textbook Council," *Middle East Quarterly* (Summer 2003), http://www.meforum.org/article/559; William J. Benetta, "Houghton-Miflin's Islamic Connection," *The Textbook Letter*, July 2000–August 2000, http://www.textbookleague.org/113centu.htm; and "Islam: A Simulation of Islamic History and Culture, 610–110," undated, *The Textbook League*, http://www.textbookleague.org/filth.htm.

84. Gilbert T. Sewell, "Islam in the Classroom: What the Textbooks Tell Us," *American Textbook Council*, 2008, http://www.historytextbooks.org/islamreport.pdf.

85. Brooklyn Academy of Music, Spring Season 2009, "Muslim Voices, Arts and Ideas," http://www.bam.org/viewdocument.aspx?did=2820.

86. Advisory Committees, New York City's First Muslim Arts Festival, http://muslimvoicesfestival.org/about/committee; Feisel Abdul Rauf, "Obama vs. Osama in the Muslim World," *Washington Post*, Mar. 27, 2009, http://newsweek.washingtonpost.com/onfaith/panelists/feisal_abdul_rauf/2009/03/why_obama_should_speak_to_the_muslim_world.html; Beila Rabinowitz and William Mayer, "Khalil Gibran School Advisor Khalid Latif Threatened NYU with Jihad over Danish Cartoons," *Militant Islam Monitor*, May 17, 2007, http://www.militantislammonitor.org/article/id/2910.

87. Qawalli and the Art of Devotion, "Muslim Voices Festival," http://muslimvoicesfestival.org/resources/qawalli-and-art-devotion; Hussein Rashid, "Music and Islam: A Deeper Look," http://muslimvoicesfestival.org/http:/%252Fwww.muslimvoicesfestival.org/resources/music-and-islam-deeper-look; Youssou N'Dour, "Music," (including Qur'anic recitation), http://muslimvoicesfestival.org/event/youssou-n%27dour; "Creators of New York Masjid," http://muslimvoicesfestival.org/artist/creators-new-york-masjid; Edward Grazda, "The Mosques of New York City," http://muslimvoicesfestival.org/artist/edward-grazda; "America at a Crossroads: The Mosque in Morgantown," http://muslimvoicesfestival.org/event/america-crossroads-mosque-morgantown; Jaqueline Ganem, "Writing the word of God: calligraphy and the Qur'an," http://muslimvoicesfestival.org/resources/writing-word-god-calligraphy-and-quran; "The seen and the hidden: (dis)covering the veil," http://muslimvoicesfestival.org/events/associate-partner-events.

88. "Faith, Hate and Charity," BBC, July 30, 2006, http://www.bbc.co.uk/pressoffice/pressreleases/stories/2006/07_july/30/panorama.shtml, cited by Rachel Ehrenfeld and Alyssa A. Lappen, "Tithing for Terrorists," *National Review*, October 12, 2007, http://article.nationalreview.com/?q=MWEwMDg1ZThjM2FmYzU1MTU5Y2Q3MTBhY2I2YjM5NTc.

89. Abd al-Rahman al-Rashed, "Follow the Money," *Al-Sharq al-Awsat*, October 20, 2004, cited at *Intelligence and Terrorism Information Center at the Center for Special Studies* (C.S.S.), November 2004, http://www.terrorism-info.org.il/malam_multimedia/html/final/eng/sib/12_04/financing.htm.

90. Ehrenfeld and Lappen, "The Truth about the Muslim Brotherhood."

91. "Future of Islamic Finance Seems Bright," *Zawya*, October 18, 2008, http://www.zawya.com/Story.cfm/sidGN_18102008_10252693/Future%20of%20Islamic%20finance%20seems%20bright/; "All the Riches are Ours," *Investors Business Daily*, October 15, 2008, http://www.ibdeditorials.com/IBDArticles.aspx?id=308961787242329.

92. Rachel Ehrenfeld and Alyssa A. Lappen, "Financial Jihad," *Human Events*, September 22, 2005, http://www.humanevents.com/article.php?id=9235.

93. William L. Rutledge, "Regulation and Supervision of Islamic Banking in the United States," New York Federal Reserve Board Executive Vice President, to Arab Bankers' Association of North America, April 19, 2005, http://www.arabbankers.org/download/123321_U127360__71877/Rutledge%20Presentation.pdf.

94. Timur Kuran, *Islam and Mammon: The Economic Predicaments of Islamism* (Princeton: Princeton University Press, 2005), pp. x, 13, cited by Alyssa A. Lappen, "Shari'a Finance," *FrontPage Magazine*, November 14, 2007, http://www.frontpagemagazine.com/Articles/Read.aspx?GUID=1E90E478-FA24-45F9-A43D-F47D8C4B9CE2.

95.

96. Mohammad Nejatullah Siddiqi, "Towards a Grass-roots Based Islamic Finance for All," June 16, 2001, http://www.siddiqi.com/mns/speech_16June2001.html.

97. Mohammad Nejatullah Siddiqi, "Islamic Finance and Beyond: Premises and Promises of Islamic Economics," http://www.siddiqi.com/mns/IFandBeyond.html.

98. Mahmoud El-Gamal, "Incoherent Pietism and Shari'a Arbitrage," May 23 2007, http://www.ft.com/cms/s/01ccc914-0553-11dc-b151-000b5df10621,dwp_uuid=ead739d6-0860-11dc-b11e-000-b5df10621,Authorised=false.html?_i_location=http%3A%2F%2Fwww.ft.com%2Fcms%2Fs%2F1%2F01ccc914-0553-11dc-b151-000-b5df10621%2Cdwp_uuid%3Dead739d6-0860-11dc-b11e-000-b5df10621.html&_i_referer=http%3A%2F%2Fwww.frontpagemagazine.com%2FArticles%2FRead.aspx%3FGUID%3DC64342C1-C28F-4BED-865 -B69E78684D38, cited in Alyssa A. Lappen, "A Secular Market Nightmare," *FrontPage Magazine*, May 9, 2008, http://frontpagemag.com/articles/Read.aspx?GUID=C64342C1-C28F-4BED-8658-B69E78684D38.

99. Alyssa A,. Lappen, "Beware Fool's Gold—and Shari'a Finance," *FrontPage Magazine*, January 21, 2008, http://www.frontpagemag.com/Articles/Read.aspx?GUID=99BA1C91-19C9-4694-B70D-9CCDF1BAEC59.

100. Andrew Norfolk, "Our Followers 'Must Live in Peace until Strong Enough to Wage Jihad,'" *Times Online*, September 7, 2007, http://www.timesonline.co.uk/tol/comment/faith/article2409833.ece.

101. "Islamic Finance Suffers from Growing Pains," June 30, 2008, http://www.efinancialnews.com/assetmanagement/index/content/2451040585; "Grappling with Problems of Success," June 18, 2008, http://www.zawya.com/Story.cfm?id=ZAWYA20080619083913&pagename=sukukmonitor.

102. Norfolk, "Our Followers must live in Peace."

103. Paul Sperry, "Shari'a Showdown on Wall St.," *FrontPage Magazine*, July 9, 2008, http://frontpagemag.com/Articles/Read.aspx?GUID=D0A52215-262C-4438-A3CD-8073D0DE26CB.

104. DeLorenzo bio, *American Muslim*, October 6, 2005, http://www.theamericanmuslim.org/tam.php/features/articles/delorenzo_dr_yusuf_talal/.

105. Patrick Poole, "What Virginia's Islamic Academy Doesn't Want You to Know," *Pajamas Media*, June 13, 2008, http://pajamasmedia.com/blog/what-virginias-islamic-saudi-academy-doesnt-want-you-to-know/.

106. Usl al Fiqh al Islami, http://sunnah.org/fiqh/usul/usul_fiqh_alwani/Default.htm; and http://www.kvisionbooks.com/product_info.php/2_Spirituality_Athkar/Remembrance_and_Prayer_The_Way_of_Prophet_Muhammad/.

107. Fiqh Council of North America backgrounder, *Investigative Project*, http://www.investigativeproject.org/FCNA-CAIR.html;   http://www.djindexes.com/mdsidx/?event=showIslamicOverView#delorenzo.
108. Ahmed-Ullah, Barker, Cohen, Franklin and Roe, "Hardliners Won Battle"; "Struggle for the Soul of Islam," http://www.chicagotribune.com/news/specials/chi-islam-specialpackage,1,2843820.special; Jeff Borgardt, "Mosque Terror Allegations Not Pretty," *Desplaines Valley News*, February 19, 2004, http://www.desplainesvalleynews.com/mosque_terror_allegations.htm; "Islamization of North America, NAIT and the DJII Fund," *Militant Islam Monitor*, January 12, 2006, http://www.militantislammonitor.org/article/id/1544.
109. Ahmed-Ullah, Barker, Cohen, Franklin and Roe, "Hardliners Won Battle"; "UnIndicted Co-Conspirators"; DJII Fund Directors, http://www.investaaa.com/pdfs/dow_Board_of_Directors.pdf.
110. North American Islamic Trust Board Members, http://www.isna.net/ISNAHQ/pages/Board-of-Directors.aspx.
111. Abdullah Idris Ali Biography, http://www.alimprogram.com/scholars/idris.shtml; "UnIndicted Co-Conspirators."
112. Ali Bio; "Al Haramain Islamic Foundation-All Offices," U.S. Designation Date, June 19, 2008, http://www.ustreas.gov/offices/enforcement/key-issues/protecting/charities_execorder_13224-a.shtml.
113. "Islamization of North America."
114. "ISNA: The Islamic Society of North America," August 24, 2004, http://www.militantislammonitor.org/article/id/254.
115. Alex Alexiev, "Jihad Comes to Wall Street," April 4, 2008, *National Review*, http://www.militantislammonitor.org/article/id/3414.
116. DJII Fund Directors; IMANX profile, *Yahoo Finance* http://finance.yahoo.com/q/pr?s=imanx.
117. Akram, "An Explanatory Memorandum on the General Strategic Goal for the Group in North America, 5/22/1991."

INDEX